The Legacy of Christopher Columbus in the Americas

The LEGACY *of* CHRISTOPHER COLUMBUS *in the* AMERICAS

New Nations and a Transatlantic Discourse of Empire

Elise Bartosik-Vélez

Vanderbilt University Press
NASHVILLE

© 2014 by Vanderbilt University Press
Nashville, Tennessee 37235
All rights reserved
First printing 2014
First paperback edition 2016

This book is printed on acid-free paper.

Library of Congress Cataloging-in-Publication Data on file
LC control number 2013007832
LC classification number E112.B294 2014
Dewey class number 970.01/5

ISBN 978-0-8265-1954-2 (paper)
ISBN 978-0-8265-1953-5 (cloth)
ISBN 978-0-8265-1955-9 (ebook)

For Bryan, Sam, and Sally

Contents

Acknowledgments ix

Introduction 1

CHAPTER 1
Columbus's Appropriation
of Imperial Discourse 15

CHAPTER 2
The Incorporation of Columbus
into the Story of Western Empire 44

CHAPTER 3
Columbus and the Republican Empire
of the United States 66

CHAPTER 4
Colombia: Discourses of Empire
in Spanish America 106

Conclusion: The Meaning of Empire
in Nationalist Discourses of the United States
and Spanish America 145

Notes 153
Works Cited 179
Index 195

~ Acknowledgments ~

Many people helped me as I wrote this book. Michael Palencia-Roth has been an unfailing mentor and model of ethical, rigorous scholarship and human compassion. I am grateful for his generous help at many stages of writing this manuscript. I am also indebted to my friend Christopher Francese, of the Department of Classical Studies at Dickinson College, who has never hesitated to answer my queries about pretty much anything related to the classical world. His intellectual curiosity and commitment to academic inquiry is inspiring. I thank him for meticulously reviewing many of the translations from Latin in this book and for making helpful comments on the drafts of my essay regarding Peter Martyr.

I wish to thank Eli Bortz at Vanderbilt University Press for his faith in this project. I also thank Sue Havlish, Joell Smith-Borne, and copyeditor extraordinaire Laura Fry at Vanderbilt. I am also grateful to Silvia Benvenuto for the index. A special thanks to the anonymous readers whose careful reading significantly improved this book.

Thank you to Ken Ward, librarian at the John Carter Brown Library, for scrounging up all kinds of gems for the sake of intellectual inquiry and friendship. I am also grateful to Cristóbal Macías Villalobos at the Universidad de Málaga for helping me understand more about the Romans and their language.

I wish to thank Dickinson College and the Dickinson College Research and Development Committee for its generous financial support of this project and to my colleagues at Dickinson who make this a vibrant intellectual community. Thank you to Kristin Beach and Ursala Neuwirth, my Dana Research Assistants funded by Dickinson. I am grateful to the library staff at Dickinson, especially Tina Maresco and everyone in the interlibrary loan office. Thank you also to the cheerful and efficient Jennifer Kniesch, Visual Resources Librarian at the Art and Art History Department, for helping me locate images and secure permission to use them.

I have benefited much from the generosity and insight of many fellow colleagues who have willingly shared material and/or their work over the years, including Scott Breuninger, Lina del Castillo, Karen Racine, and fellow Columbus scholars Jenny Heil and Carol Delaney.

I thank many friends and colleagues who have shared their expertise with me at various points in the development of this book, as well as those who have commented on various bits (long or short) of the manuscript. These include Sandra Alfers, David Boruchoff, Deirdre Casey, Stelio Cro, Lucile Duperron, Stephen Fuller, Heather Hennes, Christopher Lemelin, Jim Muldoon, Tony Moore, Sharon O'Brien, Jeremy Paden, Linda Shoppes, Joel Westwood, Bob Winston, Amy Wlodarski, Margarita Zamora, and Nadine Zimmerli.

To my dispersed circle of friends throughout the world, some also included above, I am a better person for your friendship: Katie, Jeff, Becky, Nancy, Tara, Victoria, Dana, Isabel, Ángeles, Emily, Sarah, Jimmy Mac, Bobby, and Jorge. Thank you to my parents, Barbara and George. I could not have written this book without years of support and encouragement, not to mention countless hours of shared laughter and parenting, from my best friend Bryan. And to Sam: thank you for wanting to learn and for reminding me to look at the sky.

The Legacy of Christopher Columbus in the Americas

～ Introduction ～

Why is the District of Columbia, the capital of the United States, named after Christopher Columbus, a Genoese explorer commissioned by Spain who never set foot on the future US mainland? Why did Spanish Americans in 1819 name the newly independent republic "Colombia" after Columbus, the first representative of the Spanish Empire from which political independence was recently declared? This book answers these questions.

Christopher Columbus introduced the Old World to the New World and thereby changed the course of history and marked the beginning of modernity.[1] His accidental "discovery" of the New World in 1492 began the process by which European culture and institutions were transmitted to the Western hemisphere, which in turn also deeply influenced Europe. It also initiated the overseas extension to the greater Atlantic world of long-standing European imperial rivalries and caused the forced migration of massive numbers of people, the genocide of indigenous peoples and cultures, the ecological modifications of plants and animals, and the environmental destruction of New-World landscapes. Such is Columbus's legacy.

At the end of the fifteenth century, Portugal and the Crown of Castile, the distinct state formed in 1230, had long been developing programs of overseas expansion along the coast of Africa. If it had not been Columbus in 1492, it would likely have been some other adventurer who would have claimed the New World for the Old at some point, probably in the sixteenth century. But it was Columbus who first took possession for Castile of the island of Guanahaní on 12 October 1492, and he thence became the emblem of Spain's overseas empire, the largest the world had ever seen up to that point. In more general terms, he became a symbol of Europe's imperial conquest and colonization of the rest of the Western world.

Columbus's association with empire, something he consistently emphasized in his own writings, remained intact after his death, as many authors who wrote about him portrayed him as an imperial servant, some even describing him as a new version of Aeneas, Virgil's famous founder of Rome. The main argument of this book is that centuries after Columbus's death in 1506, the figure of Columbus was appropriated by nationalists in the Americas in ways that reveal how they viewed their new independent nation-states in relation to old political typologies of empire. The embrace of Columbus as an imperial figure in New-World republics that claimed political independence from Old-World empires shows the ideological imperial underpinnings of their new nation-states.

Placing the figure of Columbus, as he appears in the Americas in nationalist discourses of the eighteenth and nineteenth centuries, within the context of the centuries-long tradition of Columbus interpretation preserves the crucial association between Columbus and empire that the admiral himself sought to forge and that writers after him perpetuated. In turn, this allows us to view the independence and early republican periods of the region through an "empire-based lens," which reveals how American representations of Columbus worked to integrate older discourses of empire alongside newer discourses about the nation-state. In this context, to take one example, the naming of the District of Columbia, the capital of the United States, after Columbus in 1791 reflects the significance of empire in the construction of the new nation-states of the Americas. Empire was indeed on Americans' minds. In fact, the desire for territorial expansion and the belief in the right to expand westward over the whole American continent was evident even in the charters of five of the original thirteen English colonies that designated their western boundaries as the Pacific Ocean. Later, George

Washington famously called the United States a "rising empire." Thomas Jefferson, agreeing with that view, wrote in 1786, "Our confederacy must be viewed as the nest from which all America, North and South, is to be peopled."[2] As historian Eran Shalev has recently shown in his well-documented study, *Rome Reborn on Western Shores: Historical Imagination and the Creation of the America Republic*, the dominant notion of empire in the imagination of these early Americans drew on the Roman experience, the very same that was important in Columbus's day.

The figure of Columbus was employed differently in the rhetoric of revolutionaries and nationalists of Anglo and Spanish America. Columbus, understandably, had a much longer history in the Hispanic world, where there was no need, as was the case in British America, to construct elaborate myths to incorporate him in the nationalist historiographies of the late eighteenth and early nineteenth centuries. Columbus was Spain's first representative in the New World. Many Spanish American Creole revolutionaries in the late eighteenth century, whose legitimacy largely depended on their Spanish heritage, ironically claimed the Italian Columbus as their racial and spiritual forefather. This kind of identification with Columbus is absent in the more mythological Columbus invoked by British Americans who constructed a national symbol that allowed them to cut conceptual ties with their mother country. The tortuousness of the constructed myth of Columbus in British America, the very visibility of the scaffolding on which the myth is built, results in a more powerful story than the more easily constructed myth of Columbus in Spanish America. In this way the Columbus story in the two regions adheres to the distinction drawn by Aristotle between poetry and history, poetry being more powerful—more true—than history because of poetry's artifice and because of its powerful transformation of the particular into the universal. Partly because of this, the Columbus myth in British America is stronger and a more compelling component in the dominant narrative about national origins than in similar narratives of

Spanish America. This helps explain why this book follows the Columbus legacy in the United States until its climax at the 1893 World's Columbian Exposition in Chicago but limits its discussion of the legacy of Columbus in Spanish America to the early independence period. At the end of the nineteenth century in Spanish America, the legacy of Columbus was not nearly as important in nationalist narratives as it was in the United States.

The differences with regard to the manner in which Columbus was employed in nationalist discourses of British and Spanish America are also related to different understandings of the term "empire" in the two regions, as I discuss in this book's Conclusion. The term "empire" in the United States, from its inception, had connotations associated with the drive to territorial expansion that was at the heart of US policies regarding the Louisiana Purchase, the War of 1812, the Monroe Doctrine, the constant wars against Native Americans, the Mexican American War, and a host of other policy decisions that either indirectly supported or directly led to the acquisition of new territory. In the new nation-states of Spanish America, there was no such systematic drive to acquire new territory, and the term "empire" was understood by early nationalists in a much more nebulous sense related to the exercise of power.

Despite these differences, both Spaniards and English in the New World viewed themselves as successors of the Roman Empire, as well as Western empire in general. And in the postcolonial era in both Anglo and Spanish America, the Western narrative of the *translatio imperii* (the transfer of empire) was employed to legitimate the construction of the nation-state.

According to the standard story in the West about the *translatio imperii*, occidental empire—and Western civilization itself, the dominant version of which accompanied empire—was believed to move progressively from east to west.[3] The specific trajectory of empire depended on who told the story, but in most versions empire was said to begin in Asia, then move to Greece, and then to Rome. The itinerary of empire after Rome varied. It often included Germany, where Charles I was crowned Roman Emperor by Pope Leo III in 800, and then France, England, and/or Spain. Eventually, inhabitants of the New World, and certainly the early nationalists of the eighteenth and nineteenth centuries, claimed to inherit Western empire. I discuss in Chapter 2 how, almost immediately after his death, Columbus was cast as a protagonist in this narrative of domination and power. I explore in Chapters 3 and 4 the role of Columbus in the *translatio imperii* narrative as it was articulated in British and Spanish America.

The definitions of "empire" suggested by the various articulations of the *translatio imperii* in both Europe and the Americas are admittedly obscure. I consider these narratives not as a political scientist—that is, as conforming to specific political typologies—but as a student of intellectual and cultural history. As such, while they certainly have a foot in the rational world—they rhetorically underwrite discourses of power that have real implications—they themselves do not rationally trace historical events. Rather, they are mythic. They frequently invoke "empire" as an idea in the popular imagination that relates, often quiet vaguely, to the exercise of power and dominion, as well as to grandeur and great territorial expanse. The term "empire" in narratives of *translatio imperii* connotes the domination of one people over large swaths of territories and peoples. It involves a dominant culture that is imposed via the *translatio studii* (the transfer of culture) along with the *translatio imperii*.

The significance of Rome, both the Roman Empire and the Roman Republic, and its legacy in Western culture looms large in the meaning of "empire" as it is employed in this book. Also important is Virgil's *Aeneid* as the paradigmatic articulation of the *translatio imperii* story.[4] Written during Augustus's principate, the epic relates the history of the legendary founding of Rome, which, according to Jupiter in the story, is destined to have an empire without end.[5] The *Aeneid* is relevant to the legacy of Columbus because Columbus's self-characterizations as a servant of empire were taken up by historiographers and poets who then incorporated him into Virgil's classical narrative about the rise to power of one culture over others. These accounts, some of which were produced in the Americas, portrayed Columbus as a conquering neo-Aeneas.

The figure of Columbus fits easily within narratives of one group of people conquering and dominating another. Given his fame as the agent who set in motion Europe's conquest of the New World, Columbus as a historical actor is inherently imperial. The figure of Columbus, as he was commonly interpreted by generations of historiographers and literati, never lost its association with empire. And it is this association, I believe, that New-World nationalists effectively exploited as they employed the figure of Columbus in the eighteenth and nineteenth centuries.

The broad geographical and (often) chronological perspective employed by so-called transatlantic historians allows for an understanding of American phenomena, such as narratives about Columbus, in relation to their Old-World contexts. John Elliott's masterful *Empires of the Atlantic World: Britain and Spain in America, 1492–1830* is illustrative of this approach, as is the work of Jorge Cañizares-Esguerra (*Puritan Conquistadors: Iberianizing the Atlantic, 1550–1700*) and Anthony Pagden (*Lords of all the World: Ideologies of Empire in Spain, Britain and France, c.1500–1800;* and *Spanish Imperialism and the Political Imagination*). Some scholars of "Atlantic" history, like Elliott and Pagden in *Lords of all the World*, compare and contrast the experiences of different regions and cultures in the Americas, as is also the case in this book. Elliott, for example, in his study of the British and Spanish colonial systems in the Americas, consistently contrasts the British and the Spanish experience, thereby shedding light on the specific articulations of both empires. Elliott's work can be viewed as a contemporary response to Herbert Bolton's 1932 call for an "epic of Greater America," one that would show "the larger aspects of Western Hemispheric history."[6] Departing from Bolton's call for more scholarship that focuses on the hemisphere, scholarship in the field of "inter-Americanist" literary studies (sometimes called "hemispheric studies") has a long and vibrant tradition to which this book contributes. It includes studies written by Alfred Owen Aldridge (*Early American Literature: A Comparatist Approach*), Djelal Kadir (*Columbus and the Ends of the Earth: Europe's Prophetic Rhetoric as Conquering Ideology*), Lisa Voigt (*Writing Captivity in the Early Modern Atlantic: Circulations of Knowledge and Authority in the Iberian and English Imperial Worlds*), and most recently, Ronald Briggs (*Tropes of Enlightenment in the Age of Bolívar: Simón Rodríguez and the American Essay at Revolution*). Like the work of these scholars, this book seeks to trace not only European thought in the Americas, but also how that thought has been adapted and expressed differently in British and Spanish America.

Recent efforts to acknowledge and better understand the presence of empire in US history and culture, which are at the heart of "New Americanism," also give us reason to view Columbus as he was employed during the post-independence periods of the Americas: as a figure of empire. "New Americanism," first promoted in the work of scholars such as Donald Pease and Amy Kaplan, departs from a critique of the use of the nation-state as the dominant unit of scholarly analysis.[7] Historian Antoinette Burton refers to this scholarship as "new imperial studies," and her description of it emphasizes the continuity between empire and nation: this kind of work, she writes, "seeks to recast the nation as an imperialized space—a political territory that could not, and still cannot, escape the imprint of empire."[8] "Early (US) Americanists," those who study the British colonial period and the early republic in North America, as well as Latin Americanists of all kinds have traditionally viewed "postcoloniality" as an important historical reality.[9] But it has been only in the last twenty years or so that scholars working in (US) American Studies have begun to systematically explore the continuities between pre- and post-independence periods. And although "new imperial" and "New Americanist" scholarship has created a better understanding of the US nation as empire, it has yet to revisit the significance of Columbus as he appears in the eighteenth and nineteenth centuries. Our view of Columbus has therefore remained impeded by nation-centric methodologies that exclude the supranational contexts in which the meanings of Columbus have been constructed. This book seeks to correct this problem.

In addition to adopting a comparative lens and one that does not privilege the nation-state, this study also employs the methodological assumption that a full understanding of the meaning of Columbus as he was represented in the Americas requires that we begin by considering Columbus's own texts. Although the afterlife of Columbus has been the subject of many scholarly works, none have considered Columbus's own part in constructing his image.[10] Moreover, very few have used a comparative lens, which is also necessary for a complete view of the figure of Columbus in the Americas, as that figure has been constructed in a variety of languages and traditions. Some scholars working solely with English texts would have us believe that the word "Columbus" (meaning the English version of Columbus's name, not the Italian Colombo or the Spanish Colón, by which he was always referred to in Spanish documents) came into existence as separate from the historical person Columbus, the mariner who grew up in Genoa, then lived in Portugal, and then Spain. William Spengemann, for example, in his engaging study of Columbus's textual appearances in English, refers to "Columbus" as invoked by Ralph Waldo Emerson in the essay "Experience." Spengemann writes, "Emerson's *Columbus* is just a word, a particular selection and arrangement of letters that was adopted long after the navigator's death."[11] Actually, it was only forty-seven years after Columbus's death that the English word "Columbus" was first employed, as Spengemann himself notes, in Richard Eden's partial translation of Sebastian Münster's Latin *Cosmographiae*, which was Münster's translation of his own German work *Cosmographia: Beschreibung aller Lender*. This original German text related Columbus's voyage to the New World and was itself largely based on Peter Martyr's Latin account in the *Orbe novo*. Spengemann appears to discount the significance of the multiple versions: Eden's translation of Münster's work was an English translation of a Latin translation of a German text about Columbus that, in turn, drew heavily from another Latin text about the actual historical figure.

This book's argument is grounded in the firm belief that intertextuality matters, and there is a connection between the historical person Columbus and the manner in which others have interpreted him through the centuries. Hence, I disagree with Spengemann's statement that "Insofar as *Columbus* is an English word whose meanings, including its various referents, consist entirely in other English words, its history is also distinct from those of the Spanish Colón, the French Colomb, the German Kolumbus, the Italian Colombo, and the Portuguese Colom."[12] I acknowledge that different people have interpreted Columbus differently, according to their own agendas. My point is that a tradition of interpretation is at the core of the great majority of representations of Columbus, including Eden's 1553 English translation of Münster's text and the majority of the representations of Columbus produced in the Americas in the eighteenth and nineteenth centuries. This, in addition to showing the interconnected nature of cultural production in the Atlantic world, undergirds the argument that American discourse about Columbus is most accurately interpreted within the context of this tradition of textual production. Hence, when Columbus appears in texts published in the independence or early republican periods in the Americas, the hermeneutical task ideally involves answering questions about the relationship between empire and nation.

Tracing and understanding the tradition of Columbus interpretation and its variations require that one work in multiple time periods and across linguistic and "national" disciplines. The consequences of not doing so are evident in Spengemann's inability to explain the popularity of Columbus in the United States: "If

Anglo-America demanded a history beginning in a single, identifiable individual human action," Spengemann asks, "how did *Columbus* get chosen over other, seemingly sounder alternatives as the site for this elaborate construction?" His answer: "It is a mystery."[13]

This book argues otherwise. I believe that Columbus's appropriation of a discourse of empire that was circulating in the Spanish court during the late fifteenth century was the first brick in the edifice that became his historical persona as a figure of empire (see Chapter 1). The historiographers and writers who wrote about him, the subject of Chapter 2, perpetuated this characterization. They incorporated Columbus as the protagonist in the Western stock narrative about the conquering and dominance of one society, deemed "civilized," over others deemed less so. By the time revolutionaries in the New World were imagining their own politically independent societies, Columbus had long been a symbol of empire in the Western imagination. The appropriation of Columbus by nationalists in the Americas is of a piece with the manner in which they welded together ideas about empire and the nation-state. In the United States, the drive to empire in the sense of great territorial expansion was a very real force in the early republic. As Patricia Limerick has argued, at the heart of the national mission was an appetite for conquest and colonization.[14] There could be no more fitting symbol of that mission than Columbus, the paradigmatic conqueror. In Spanish America, where there was no such systematic project of territorial expansion, revolutionaries also appropriated the *translatio imperii* narrative. Instead of aspiring to empire in the sense of large expanses of territory, they aspired to the kind of spiritual quality and glory associated with the great empires of the past—in particular, Rome. Columbus became their national symbol, despite the fact that the historical Columbus was the first representative of the colonizing force that dominated the region for so long, largely because of his association with empire.

Let me be clear that I am not suggesting that the manner in which Columbus portrayed himself, or the manner in which subsequent historiographers portrayed him, set in stone all future interpretations. Columbus has been interpreted, for example, as the germ of rugged individualism and liberty in the United States. In much of the Americas, Columbus is praised as a St. Francis figure, a bringer of Christ to the Americas. My argument is that a great many representations of Columbus, over the centuries and in a variety of cultural contexts, tap into Columbus's status as a figure of empire. I also note that many of the contexts in which Columbus appears are about empire. When the story of empire in the Americas has sought a protagonist, it has often found one in Columbus.

The term "Columbia" and its many variants, such as "Colombia," "Colomba," and "Colombona," clearly illustrate the extent to which the figure of Columbus has circulated across political and linguistic borders. To trace the appearance in English of "Columbus," or "Columbia," with no regard for what came before in other languages, creates the illusion that writers in English lived in a bubble and did not read works in other languages. It also ignores the imperial implications that were present in the first formulation of the term, believed to have been suggested by Bartolomé de las Casas, who argued in the sixteenth century that the New World should be named after Columbus instead of Amerigo Vespucci. Las Casas suggested the names "Columba" or "Columbo," and he did so very much with the expanded empire of Christendom in mind.[15] Citing both the Bible and Aristotle, Las Casas argues that the admiral's name reveals that he was destined to expand the empire of Christ:

> So it was that he was named Christopher, that is to say *Christum ferens*, which is Latin for the bearer or carrier of Christ, and he signed his name in this way on a number of occasions and, indeed, he was the first to open up the routes across this Ocean

> Sea and to make the blessed name of our savior, Jesus Christ, known in these remote lands and kingdoms, of which hitherto they had known nothing; and it was he who was adjudged worthy above all others to bring these numberless peoples who had lain in oblivion throughout so many centuries to the knowledge and worship of Christ. His family name, Colón, means "new settler," a fitting title for a man whose industry and whose labors led to the discovery of numberless souls who, through the preaching of the gospel and administering of the blessed sacraments, have come and continue every day to come in triumph to the great city descending out of heaven. The name suited because he brought the first settlers from Spain . . . to found colonies, or new settlements of incomers, among and alongside the indigenous inhabitants of these immense territories and to build a new, mighty, vast, and most noble Christian church and earthly republic amongst them.[16]

Note here Las Casas's emphasis on the "remote lands and kingdoms" that Columbus brought within the fold of Christendom. As the first "new settler," Columbus led the effort "to build a new, mighty, vast" church "and earthy republic." That "republic," in Las Casas's eyes, was led by Queen Isabel and King Ferdinand, who had been designated the Catholic kings by Pope Alexander VI for their service against the infidel; it was without a doubt an empire.

Las Casas's Columbus was a complex figure. Santa Arias has noted how the author, in his *Historia de las Indias*, compares the admiral to the heroes of the Roman Empire.[17] Las Casas also blames Columbus for setting in motion the disastrous consequences of Spanish colonization, which Las Casas later condemns in his *Brevísima relación de la destrucción de las Indias*. Nevertheless, Las Casas ultimately represents Columbus as an imperial figure responsible for establishing Spain's empire of Christ in the New World, something that Las Casas never faltered in supporting despite his fame for challenging the Spanish methods of conquest. Columbus's status as hero of Spain's Christian empire, I would argue, is present in Las Casas's preferred name for the Americas: *Columba* (or *Columbo*).

Many of Las Casas's countrymen, eager to defend the legitimacy of the Spanish Empire, agreed that the name "America" denied Columbus the glory he deserved and was a potential threat to Spain's authority in the New World, which was increasingly under attack during the sixteenth and seventeenth centuries. As Olga Cock Hincapié notes, a variety of authors in Spain and Spanish America, especially in the seventeenth century, followed Las Casas's lead, suggesting that the New World be named after various forms of Columbus's name. For example, in his *Monarquía de España* (published in 1770 but completed in 1601), Pedro Salazar de Mendoza proposes the name "La Colonea"; fray Tomás Malvenda suggests the adoption of "Colonia," "Colonea," "Nuevo Orbe Colonio," or "Coloneo" (*De antichristo*, 1604); Francisco Mosquera de Barnuevo suggests the names "Colonia" or "Colónica" in his *Numantina* (1612); and Juan de Solórzano Pereira (*Disputationem de Indiarum Iure*, 1629; and *Política Indiana*, 1648) and fray Antonio de la Calancha (*Crónica moralizada*, 1638) opt for the names "Colonia" or "Columbania." These historians' preference for the name "Colonia," or some variant thereof, reveals the close association they maintained between Columbus and the exercise of Spanish imperial power abroad.[18]

The argument that the New World should be named after Columbus also appeared in English in the seventeenth century when Englishman Nicholas Fuller wrote in 1612 that America would be better named "Columbina."[19] In 1738, the name "Columbia" was used in a summary of Parliamentary debates, probably written by Samuel Johnson, to denote the British colonies in America. (He used "Lilliput" to denote England.) This summary was reprinted on the other side of the Atlantic three years later, on 30 November 1741, in the *Boston Evening Post*.[20] The belief that some form of Columbus's name should designate the American continent, originally expressed in Spanish by Las Casas in the sixteenth century, was repeated in the British colonies at the end of the seventeenth and in the eighteenth centuries.[21]

The circulation of the term "Columbia" and its variants across temporal and linguistic boundaries, along with the similar circulations of texts (and their translations) about Columbus and his activities in the New World, demand that we open our field of inquiry. Let us consider, for example, the many representations of Columbus at the 1893 World's Columbian Exposition or Simón Bolívar's purported conversation with the "God of Columbia" atop Mount Chimborazo. These should not be severed completely from previous representations of Columbus, including those he himself crafted. This is not to say that the meaning of every exemplar in which Columbus has been represented is predetermined. The change in Columbus's fortunes in the late twentieth century, as he went from hero to villain in the eyes of many in the Americas, attests to this not being the case. But the proliferation of negative portrayals of Columbus in the late twentieth century is best understood by viewing him according to the dominant interpretative tradition that starts with his own writings. As a figure of empire, Columbus has since the late twentieth century become a logical target of those resisting new forms of empire and increased internationalization of capital and power. Similarly, if we carefully consider the interpretive tradition about Columbus that began with his own writings, it becomes clear that it is not "ironic" that Columbus was both a symbol of an Old-World empire and a New-World republic.[22] Rather, it makes perfect sense.

~ I ~

Columbus's Appropriation of Imperial Discourse

Christopher Columbus has long been the subject of disagreement among historians. The protracted debate about his origins, whether he was Genoan, Spanish, Jewish, Catalán, etc., is merely the tip of the iceberg that seems to have had a special attraction for the public at large over the years. Beneath that popular debate, there are other disagreements among historians regarding Columbus's character. Some have emphasized his ardent religious faith, others his scientific curiosity and his skill as a mariner, and still others his drive to acquire wealth and power. In nearly all historical studies, the writings of Columbus are quoted to support the argument at hand. In this book, however, I would like to start by considering how Columbus represented himself in writing over time. He left behind a large corpus of writings in which he portrayed himself and his "enterprise" in a particular and consistent manner. The earliest historiographers who wrote about Columbus, including Peter Martyr, Bartolomé de las Casas, and Columbus's son Ferdinand, all consulted the corpus of Columbus's writings. The evidence suggests that the manner in which Columbus portrayed himself in writing influenced those who wrote about him and that they continued, and enhanced, the same characterization that he himself initiated.

Columbus appears to have been very savvy in regard to the politics of self-fashioning. Given his knowledge of court practice and procedure, he was likely aware that after 17 April 1492, when the king and queen signed the *Capitulaciones de Santa Fe*, the document that officially sanctioned his enterprise, whatever he wrote to the Crown would be preserved in royal archives. In addition, because he was politically astute he probably realized that the manner in which he represented himself would set the tone for future representations written by others. The extant documents in the historical record believed to have been written by Columbus suggest that he employed a very conscious strategy of self-promotion, mutating his persona and the manner in which he portrayed his enterprise in response to the exigencies of the moment. While Columbus modified his rhetorical strategy according to the occasion, we observe at least one constant in his self-representations: he always appears as a loyal servant of Ferdinand and Isabel and their imperial agenda. From 1492 to the end of his career, Columbus portrayed himself and his enterprise as fundamental to Spain's drive to universal Christian empire.

The Discourse of Empire in Late Fifteenth-Century Spain

Before discussing how empire was understood during this period in Spain, it should be noted that no official document issued during the reign of Ferdinand and Isabel refers to their territorial possessions in Europe and the New World as an "empire." Rather, the preferred term was the "Spanish Monarchy," which claimed dominion over a number of distinct "kingdoms" that together comprised the composite monarchy commonly known as "las Españas." Thus Ferdinand and Isabel were officially the "King and Queen of Castile, León, Aragon, Sicily, Granada, Toledo, Valencia [etc.]." Their kingdoms in the New World, incidentally, fell under the authority of the Crown of Castile. Notwithstanding the absence of the term "empire" in official language, the notion of empire was very much present in the Spanish imagination at the end of the fifteenth century. For example, a sonnet written by a courtier in January 1492, before Columbus left on his first voyage westward, proposed that the "I" in "Isabel" stood for "imperio," (empire).[1] We also find evidence of the importance of empire in the Spanish worldview commonly repeated in contemporary comparisons of Spain to the Roman Empire.

The Spanish imperial tradition drew its inspiration from both the Bible and imperial Rome, and it was inexorably linked with Spain's unique crusading tradition.[2] It is in the context of the crusading tradition in Spain, in which the Reconquista was firmly rooted, that Columbus interpreted his enterprise as a contribution to the empire of Ferdinand and Isabel. When European princes launched the Crusades to conquer Jerusalem in the eleventh century, the goal of regaining the Iberian Peninsula from the Muslims, who had occupied it since the eighth century, assumed special meaning. Isidore of Seville (c. 560–636) had already asserted in his *Historia de regibus Gothorum, Wandalorum, et Suevorum*, a book Isabel possessed, that Spaniards were an elect people inhabiting a holy land. This sentiment was pervasive when the Crusades were launched; regaining Spain was viewed as analogous to regaining the heart of Christendom. The kings who led the Iberian reconquest facilitated the conflation of Spain and Jerusalem, and Spain and Christendom itself. After Jerusalem was taken by Muslims in 638, European Christian kings, including those of Castile, became obsessed to varying degrees with its recapture.

The importance of Jerusalem in Spain and its connection to the notion of universal empire within the rhetoric of the reconquest bears repeating.[3] As Liss notes, "Jerusalem, Christendom's core, [was] often coupled in Castilian prophecies and sermons with Spain's future greatness, even with achievement of world empire. Jerusalem, like Spain having once been destroyed, served as its analogue, the lodestar of Castilian chivalric ideals and messianic hope, the ultimate goal of reconquest. Its restoration to Christian rule was an obligation laid by God upon Castile's monarch."[4] In Ferdinand and Isabel's day, the final goal of the reconquest was commonly viewed as regaining Jerusalem. As long as the heart of Christendom was in the hands of the infidel, many believed the Christian Empire would not be complete.

Although the concept of a universal Christian empire was just one of several understandings of empire at the end of the fifteenth century,[5] it was of crucial importance in the dominant political discourse during the reign of Ferdinand and Isabel. The reconquest had been described for centuries in terms of Christendom's fight against the heathen for universal rule. Ferdinand and Isabel's final victory over the Moors in Granada in 1492 quickly became one of the seminal symbolic events of their reign; chroniclers declared that they were destined to expand their territory and conquer the infidel outside the peninsula. Many expressed the desire to conquer Africa. Before her death in 1504, Queen Isabel, in fact, stated in her will her desire that the Africa crusade be pursued. Pope Alexander VI had approved of an African crusade in 1494, but no action was taken for a decade, despite the prophecies and stories about it that had been circulating at court even before Granada was seized.[6]

The idea of universal rule is complicit with both biblical and Roman traditions. Alfonso X (1221–84) contended that Spain was heir to the Roman Empire and would rule over the last world empire described in the book of Daniel. In doing so, Alfonso believed, Spain would fulfill Virgil's prophecy that Rome was destined to rule the world.[7] Alfonso based his claim to empire on the widespread belief in the *translatio imperii* (literally, the transfer of empire), according to which empires move throughout history from east to west. He asserted that the imperial lineage started with Jupiter, passed through Aeneas, Alexander the Great, and the Roman Caesars to the Holy Roman Emperors, Frederick I Barbarossa, and Frederick II, and then ended with himself. Spanish humanist Antonio de Nebrija also expressed the belief in *translatio imperii*, claiming in 1492 that Spain was heir to an empire that had successively moved westward. In the Spanish context, added to this belief in the *translatio imperii* was a series of popular prophecies attributed to Merlin and the sibyls, which foretold of a final emperor who would defeat the Muslims, recapture Jerusalem, and claim world dominion.[8]

Queen Isabel possessed a compilation of these prophecies, in addition to Alfonso X's histories. She promoted the image of herself and Ferdinand as the heirs who would fulfill Spain's sacred destiny. Her doing so was not surprising; her predecessors were proclaimed to have had this role as well. Liss stresses the common belief at the end of the fifteenth century in Spain's future universal rule: "Against this extended background, the fall of Granada in 1492, along with the departure of the Jews and imperial expansion enabled by Columbus, could not but appear to confirm Spain as final world empire and ratify the messianic role of its rulers."[9]

Liss surmises in a footnote that an Italian like Columbus "could be so attuned to providentialist aspects of Isabeline ideology and their scriptural associations" because he would have been exposed to a "common Western stockpile" of stories regarding the imperial tradition.[10] There was no doubt a common bank of ideas, beliefs, and legends about empire, and Columbus clearly tapped into this discourse. However, as I argue at the end of this chapter, although Columbus was particularly bold in interpreting his enterprise according to the Spanish imperial tradition, he does not appear to have been knowledgeable about the *translatio imperii* tradition. Indeed, Columbus quotes Seneca's *Medea*, a text whose imperial meanings were often exploited after Columbus's death to promote imperial agendas, but he ignores the text's allusions to empire. His appropriation of the imperial tradition largely honed in on its medieval aspects as they played out on the Spanish stage. This involved a set of beliefs tied conceptually to religion and imperial Rome as read through Alfonso X and patristic thinkers like Augustine and Isidore of Seville. I do not suggest that Columbus read their works—that is unlikely—but I believe the manner in which he wrote about his enterprise confirms that he was well versed in a Spanish imperial discourse in which the notion of a universal Christian empire loomed large. To be sure, Columbus was no humanist, and there is no evidence to suggest that he saw his enterprise as it related to the *translatio imperii* in the manner that, for example, the Milanese humanist Peter Martyr did, as I discuss in Chapter 2.

Columbus's Appropriation of Spanish Imperial Discourse

During the approximately seven years Columbus spent in Spain lobbying the Court to support his voyage, he appears to have listened attentively to popular narratives about Ferdinand and Isabel's destiny as rulers who would, after their predicted victory over the Moors in the reconquest, lead a final crusade against Islam, win the Holy Land for Christendom, and establish a universal monarchy. Throughout his career at the Spanish court, starting with his earliest writings, Columbus consistently portrayed his enterprise as an integral part of this narrative, not as a mere commercial venture but as an extension of the victory at Granada and as a further step on the road to achieving universal Christian empire.

Columbus was likely the first to interpret his enterprise as an extension of the reconquest, although it should be noted that this interpretation quickly became common. In fact, it was sanctioned soon after Columbus's return from the first voyage by no less than Pope Alexander VI whose bull *Inter caetera* (3 May 1493) granted Ferdinand and Isabel ecclesiastical jurisdiction over the newly discovered Indies.[11] *Inter caetera* frames Columbus's "discovery" as an extension of the Spanish reconquest. It begins by reviewing the history of Ferdinand and Isabel's crusade against the infidel. Judging the king and queen to be earnest in their previous battles against the barbarians and declaring them victorious in their seizure of Granada, the bull grants them the authority to carry Christ beyond the bounds of the peninsula to the Indies. In other words, the reconquest of the peninsula and the conquest of the Indies are interpreted in this papal document as part of the same project, the former serving as the proving ground for the latter. Perhaps the most well-known formulation of this interpretation was penned in the early 1540s by historian Francisco López de Gómara: "Conquests of the Indians began when conquests of the Moors had ended, so that Spaniards might always be at war with infidels."[12]

Modern scholars have continued to emphasize the connection between the reconquest and the conquest of the Indies—and the sanctioning of Columbus's voyage in particular. The venerable John Elliott, for example, writes: "The close coincidence between the fall of Granada and the authorization of Columbus's expedition would suggest that the latter was at once a thank-offering and an act of renewed dedication by Castile to the still unfinished task of war against the infidel."[13] As James Muldoon and Luis Weckmann have argued, there are more continuities between the medieval and early modern periods than are generally recognized.[14] Spain's conquest of the Americas is most accurately understood in relation to, not separate from, its recent (and not so recent) historical experience. The invasion of the New World was, in Elliott's words, a "natural culmination of a dynamic and expansionist period in Castilian history which had begun long before."[15]

We would do well, however, to remember that in the first moments of the Columbian project—that is, before Columbus set sail in August 1492—there was no explicit or natural connection between it and the reconquest. If we assume that this connection existed since the very beginning of the venture, we risk missing the fact that it was Columbus who first rhetorically hitched his enterprise to the reconquest narrative. While it might have been an obvious association to make, the sovereigns clearly had not made it in 1492. That Columbus managed so skillfully to craft this association when, as Elliott observes, he "himself did not belong to the tradition of the *Reconquista*,"[16] points to his savvy as an observer of the Spanish political and rhetorical landscape. That he did so by emphasizing the contributions of his enterprise to the medieval notion of universal Christian empire illustrates Columbus's medieval mindset. It was left to others, as I shall argue, to reinterpret Columbus's connection to empire in a manner that revealed the sensibilities of the early modern era.

The Crown did not at first incorporate the Columbian enterprise within its overall strategy and political discourse about universal Christian empire. In fact, it likely rejected Columbus's interpretation, which did incorporate the enterprise in this manner when he first suggested it.[17] According to the *Capitulaciones* signed by the king and queen in April 1492, Columbus's enterprise was strictly a commercial venture that had nothing to do with either religious matters or territorial expansion.[18] Although the formulaic introductory sentence of the *Capitulaciones* mentions "the help of God," there is no further mention of God or religious matters in the text that follows. Zamora is puzzled by this omission in light of the religious charge of the dominant political discourse generated by the Crown: "Such silence," she writes, "is quite perplexing given that these were the official documents by which the Reyes Católicos (Catholic Monarchs) authorized an embassy to foreign lands. For according to medieval kingship theory, Christian kings were expected to be missionaries and crusaders on behalf of the Church, and this was precisely how Ferdinand and Isabella conceived and justified their actions in the reconquest of the Iberian Peninsula from the Moors."[19]

Based on the prediscovery documents generated by the Crown, it would appear that the sovereigns viewed Columbus's venture as separate from their greater imperial strategy. Although the economic and the religious were never separate spheres—indeed, the quest for profit was justified by religious arguments—Castile, Aragon, and Portugal had all been focusing on trade-building ventures before 1492.[20] This is not to say that there was a lack of "missionary purpose" in Ferdinand and Isabel's sanctioning of maritime expansion,[21] yet early on in the process of the conquest and colonization of the Indies, the desire to evangelize was not backed up in practice. The material interests of both Spain and Portugal appear to have outweighed their desire to promote the spiritual.[22] As J. R. S. Phillips concludes, Spanish "missionary efforts lacked organization and vigor, and their expansion was essentially opportunistic; they looked for whatever might be found that would be profitable."[23]

In April 1492, when the sovereigns agreed to support Columbus, no one could have predicted the scope of Columbus's discoveries or their importance in Ferdinand and Isabel's reign. If this had been possible, the *Capitulaciones* surely would have been a different document. But let us not permit our reading of the past to be influenced by our knowledge of the outcome. The Crown had no reason to consider Columbus's proposed voyage as integral to its overall mission. While it would be a mistake to conclude that the Crown considered Columbus's project to be unimportant in April 1492, we can conclude that it was not integral to royal strategy or ideology, as had been the campaign to conquer Granada.

It was Columbus who first portrayed his enterprise as something greater than a commercial venture, and it was Columbus who first used the language of the reconquest, a language which drew from the Spanish discourse of universal Christian empire, to describe his venture. We see this rhetorical strategy at work in the document that has long served as the prologue to the *Diario*. Here, Columbus virtually ignores the commercial purpose of his commission as laid out by the *Capitulaciones* and instead interprets it as a logical continuation of the reconquest. The prologue was likely written with considerable care, as Columbus surely would have foreseen that it would be stored in royal archives. The notion of Columbus's deliberateness is important because the most obvious rhetorical strategy of the prologue involves an erroneous chronology that is almost surely no mistake, given that its rhetorical effect is to link Columbus's enterprise with the recent victory over the Moors at Granada and the expulsion of the Jews. Columbus repeats several times the year 1492, asserting in one instance that the sovereigns decided to commission Columbus "in this present year 1492, after your Highnesses concluded the war with the Moors" and "after having expelled all the Jews from your kingdoms and possessions."[24] According to the prologue, the victory over the Moors, the expulsion of the Jews, and the decision to send Columbus to the Indies all occurred in Granada in January 1492. In reality, Granada fell in January, the expulsion decree was signed in March before the sovereigns entered Granada, and the *Capitulaciones* were signed in April—not in Granada but in Santa Fe. Columbus's inaccurate version of these events incorporates his enterprise into the narrative of the reconquest that culminated in the final victory over the Moors and the expulsion of the Jews—a victory that was commonly interpreted as a necessary step in the progression of Ferdinand and Isabel's reign to universal, Christian dominion. As Milhou concludes, "The seizure of Granada, the expulsion of the Jews, and the political and missionary expedition to Cathay are presented in the prologue on the same plane as events of equal importance that all contribute to the extension and triumph of Christendom."[25]

An additional detail of the prologue that links Columbus's project to the evangelical mission of the Catholic kings is its description of their reasons for supporting Columbus. While the first royal motive provided in the prologue conforms in spirit to the mercantile expectations of the *Capitulaciones* ("to see those princes and peoples and lands and their attitudes and everything else about them"), the second motive ("to take stock of how one could go about converting them to our holy faith") adds an element absent in the *Capitulaciones:* evangelization.[26] According to the prologue, the sovereigns' desire to commission Columbus is allegedly tied to their status as "Catholic Christians and princes who love the holy Christian faith and spread it, being enemies of the sect of Mohammed and of all idolatries and heresies."[27]

The monarchs decided to support Columbus, the prologue states, after he informed them that the Gran Can of the Indies and his ancestors "many times . . . had sent to Rome for men learned in our holy faith who might instruct them in it (yet the Holy Father never provided them, letting so many people go to perdition through falling into idolatries and accepting sects which carry them to ruin)."[28] Claiming that Ferdinand and Isabel respond to those seeking instruction in the faith and that the pope does not do so, Columbus brazenly insinuates that the Spanish sovereigns are more fit shepherds of Christendom than the pope himself.

The *Diario*, the original log[29] of Columbus's first voyage, also describes the Columbian enterprise with the language of Spain's religiously charged discourse of empire.[30] A key passage from the *Diario* that depicts the voyage as more than a mere commercial venture is found in the entry dated 26 December 1492. In all of the writings attributed to Columbus, this passage probably contains the earliest mention of the reconquest of Jerusalem:

> The Admiral again writes that he hopes to God that when he returns from Castile, as he intend, he should find a barrel of gold obtained in trade by those he will leave there and that they should have found the gold mine and the spices in sufficient quantity that within three years the Sovereigns could plan and carry out the conquest of the Holy Sepulcher, for, he says, "I swore to Your Highnesses that all profits from this enterprise of mine should be spent for the reconquest of Jerusalem, and Your Highnesses smiled and said it pleased You and that You had already harbored that desire."[31]

Jerusalem in this passage of the *Diario* is a crucial symbol in the Spanish narrative of universal Christian empire. Given the meaning of Jerusalem in the rhetoric of contemporary Spain, the assertion in the *Diario* (whether it is true or not) that Columbus had already urged the sovereigns to use the profits of his voyage to finance a final crusade serves to incorporate it into the already circulating discourse about Spain's final crusade to Jerusalem.

Columbus also interpreted his enterprise in religious terms and as part of the royal imperial mission in his 4 March 1493 letter to Ferdinand and Isabel. The imperial frame in this letter is starkly absent in another letter that is often believed to be written by Columbus but is more likely a royally sanctioned revision of Columbus's March 4 letter. According to Demetrio Ramos Pérez and Margarita Zamora, this second letter, addressed to Luis de Santángel and Gabriel Sánchez, was likely composed for purposes of propaganda.[32]

If the March 4 letter is Columbus's "original" letter and the Santángel/Sánchez letter is a royally sanctioned revision of that original, a comparison of the two letters suggests that the court was slow to agree with Columbus's interpretation—what we might call his "imperial interpretation"—, even rejecting it immediately after the discovery and before the court had devised a comprehensive public relations strategy. If we follow Zamora's exhortation to consider as dialogic the documents generated by Columbus and the Crown, the Santángel/Sánchez revision of Columbus's March 4 letter can be understood as a royal response to Columbus that rejected his interpretation of the project.[33]

The majority of the March 4 letter addresses the mercantile interests of the Crown, as specified in the *Capitulaciones*, by reporting on the fertility of the land and its general features, the mild nature of the natives, the plethora of good harbors, and how best to navigate the area. Several passages in the March 4 letter, however, construe the Columbian enterprise in terms of its contribution to the preexisting royal imperial agenda. The first sentence of the letter, for example, is similar to the prologue of the *Diario* in that it represents Columbus's voyage as an extension of the reconquest: "That eternal God who has given Your Highnesses so many victories now gave you the greatest one that to this day He has ever given any prince."[34] The reference to "so many victories" already granted by God alludes to the reconquest, a series of military victories that culminated in the seizure of Granada and the subsequent imposition of religious orthodoxy, both of which were interpreted as part of the narrative of consolidation of Christian empire. Columbus refers to his own voyage of discovery as "the greatest [victory]," of even greater importance than the victory at Granada. Columbus's position as the protagonist in this transoceanic expansion of the reconquest is then emphasized by the fact that the next sentence begins with the first person pronoun "I" and that the same "I" is repeated twice more within that sentence. ("*I come* from the Indies with the armada Your Highnesses gave me, to which [place] *I traveled* in thirty-three days after *I departed* from your kingdoms."[35])

Not only does the corresponding sentence in the Santángel/Sánchez version de-emphasize the presence of Columbus (while it contains several verbs conjugated in the first person, it contains only one first-person subject pronoun, "yo," in the original Spanish), it also omits the allusion in the March 4 letter to the reconquest, thus removing Columbus's innovative "empire frame." With a businesslike tone that characterizes the whole of the Santángel/Sánchez letter, the first line reads: "My Lord, since I know you will take delight in the great victory Our Lord granted me on my voyage, I am writing you this letter, from which you will learn how in thirty-three days I went from the Canary Islands to the Indies."[36] While the discovery here is said to be a "great victory" given to Columbus by God, the deletion of the March 4 letter's reference to the reconquest erases the link established in the original version between this "victory" made possible by Columbus and the imperial agenda of the Catholic kings.

This is not the only instance when an allusion to the expansion of Ferdinand and Isabel's Christian Empire in the March 4 letter is omitted in the royally sanctioned Santángel/Sánchez version. The March 4 letter contains the following passage (unfortunately damaged in the original document) about evangelization that is absent from the Santángel/Sánchez letter: "But Our Lord, who is the light and strength of all those who seek to do good and makes them victorious in deeds that seem impossible, wished to ordain that I should find and was to find gold and mines and spicery and innumerable peoples . . . numbers disposed to become Christians and others so that Christians . . ."[37] Despite the lacunae in the original document, it is certain that the subject at hand is the conversion of the natives. This is the first mention of evangelization perhaps anywhere in Columbus's writings. The description of the natives as "disposed to become Christians" toward the end of a phrase that begins by listing the specific goods that God wished Columbus to find in the Indies illustrates the manner in which the March 4 text discursively adds the religious interpretation to the commercial interpretation of the voyage that had been laid out by the Crown in the *Capitulaciones*. Although the anonymous editor of the Santángel/Sánchez letter included a slightly modified version of the beginning of the sentence ("the eternal God Our Lord, who gives to all who follow His ways victory in seemingly impossible undertakings"[38]), this version omits the description found in the "original" text of the natives as inclined to convert. The subject of evangelization thus appears of greater significance in the original March 4 version. The omission of the reference to evangelization in the royally sanctioned Santángel/Sánchez version suggests that the royal editor, and perhaps the court itself, was not yet interpreting the Columbian project as part of the same royal agenda that had underwritten the reconquest.

Also deleted from the letter to Santángel/Sánchez is the passage in the March 4 letter that most stridently incorporates the Columbian enterprise within the narrative of universal Christian empire. Here Columbus recommends using the proceeds of his discoveries to finance a crusade in order to wrest Jerusalem from Islamic control:

I conclude here: that through the divine grace of He who is the origin of all good and virtuous things, who favors and gives victory to all those who walk in His path, that in seven years from today I will be able to pay Your Highnesses for five thousand cavalry and fifty thousand foot soldiers for the war and conquest of Jerusalem, for which purpose this enterprise was undertaken. And in another five years another five thousand cavalry and fifty thousand foot soldiers, which will total ten thousand cavalry and one hundred thousand foot soldiers; and all of this with very little investment now on Your Highnesses' part in this beginning of the taking of the Indies and all that they contain, as I will tell Your Highnesses in person later. And I have reason for this [claim] and do not speak uncertainly, and one should not delay in it, as was the case with the execution of this enterprise, may God forgive whoever has been the cause of it.[39]

In this passage Columbus reinvents his enterprise as integral to Ferdinand and Isabel's divinely sanctioned plan to regain the symbolic center of Christendom and establish an *imperium sacrum*. He even claims, contrary to the terms of the prediscovery documents generated by the Crown and despite a lack of evidence elsewhere in his own writings, that such a religious crusade was the original rationale for his voyage.[40] Columbus later repeats this claim in his 1502 letter to Pope Alexander VI.[41] In both of these instances, as well as in the prologue to the *Diario*, Columbus revises history and interprets his discoveries as part of the Catholic kings' predestined drive to universal empire. In this way, Columbus granted his discoveries more significance than they had previously been granted by the Crown.

The reason the royal editor of the Santángel/Sánchez version deleted this passage is a matter of speculation. Obviously the court would not have appreciated Columbus's bold admonition that it should not dawdle with regard to the crusade to Jerusalem, as it had done with respect to his own voyage. Yet why would the Santángel/Sánchez version not include Columbus's reference to the Jerusalem crusade when this would have granted the discovery more gravitas given the importance of Jerusalem in the current ideology of reconquest and empire? Zamora conjectures that "the Crown may have felt the commitment to evangelization proclaimed in the letter was sufficient to ensure that the church would be well-disposed toward the enterprise without the additional, and much more costly, commitment to a campaign for the Holy Land."[42] It is true that the sovereigns had not yet petitioned the pope for a bull that would grant them dominion in the Indies. Perhaps they were hesitant to publicize Columbus's voyage in this light, especially given that the right to the territories Columbus found had already been disputed by Portuguese King João II, who was preparing a fleet to find the Indies.[43] Yet if one of the major purposes of the widespread publication of the Santángel/Sánchez letter was to pave the way for smooth negotiations with the pope, as Ramos Pérez argues, this omission is puzzling.[44] In effect, the royal editor's deletion of the March 4 letter's reference to Jerusalem served as a royal rejection of Columbus's attempts to interpret his enterprise within the prevailing rhetoric of reconquest and imperial expansion by emphasizing its religious consequences.

Another relevant passage that appears in the March 4 letter to Ferdinand and Isabel but not in the Santángel/Sánchez version portrays the discoveries as a feat to be celebrated by "all of Christianity." Its subtext emphasizes Columbus's contributions to the aggrandizement of Christian empire:

> Most powerful sovereigns: all of Christendom should hold great celebrations, and especially God's Church, for the finding of such a multitude of such friendly peoples, which with very little effort will be converted to our Holy Faith, and so many lands filled with so many goods very necessary to us in which all Christians will have comfort and profits, all of which was unknown nor did anyone speak of it except in fables. Great rejoicing and

celebrations in the churches [damaged] . . . Your Highnesses should order that [many] praises should be given to the Holy Trinity [damaged] your kingdoms and domains, because of the great love [the Holy Trinity?] has shown you, more than to any other prince.[45]

In previous passages of the March 4 text the religious interpretation is tacked on to the commercial. In these instances Columbus first complies in writing with the responsibilities assigned to him by the *Capitulaciones*, and only after that does he discuss religious matters that grant his enterprise greater significance. In the passage cited above, however, the religious interpretation appears first: Christendom should celebrate first because Columbus found so many pagans to convert and only secondly because he also found desirable material goods.

The editor of the Santángel/Sánchez version maintained this order of the religious first and then the commercial second in the following key passage near the end of that letter:

> In this way, then, Our Redeemer granted to our most illustrious King and Queen and to their famous realms this victory in a matter of such great importance, for which all Christendom should rejoice and celebrate and give solemn thanks to our Holy Trinity with many solemn prayers for the great exaltation that will ensue from the addition of so many people to our holy faith and, besides, for the temporal goods, as not only Spain but all Christians will find in it respite and profit.[46]

This passage declares the significance of Columbus's enterprise with regard to Christian empire. The exaltation, literally the expansion (enxalçamiento), of Christendom is granted more importance than the temporal benefits of the discovery by the phrase "and, besides," in that Christendom "should rejoice and celebrate and give solemn thanks" first because so many pagans will turn to Christ, and *only thereafter* (y después) because of the "temporal goods" that will result from the discoveries. This may be the first instance in which the Crown can be said to have leaned toward interpreting Columbus's voyage according to the ideology of Christian empire that had propelled the reconquest and motivated contemporary chroniclers to predict that Ferdinand and Isabel would continue their Christian conquests abroad after the fall of Granada.

It was not until the Crown's "instructions" to Columbus dated 29 May 1493 that the sovereigns appear to adopt an interpretation of the Columbian enterprise similar to that which had been proposed in Columbus's March 4 letter, the prologue to the *Diario*, and the *Diario* itself. Their first "instruction" in the May 29 document addressed to Columbus suggests that the king and queen now saw his venture as part of their greater imperial project:

> Firstly, it hath pleased God, Our Lord, in His abundant mercy to reveal the said Islands and Mainland to the King and Queen, our Lords, by the diligence of the said Don Christopher Columbus, their Admiral, Viceroy and Governor thereof, who hath reported it to Their Highnesses that he know the people he found residing therein to be very ripe to be converted to our Holy Catholic Faith, since they have neither dogma nor doctrine; wherefore it hath pleased and greatly pleaseth Their Highnesses (since in all matters it is meet that their principal concern be for the service of God, Our Lord, and the enhancement of our Holy Catholic Faith); wherefore, desiring the augmentation and increase of our Holy Catholic Faith, Their Highnesses charge and direct the said Admiral, Viceroy and Governor that by all ways and means he strive and endeavor to win over the inhabitants of the said Islands and Mainland to be converted to our Holy Catholic Faith.[47]

According to this first royal "instruction" dictated to Columbus, the intention of the king and queen "in all matters," that is with regard to the entire enterprise, is to promote "the service of God, Our Lord, and the enhancement (*ensalzamiento*) of our Holy

Catholic Faith." That this differs significantly from the tenor and content of the *Capitulaciones* is surely no coincidence. Alexander VI had just issued the 4 May bull charging the Catholic kings with the responsibility of converting the inhabitants of these new lands. Morison notes that the *Inter caetera* was sent from Rome "to Spain on May 17, and doubtless arrived before the end of the month."[48] It is in this context that the sovereigns, in these instructions dated 29 May, attribute their pleasure first and foremost to the fact that the inhabitants of the discovered lands are disposed to convert. And because the sovereigns wish for the "augmentation and increase of Our Holy Catholic Faith," they authorize Columbus in this document to take whatever measures necessary to convert the foreign peoples he encounters. This first of eighteen instructions establishes evangelization as the highest priority of the Crown with regard to Columbus's project. It is worth noting, however, that only five clerics (out of a total of approximately twelve hundred people) accompanied Columbus on the second voyage to the Indies, a number that suggests that the sovereigns did not yet fully back up with concrete action their royal rhetoric about the high priority they now granted to evangelization.

Not only was Columbus the first to interpret his enterprise in religious terms, he was also keen to point out the vastness of the territory he had discovered.[49] Territorial expansion, of course, was an essential component of the royal agenda during the reconquest and a requirement for achieving universal Christian empire. While others were encouraging the sovereigns to continue the reconquest by invading Africa or the Levant, Columbus was merely redirecting westward (or, according to Nicolás Wey Gómez, southward[50]) the arrow on the map that pointed to the territory to be incorporated into the empire. In a 1495 letter written to the sovereigns, Columbus suggests that he has discovered the last of the ecumene that had been previously unknown to Europe. Thus he names the easternmost point of Cuba (which he called Juana), Alpha and Omega, the beginning and the end.

Between this point and the western-most point of Spain, he states, "is contained all the peoples of the world,"[51] a bold claim if one is thinking in terms of universal dominion. Already in a letter dated January 1494, Columbus had promised the king and queen continual territorial expansion: "every year," he states, "we shall be able to significantly enlarge the map, because new discoveries will continue to take place."[52] In this same letter, he also stresses the great size of the territory he has discovered, as in his letter to the sovereigns regarding the third voyage, where he writes, "I believe that this land that Your Highnesses have caused to be discovered is huge and that there are many more to the south."[53] Several passages in his writings dating from the third voyage and after declare that he has made possible unprecedented territorial expansion, the kind never seen by any of the previous Spanish princes, none of whom, he is sure to point out, had ever gained territory outside the peninsula.[54] In 1501, Columbus assures Queen Isabel, "I am inclined with all of my senses to give you rest and happiness and to increase your realms."[55]

In several instances Columbus compares the territory he won for Castile to that of the Greek and Roman Empires, the paradigmatic empires with which Columbus conceptually competes.[56] Attempting to transcend the classical empires of the past, he defends his venture to the king and queen and against his critics, writing: "I call on he who has read the histories of the Greeks and Romans to testify if with so little effort they enlarged so much their territory as now Your Highnesses have enlarged the territory of Spain with the Indies."[57] In another instance, Columbus insinuates that because of his efforts, the Catholic kings are achieving what the Romans and the Greeks only strived to do: "I had read that the lords of Castile had never gained lands outside Castile itself, and that this was another world, the one for which the Romans, Alexander and the Greeks strove to gain."[58] It is in accordance with this line of thinking that Columbus characterizes his journals that he kept about his voyages as being "in the form and style of Caesar's Commentaries."[59] On the surface, this comparison refers to the straightforward, unembellished literary style for which Augustus's work was known. On a deeper level, however, the comparison suggests that Columbus was expanding the empire of Castile just as Julius Caesar had done for Rome.

When Columbus came under increased scrutiny for his maladministration of Spanish settlements in the Indies, he did not waiver in his interpretation of his enterprise in terms of its contribution to the attainment of universal Christian empire. The tenor of his rhetoric, however, intensified as he began to appropriate the prophetic and then the apocalyptic tradition.[60] Before the third voyage (1498–1500), as I have shown, Columbus described his project as an extension of the imperial mission of the Catholic kings who had underwritten the reconquest. He placed his conquests in the Indies on the same ideological level as the conquest of Granada. As the challenge to his privileges and status grew, he escalated the rhetoric he used to describe his venture by resorting to the prophetic tradition, which was well known in Columbus's day and had been used by many to interpret the reconquest. Based on the common belief that biblical prophecies would necessarily be fulfilled before the end of time, Columbus began in his 1498 relation to the king and queen about his third voyage to argue that his discoveries played a crucial role in the unfolding of God's divine plan: they were the fulfillment of biblical prophecies regarding the conversion to Christianity of all the peoples of the earth, who would also be incorporated into the Christian Empire.

It is in the *Book of Prophecies*—compiled after Columbus had been arrested on Hispaniola in October 1500 and forcibly returned to Spain in chains—where this strategy of representation reaches an extreme. The original title provided by Gaspar Gorricio, the Carthusian monk who helped draft the document, differs from the collection's current title (provided by Columbus's son Ferdinand) and clearly points to the argument at the heart of the document—Columbus's discoveries had been prophesied and are, therefore, part of God's divine plan: "Book or collection of *auctoritates* (authoritative writings), sayings, opinions, and prophecies concerning the need to recover the Holy City and Mount Zion, and the finding and conversion of the islands of the Indies and of all people and nations."[61] As Gorricio's title suggests, the *Book of Prophecies* is a reprisal of many of the themes that are present in Columbus's earlier writings, including the final crusade to conquer Jerusalem. According to one of the prophecies cited in the book, "someone from Spain would recover the wealth of Zion."[62] That Columbus felt this prophecy was important for his self-representation is clear in his repetition of it not only in his 1503 letter to the sovereigns written from Jamaica, but also at the end of his letter that appears to have been meant to introduce them to the *Book of Prophecies*, where he reminds them that "the Calabrian abbot Joachim said that whoever was to rebuild the temple on Mount Zion would come from Spain."[63]

Columbus's self-portrayals as Christ-bearer, promoted by his signing letters "Xρo ferens" (Christ-bearer) after he returned to Spain from his third voyage, overlapped toward the end of his career with his self-portrayals as a martyr for the empire of Christendom. With increasing clarity, he represented himself as a victim of his high ideals and the ingratitude of Spaniards.[64] Only God, in Columbus's ultimate rendering, understands the cost Columbus paid to give an overseas empire to the Crown of Castile. It is in this sense that Columbus cast himself as a martyr. I return to this later, as this self-fashioning was the basis of the so-called "Columbian legend," which was taken up by Spanish American revolutionaries who eventually advocated independence from Spain. For now, we note that Columbus's long list of complaints began with his unfair treatment in the Spanish court by those who doubted his plan. For example, in what Consuelo Varela labels a "fragment of a piece of writing in the Log Book,"[65] apparently written after his discovery, Columbus first mentions his "toils and perils" and then says, "May it please God that the detractors of my honour may be abased, who with so much dishonesty and malice have made a mockery of me and defamed my enterprise without knowing either my statements or what advantages and increase of dominion would accrue to their Majesties."[66] This kind of complaint, which appears in many of Columbus's subsequent writings, emphasizes both Columbus's loyalty to the Crown, something that had always been subject to question by many Spaniards because he was a foreigner, as well as his dedication to expanding the Crown's empire.

He complains with increasingly frequency about the character of the Spanish colonists, whom he views as greedy and immoral and who do not, as he does, sincerely support the imperial project of the Catholic kings (i.e., the expansion of Christendom).[67] As early as January 1494, in the report to the king and queen that he sent back to Spain with Antonio Torres, Columbus requested that Torres, on his behalf, ask them to more carefully select colonists: "Tell Their Highnesses, entreating them as humbly as possible on my account, to have the goodness to consider . . . that for the peace and tranquility and harmony of the people here they appoint in their service people who get along with one another and who value more the reason for which they were sent than their own personal interests."[68] Columbus draws a stark contrast between these disloyal settlers and himself, beginning this report by emphasizing his own loyalty to the Crown. Here, he calls Ferdinand and Isabel "my natural sovereigns, in whose service I wish to end my days."[69] In contrast, he portrays the Spaniards who come to the Indies as disloyal. For example, in his letter to Doña Juana de la Torre, he describes them as a "dissolute people, who have no fear of God or of their king and queen, and who are full of folly and malice."[70] The "maintenance of justice and the extension of the [dominions] of [Your] Highnesses," he complains, "up to now has brought me to the depth."[71] He also claims in this letter that the Spaniards in Spain, including those at court, misunderstand him. "If I had violently seized the Indies or the land made holy because in it there is today the fame of the altar of St. Peter, and had given them to the Moors, they could not have shown greater enmity towards me in Spain. Who would believe such a thing of a land where there has always been so great nobility?"[72] Columbus argues that instead of seeing him as having conquered a foreign people and established an empire in the tradition of the great imperial conquerors of Rome, Spaniards see him as a small-time governor of a foreign province.[73] In what Varela thinks is likely a draft of a letter to the members of the Council of Castile, Columbus's thoughts on this point are at their sharpest:

> I have lost (in these labours) my youth and the part of these things which belongs to me, and likewise the honours; but it should not be [so] outside of Castile where my deeds shall be judged, and I shall be judged, as a Captain who went to conquer from Spain to the Indies and not as a governor of a city or of a people already under government, but to place under the sovereignty of Their Majesties a people savage, warlike and who live among the hills and mountains.[74]

We note the contrast Columbus draws between how he is perceived in Spain and how he will be perceived outside of Spain. Many American appropriations of Columbus in the late eighteenth and early nineteenth centuries echo this accusation that Spain was unjust toward the admiral.

Columbus's Allusions to Seneca's *Medea*

Although Columbus consistently portrayed himself throughout his career as a figure of empire, no evidence in his writings suggests that he had read or was deeply knowledgeable about the work of authors who articulated the Western tradition of *translatio imperii et studii*. Columbus's allusions to empire appear to result from his intuitive apprehension of a popular discourse about empire, as opposed to his conscious desire to invoke this tradition.

An analysis of Columbus's allusions to Seneca's tragedy *Medea* supports this point. Although the *Medea* is replete with allusions to empire in its relation of the myth of Jason and the Argonauts, allusions which were later exploited for political purposes in the royal courts of Europe, Columbus's use of the *Medea* is devoid of any imperial dimension.[75]

Here it is appropriate to provide some background about the *Medea* story and how it later played into imperial discourse in Spain. According to the Argonautic legend, Jason and his crew sacked Troy on their way to Colchis, where they would retrieve the Golden Fleece. Virgil incorporated this story about the first destruction of Troy into the *Aeneid*, the canonical foundation story of Rome, rendering it a necessary precursor to the second destruction of Troy, the event that spurred Aeneas to leave that city and fulfill his destiny by founding Rome. In Virgil's recasting, Jason becomes the precursor of Aeneas, and his return with the Golden Fleece serves as a model for Aeneas's journey to Rome with the Penates.[76] The Fleece that Jason seeks to recapture in the original story is eventually Christianized,[77] and during the Crusades it becomes a metaphor for the recapture of Jerusalem. In 1429 Philip the Good of Burgundy formed the Order of the Golden Fleece. Philip's goal, Tanner writes, was "to unite the flower of knighthood under his leadership for a crusade to Jerusalem to defeat the Turks and recapture the Holy Sepulchre. The duke identified his crusading objectives with the capture of the Golden Fleece that had been accomplished by his mythic ancestors."[78] The Hapsburg Kings Charles V and his son Philip II, both of whom inherited sovereignty of the Order and incorporated an image of the Golden Fleece in their personal devices, relied heavily on Argonautic imagery in justifying their Trojan ancestry and their aspirations to the title of Holy

Roman Emperor. Furthermore, both Charles and Philip implicated Columbus in their versions of the pre-existing Argonautic legend. They portrayed Columbus as the new Argonaut, predicted in Seneca's *Medea*, who expanded their empire to the New World. Philip ordered that a portrait of Columbus, along with scenes of Jason's journey, be painted on a ship he named the *Argo*, which was built to lead the ships of the Christian alliance against the Turks in the 1571 Battle of Lepanto. The ship and the story it told provided Philip with an opportunity to articulate what he viewed as his right to the *translatio imperii*.

But Columbus's citations of Seneca's *Medea* ignore the imperial dimension of the text. The passage in the *Medea* that Columbus alludes to in three separate cases is found at the end of Seneca's second chorus (375–79):

> Venient annis saecula seris,
> quibus Oceanus vincula rerum
> laxet, et ingens pateat tellus,
> Tethysque novos detegat orbes
> nec sit terris ultima Thule.
>
> (There will come an epoch late in time
> when the Ocean will loosen the bonds of the world
> and the earth lie open in its vastness,
> when Tethys will disclose new worlds
> and Thule not be the farthest of lands.)[79]

In the *Book of Prophecies*, in a hand that is believed to be that of Columbus, the lines above are quoted in a slightly modified version.[80] Most notably, "Tethysque" appears as "Tiphysque," as it does in the 1491 edition of Seneca's tragedies published in Lyon that Columbus possessed. The protagonist in the version that Columbus cites is not Mother Ocean ("Tethys"), but Tiphys, the pilot of the legendary Argonaut, Jason. James Romm calls this "a fortuitous and significant corruption in the Senecan text."[81] Diskin Clay observes that "*Tethysque* is the right reading, but, for the Age of Discovery, *Tiphys* (or *Tiphis*) was the only reading possible, for it was not Tethys who was destined to reveal new worlds beyond Thule but Tiphys, the navigator of Jason, *audax Tiphys* (*Medea* 345), *Tiphys, in primis domitor profundi* (*Medea* 617)."[82] Columbus's gloss in the *Book of Prophecies* of the quote from the *Medea* suggests that his discoveries have fulfilled Seneca's prophecy: "During the last years of the world, the time will come in which the Ocean sea will loosen the bounds and a large landmass will appear. A new sailor like the one named Tiphys, who was the guide of Jason, will discover a new world, and then Thule will no longer be the most remote land."[83]

Columbus also refers to Seneca's *Medea* in the letter he wrote in 1503 to the sovereigns about his fourth voyage. Here Columbus describes how he, about to be shipwrecked and desperate for help, heard a voice that consoled him as he slept. It said:

> O fool, O man slow to believe in and serve God . . . what more did He do for Moses or David, His servants? From birth He always took great care of you; when He saw you were of an age that seemed right to him, He caused your name to resound marvelously throughout the world. The Indies . . . He gave to you. . . . *To you He gave the keys to open the barriers of the Ocean Sea, which were closed with such strong chains.*[84]

Columbus's allusions to the *Medea* help Columbus cast himself as the "new sailor," predicted in the 1491 edition of the *Medea* to break the bonds of the Ocean and "discover a new world." Rusconi explains that "Columbus was looking for any type of prediction, even in classical texts, that could conceivably refer to him; for this reason he had turned even to Seneca's *Medea*, which perhaps had seemed to him to be an account of a sea voyage toward unknown Asia."[85] Romm emphasizes the heroic nature of Columbus's self-characterization via his allusions to Seneca: "Columbus derived from the passage not only a prediction of new discoveries but a celebration of the single, heroic individual who would reveal them."[86] Yet it is clear that Columbus did not view the mariner pilot in Seneca's tragedy as anything other than one who broke the "chains" of the ocean and discovered lands previously unknown to Europeans by crossing it. For Columbus, it would seem, this was magnificent enough.

Columbus did not appear to interpret Seneca's *Medea* as part of the Western canonical narrative of empire. We would, in fact, be surprised if he saw the Argonautic myth in this light because, although Columbus's education has been disputed by some, most scholars believe that he was self-taught. He likely did not read the major texts of the humanist tradition. It is uncertain how Columbus came across the *Medea*, yet it appears that he simply interpreted this passage as a prediction regarding future ocean exploration. He did not appear to relate it to Virgil's legendary account of Rome and the Western narrative of *translatio imperii*. It was left to others, like those considered in subsequent chapters of this book, to make these connections. As we shall see, even in the nineteenth century, Seneca's *Medea* was still being quoted by the likes of Washington Irving, whose biography of Columbus begins with an epigraph quoting the lines from the *Medea* discussed here.

David Brading has noted the distinction "between the conquerors and explorers of the Indies, men more conversant with medieval romances than with the classics, and the humanists who penned the accounts which caught the imagination of the educated classes in Europe."[87] Brading's description of conquerors and explorers clearly applies to Columbus. He appropriated the imperial discourse that circulated in Spain to describe his enterprise without acknowledging the pre-existing secular imperial tradition. Rather, he relied on the imperial ideas of Catholicism, the same ideals that had inspired the Crusades. Columbus, a savvy observer of the political scene in Spain, well knew that using this contemporary imperial discourse to describe himself and his enterprise would enhance his image and status in Spain. And hence he portrayed himself consistently throughout his career as a servant of the universal Christian empire of the Catholic kings.

~ 2 ~

The Incorporation of Columbus into the Story of Western Empire

THE WEST'S MODEL NARRATIVE
OF *TRANSLATIO IMPERII*

Woodcuts of Columbus's ships illustrate the 1493 Basle edition of Columbus's popular "Letter on the Discovery." Nine years later, these same woodcuts were reused to illustrate not a text written by or about Columbus, but a popular edition of Virgil's works, first published by Sebastian Brant at Strasbourg and then reissued in Paris, Lyon, and Venice. Brant, a German humanist poet and professor of jurisprudence, was committed to popularizing the works of classical authors. Long ago in 1928, Anna Cox Brinton suggested that Brant's desire to promote the classics explains his use of a visual reference to Columbus's voyage of discovery, a contemporary legend that had inspired so many. "The extraordinary liveliness of the pictures," noted Brinton, "convinces us that to Brant's mind at least Aeneas' voyage was not so much an item of academic interest, as it was a vivid fact of the ancient world comparable only to Columbus' voyage, which was so vivid a fact of contemporary experience."[1] Brinton further explained the Aeneas/Columbus analogy:

> Men looked back through the centuries to Aeneas' westward journey with eyes aglow with the vision of the future that was opened before them by contemporary navigators. The same land

that had risen from small beginnings of Trojan colonization to dominate the Old World was now sending its seamen to explore the New World. The "grave and pious" Columbus was the typical Renaissance discoverer as Aeneas had been the voyager par excellence of all antiquity.[2]

Because Brant's edition of Virgil went through several editions, the woodcuts of Columbus's ships "dominated Virgil illustration for the first half of the sixteenth century."[3] In other words, for several decades, readers of Virgil commonly viewed Columbus's ships as they contemplated the imperialist ideology espoused in the *Aeneid*. David Scott Wilson-Okamura observes that the meaning of this kind of "quotation" of a Columbian ship in a Virgilian text "would have given the Aeneas/Columbus analogy that [these woodcuts] encoded a certain currency: as Aeneas colonized Italy, so his descendants were now colonizing the New World."[4]

The example of Brant's appropriation of the previously used woodcuts of Columbus's ships to illustrate his edition of Virgil suggests how Columbus—as a symbol of Spain's (and Europe's) conquest of the New World—was quickly incorporated into the dominant Western narrative of colonization and empire building. This narrative, the definitive version of which is Virgil's *Aeneid*, tells the story of the westward movement of empire and of Trojan descent, the Trojans being viewed in the Western tradition as paradigmatic conquerors and civilizers, the builders of the world's most prestigious empire, Rome.

The narrative of *translatio imperii et studii* defined in the Western world what "civilization" was, as well as who was civilized (and who wasn't).[5] Those who claimed to be "civilized" were invariably more powerful: they occupied the position of the narrating subject and imposed their culture, as well as their stories, on others. Such a dominant culture inevitably requires at least one large metropolitan center whose residents depend on an effective system of intensive agricultural production. The word "civilization" is derived from the Latin *civitas*, or "city," and *civis*, a "citizen" or "resident" of a city. In his book *The Founding Legend of Western Civilization*, Richard Waswo reminds us that the city was only made possible when conditions allowed for a surplus in food production. Only then could some residents be freed from tilling the land in order to work in non-agricultural sectors. A sufficient surplus in agricultural production allowed for the production of music, visual art, and literature. The very word "culture" reflects the dependence of its reference on agriculture: the word is derived from the Latin verb "to cultivate" (*colo, cultum*). Settled agricultural communities that produce enough surplus food have been, in the dominant view of the West, "civilized" (their inhabitants live in cities) and seen to produce a "high" culture. By contrast, according to this definition, nomadic communities that hunt and gather instead of till the land, or even communities that engage in small-scale subsistence agricultural production, are "savage." This definition of savage people as "culture*less*," writes Waswo, "was the fiction that enabled both ancient and modern colonialism to proceed in fact as the transmission of empire and learning (*translatio imperii et studii*), of domination and tutelage, that came largely to constitute the modern history of the world."[6]

The paradigmatic articulation of the western transfer of "civilization," "high" culture, and political power is Virgil's *Aeneid*. The epic follows Aeneas, who is destined to found Rome, as he escapes a Troy invaded by Greeks (to whom the Trojans are related, a fiction that conveniently helped to legitimize the Roman appropriation of the Greek past). Bringing his household gods, father, and son, he leads a group of Trojans as they journey around the Mediterranean in search of the land they are fated to settle. After arriving in Latium, Aeneas conquers the local population as the gods prophesied. The act of conquering is by no means unimportant. Rather, it relates to the underbelly of civilization: its required and continual forceful transmission. Civilization, according to the *translatio imperii et studii* myth, comes from elsewhere, from the east in Troy in Virgil's definitive version of the myth; it must be transmitted and imposed. New land must be conquered; new cities must be built. Virgil's epic hero, "Aeneas is not just one utterly superlative individual; he is a culture, a whole civilization and its empire. He is the means of transplanting, securing, and extending it; that means is war."[7] Aeneas fulfills his destiny: to impose (by act of war) his gods, people, and culture on Latium so that his descendants can found Rome, which Jupiter promises in the *Aeneid* will be an "Empire without end."[8] The *Aeneid* distinctly links the imposition of one society's culture over another's with the abstract concept of empire.

The *Aeneid* has long been the West's paradigmatic narrative of *translatio imperii*. In *Epic and Empire*, David Quint has shown how Virgil's epic, which itself was produced to legitimize the rule of Augustus, set the mold for future centuries with regard to the stock narrative of ascendance told by the winners of political and military conquests. In this sense, it is helpful to remember that Virgil models imperial discourse, the story an empire tells about itself and its dominion, and does not necessarily prescribe a recipe for the actual political entity of empire. The *Aeneid* is the "triumphalist narrative of empire" that writes a closed history (meaning that its teleology is already determined) of the empire from the perspective of history's winners as opposed to its losers.[9] Donna Hamilton's description of the *Aeneid* as "a colonizing text" is relevant in this regard: "Indeed [it is] the archetypical colonizing text of all time. . . . No other work has been more important to the process by which the West has naturalized the concept of colonization; its narrative of a great destiny to be fulfilled in the founding of Rome has offered itself to all of Western culture as a paradigm for the expansion and transmission of culture and ideology from one place to another."[10]

Similarly, Craig Kallendorf argues that for centuries the Aeneid provided the discursive model of authority and imperial power. He writes, "As cultural power moved from one center to the next, political authority continued to rest on explicitly Virgilian foundations." Kallendorf provides a number of historical examples that illustrate how rulers explicitly invoked the *Aeneid* in their attempts to justify their rule, including Charlemagne's assumption of the Virgilian epithet of *pius* (pious) and the Spanish Hapsburg's frequent proclamations that they were the descendants of Aeneas. Philip II, for example, ordered that the phrase from the Aeneid, "imperium sine fine dedi" (I have established an empire without end, Aen. 1.279) be inscribed on his funeral catafalque.[11] These examples indicate that Virgil's *Aeneid* has long been the West's paradigmatic narrative of the *translatio imperii*.

In this context, then, Brant's use of the woodcuts of Columbus's ships in his edition of Virgil's works is evidence that Columbus was inserted as early as the sixteenth century in this dominant narrative of the westward transmission of power and culture. Columbus was, in fact, quite a good fit in this narrative: as his own self-representations consistently emphasized, he was an emblematic figure of empire. He was the first to plant the flag of Christian princes in the New World, to proclaim his faith, and to build a city there. He was the first, in effect, to "civilize" the Amerindians. In fact, the manner in which he himself represented the natives of the New World as "a people savage, warlike and who live among the hills and mountains"[12] (i.e., who do not have large-scale agricultural production) exactly reflects the Western mindset that undergirds imperial expansion. He himself emphasized how he had expanded the Christian Empire of the Catholic kings and how he was the first bringer of its culture ("civilization") to a savage world. Others continued this portrayal of Columbus. Indeed, the manner in which the figure of Columbus has been represented through the centuries has much to do with this underlying narrative about conquest and empire building.

Peter Martyr's Columbus

The first writer to insert Columbus in this pre-existing story of *translatio imperii* was the Milanese humanist Peter Martyr d'Anghiera (1457–1526).[13] Martyr was one of the most important representatives of Renaissance humanism living in Spain during the late fifteenth and early sixteenth centuries.[14] At the age of twenty, he moved to Rome, where he circulated among the elite, enjoying the patronage of cardinals Arcimboldi and Sforza, and he consolidated his intellectual and cultural foundations in the humanist tradition, studying with the renowned Pomponius Laetus. In 1486 Martyr met the Count of Tendilla, Iñigo López de Mendoza, "the most illustrious figure of Castilian letters of the fifteenth century,"[15] who had been sent to Rome by Ferdinand and Isabel to officially pledge their obedience to the pope and to negotiate peace between the papacy and the king of Naples. After Martyr wrote a poem extolling the count's successes, the latter invited Martyr to return to Spain with him in the capacity of a man of letters. To the dismay of Martyr's friends and patrons, he accepted the invitation, later explaining in a letter to Ascanio Sforza that his future in Spain was more promising than in Italy, where success depended on noble rank, and political calamity was imminent.

It is commonly believed that Martyr met Columbus, with whom Martyr wrote he was "tied in close friendship,"[16] at the royal encampment outside of Granada. Both men witnessed on 2 January 1492 the sovereigns' triumphant entrance into Granada after it had fallen in the last battle of the Spanish reconquest of Moorish territory. Shortly after being ordained and nominated in March to the post of canon at the cathedral of Granada, Martyr sought and received an invitation to be called back to serve at court. He remained at the court until his death in 1526 during the reign of Carlos V. Martyr assumed a variety of occupations in the course of his career as royal courtier, including those of professor, royal historiographer, special ambassador, member of the Council of the Indies, and advisor on political and family matters.

Martyr was the first historiographer to write about Columbus and to recognize the significance of the first Columbian voyage by coining the term "New World." His eight-volume account of

Spain's "discoveries" in the Americas, the *Decades de Orbe Novo* that he began writing in 1493, was a primary source of information for Europeans about the Western hemisphere. Martyr's *Decades* were printed in nineteen editions, in Latin and seven vernacular languages, from 1504 to 1563.[17] It was also used as a primary source for many others who wrote about Spain's activities in the New World. The *Decades* became, in Kirkpatrick Sale's words, "the centerpiece" of a variety of other influential books about the New World, including those written by Montalboddo, Grynaeus, Münster, Ramusio, Eden, and Hakluyt.[18] The list of authors who used Martyr as a source also includes Columbus's son Ferdinand Columbus, Bartolomé de las Casas, and Antonio de Herrera, who in turn were used as sources by scores of future writers, including William Robertson (*History of America* [1777]) and Washington Irving, whose extremely popular *Life and Voyages of Christopher Columbus* (1828) was the first extensive biography of Columbus written in English.

My point in mentioning this diverse list of authors who used Martyr's *Decades* as a primary source is to suggest that his text was instrumental in framing the dominant, long-lasting discourse about Columbus as a figure of empire. Martyr's representations of Columbus in books 1–3 of the first of his eight *Decades de Orbe Novo* are mediated by the *translatio imperii* legend and its narrative *par excellence*, the *Aeneid*. His earliest portrayals of Columbus are of a neo-Aeneas forging an empire for Spain in the New World. In this way, Martyr followed the Roman and Virgilian model of the epic narration of the establishment of empire just as Spain itself followed the Roman model of colonization.

In book 2 of *Decade* 1 Martyr compares Columbus and Aeneas. Here he juxtaposes the experience of Columbus and that of Aeneas as they arrive at the site of future empire: "Our people found that there were several kings there, some more powerful than others, just as we read that the mythical Aeneas found Latium divided among the kingdoms of Latinus, Mezentius, Turnus, and Tarchon, separated by narrow borders, with the remaining territories distributed among tyrants of the same type."[19] Comparing the reality encountered by Columbus and that encountered by Aeneas, Martyr suggests that the two men both brought their cultures westward to colonize foreign territories previously ruled by many divided kingdoms. The corollary of this comparison, of course, is the prediction that Columbus will defeat and then impose order and unity on these people as he establishes his settlement. Both Aeneas and Columbus established empires in territory that had once been home to many divided kingdoms.

Book 1 ends with an unambiguous depiction of Columbus in the mode of Aeneas, the paradigmatic culture-bringer and founder of an empire. Martyr describes Columbus's preparations for a second voyage, enumerating the objects deemed necessary for starting a colony and conveying the magnitude of Columbus's project to found a city for Spain across the sea: "The Admiral also procured mares, sheep, cows and many other female animals with males of the same species for procreation; legumes, wheat, barley and other similar products, not only for eating but also for sowing."[20] Clearly, Martyr implies, Columbus is spearheading the effort to reproduce European culture and its patterns of settled agriculture in a new land. In this same section at the end of book 1, Columbus also orders that tradesmen bring "all the tools needed for their craft and, in addition, all the implements useful for the founding of a city in foreign lands."[21] The phrase "for the founding of a city in foreign lands," with the verb *condere* (to build, found, or settle), would remind Martyr's contemporary reader of Aeneas's destiny, made clear in the famous first lines of the *Aeneid:*

> Wars and a man I sing—an exile driven on by Fate,
> he was the first to flee the coast of Troy,
> destined to reach Lavinian shores and Italian soil,
> yet many blows he took on land and sea from the gods above—
> thanks to cruel Juno's relentless rage—and many losses

> he bore in battle too, before he could *found a city* (*conderet urbem*),
> bring his gods to Latium, source of the Latin race,
> the Alban lords and the high walls of Rome.[22]

In a discussion that also cites the *Aeneid*'s opening lines, James Morwood observes the importance of city building in Virgil's epic.[23] Aeneas may sometimes be seen as an oddly resigned hero—one who simply accepts the fate decreed for him by the gods, making him a hero who is merely, in the words of David Quint, "an instrument of his historical destiny"[24]—but if there is one action Aeneas performs consistently, it is building cities. "About this action," Waswo observes, "there is no dubiety, no need for planning, no debate, he does it, as it were, instinctively."[25] He begins to build cities four times in the course of the *Aeneid*.

Martyr's Columbus is also a builder of cities in the foreign lands of the Indies, particularly in books 2 and 3 of the first *Decade*. The city that Columbus builds is a symbolic site of the *translatio imperii et studii*. Consider, for example, the following passage from the end of book 2, which refers to the city of Isabela: "He himself chose an elevated place near a port to found a city, and there, in a few days, built some houses and a chapel as the short time allowed. On the day when we commemorate the feast of the Three Kings, the sacred functions were celebrated according to our rite, with thirteen priests attending as ministers, in a world, it could be said, so different, so far away, so alien to all civilization and religion."[26] Again we see in this passage the verb used so often in the *Aeneid*: *condere*. Martyr emphasizes here that the city is the stage where the culture-bringers celebrate their civilization amidst a world devoid of culture, "a world . . . so alien to all civilization." Indeed, the very act of building the city is the colonizer's first civilizing act. Its significance in Martyr's narrative is emphasized when he repeats in book 3 that Columbus built the city of Isabela: "Hence, the Admiral decided to found a city on the northern side over an elevated site."[27]

The city Columbus builds in Martyr's account serves as a base for further imperial conquest. This relation between city and conquest is manifest in the details of Martyr's narration. After recounting the founding of Isabela, Martyr describes in great detail the fertility of the area, and then he records how Columbus sent a group of thirty men to explore the region of Cipango, which he also describes in detail. Then Martyr consciously interrupts himself to return to the topic of the founding of the city: "But let us go back to the founding of the city."[28] The sentence that follows begins by describing the city's construction (noting that it was fortified with a ditch and ramparts) yet quickly transitions to the topic of Columbus's further exploration of the interior: "The city having been surrounded with ditches and ramparts so that, if the natives should attack during his absence, those who were left there could defend themselves, Columbus headed due south on 14 March, with all his cavalrymen and about four hundred foot soldiers, toward the gold-bearing region; he crossed a river, traversed a plain and climbed a mountain that borders the other side of the plain."[29] That constructing a city enables further conquest is underlined in the passage above by the image of Columbus leaving "with all of his cavalrymen and about four hundred foot soldiers, toward the region of the gold." Surely, this is not a simple reconnaissance mission but a sortie into the unconquered wilderness from the colonizer's home base, that piece of land that has already been civilized because a "city" has been built on it. From this base, Columbus, in search of booty, embarks on a mission of conquest requiring arms. This message is reiterated shortly after when Martyr writes: "When he had advanced into the gold-bearing region seventy-two miles from the city . . . he decided to set up a fortified place so that the recesses of the interior region could be explored little by little in safety."[30]

Martyr does not mention by name the first New-World settlement constructed by Columbus, the ill-fated fortress La Navidad, likely because it was a failure and did not fit within Martyr's early casting of Columbus as Aeneas. Martyr refers only to Columbus's leaving behind some of his crew ("He left thirty-eight men with that king")[31] and his attempt to provide for their safety ("Columbus made arrangements, as best he could, for the life, health and safety of those he was leaving behind").[32] In book 2, when Columbus returns to Hispaniola to find the settlement destroyed and his men killed, Martyr does nothing more than mention the fortress, describing it as "the blockhouse and the cabins our men had built for themselves, together with a rampart all around."[33] The absence of more information about the construction of the first settlement in the New World (which surely could have been replete with symbolism) might be perplexing if we did not know that Martyr likely spent years editing this first book.[34] It is probable that after learning of the grisly fate of the settlement at Navidad, Martyr deleted any description of that event that he might have initially included because the entire episode would have been inconsistent with Martyr's depiction of Columbus.

The opening sentence of *Decade* 1.1 casts the admiral as a conqueror even before his name is mentioned. Martyr suggests that those who discover previously unknown territory are exceptional. Ancient peoples, Martyr writes, esteemed as gods those "men by whose industry and greatness of spirit lands unknown to their ancestors were made accessible."[35] This sentence, which suggests Columbus is equally remarkable, is followed by one that credits Columbus with the discovery. Martyr writes, "In order to avoid doing injustice to anyone I will then start from the beginning of said venture. A certain Ligurian, Christopher Columbus. . . ."[36] Beginning this second sentence with Columbus's name, Martyr privileges the admiral as the most important actor in the discovery of the New World and establishes Columbus as the cornerstone on which Martyr's account of the discovery of the New World is based. Martyr appears to be partaking in a euhemeristic discourse that rationalized classical gods as having been in actuality exceptional mortals famous for some particular feat, a discourse popular among early Christian apologists whose work Martyr surely knew well. It is possible, though not certain, that one of these mortals Martyr had in mind was Aeneas, whose divination is predicted in the *Aeneid*.[37] According to this reading, Martyr's text begins by establishing a veiled analogy, one that it later lays bare, between Columbus and Aeneas.

The "Aeneas frame" that Martyr applies to Columbus is also hinted at, I would argue, in the first description in book 1 of Columbus as "a certain Ligurian." Scholars have proposed that this phrase illustrates Martyr's desire to disassociate Columbus from Genoa, which was aligned with France against Spain at the time the first *Decade* was composed. Ernesto Lunardi conjectures that Martyr also may have employed this reference "to emphasize the tradition of industrious and strong people to whom Columbus belongs."[38] Indeed, Ligurians in the classical tradition are known as tough mountain dwellers. In his *De lege agraria*, for example, Cicero writes: "The Ligurians, being mountaineers, are a hardy and rustic tribe. The land itself taught them to be so by producing nothing which was not extracted from it by skillful cultivation, and by great labour."[39] In this light, Martyr's description of the explorer as "quidam Ligur vir" stresses Columbus's fortitude (in addition to Martyr's knowledge of the classical tradition). More specifically, as Lunardi notes, the term "Ligur" would likely be recognized by those knowledgeable of the Latin literary tradition as a reference to Virgil's phrase in the *Georgics* (2.168), "Ligurian inured to trouble" (adsuetumque malo Ligurem). I would add that the intertextual relationship between the *Decades* and the *Georgics* that Martyr establishes with this reference is also significant. This particular phrase appears in the section of the *Georgics* known as the *laudes Italiae* (praises of Italy), where Virgil glorifies the virtuous people of Italy's different regions and then juxtaposes them to the unwarlike foreigner of the East. He then praises the Emperor Octavian for keeping that foreigner at bay: "And you, greatest Caesar, who now victorious on the furthest shores of Asia turn away the unwarlike Indian from the hills of Rome."[40] Martyr's allusion to this imperialistic passage in Virgil's poem serves to portray Columbus as a descendant of the virtuous Italian race, strength of the Roman Empire founded by Aeneas.

Martyr's defense of Columbus's foreign origins in the first book of *Decade* 1 squares with Martyr's casting of Columbus as a neo-Aeneas, the protagonist in the story of the *translatio imperii*. This Columbus is not only a Ligurian, a descendant of the hearty stock praised by Virgil as the strength of the Roman Empire, but also the agent responsible for the westward transfer of empire. His loyalty to empire, and in this case to the empire ruled by Ferdinand and Isabel, is pure and unquestionable. This comes across near the beginning of the first book when Martyr rebuts potential objections to Columbus's foreign origins. Here mutinous Spanish sailors "[felt] that they had been deceived by a Ligurian and were being dragged headlong to a place from which it would never be possible to return."[41] In response to such opposition, Martyr's Columbus threatens the crew with the charge of treason: "He kept saying that if they attempted anything against him, refusing to obey him, they would also be accused of treason against their Sovereigns."[42] It is Columbus who judges which actions are treacherous, the subtext suggesting that the admiral is more loyal to the sovereigns than the Spaniards who accompany him are.

Martyr did not long sustain his characterizations of Columbus as an Aeneas. Indeed, after 1500 (the year that Columbus was arrested)—with the exception of his brief mention of the admiral in a letter dated 19 December 1513—Martyr did not write about him for almost fifteen years, even though Columbus undertook a fourth voyage in 1503 and then died in 1506. When Martyr does return to writing about Columbus, he discusses the fourth voyage and then declares his ignorance of Columbus's fate, a claim that is difficult to believe given Martyr's privileged access to information.

Martyr stopped characterizing Columbus as an Aeneas by book 4 of *Decade* 1 for several likely reasons. He employed the notable epic tone in the first two books of *Decade* 1 as an initial response to a seemingly mythical event. These books, as Lunardi observes, "are full of the spirit of adventure and of the discovery of an unexpected reality." As the discoveries and conquest of the New World continued, however, Martyr's attitude changed, and he adopted what Lunardi views as "a more detached tone suited to a work of history."⁴³ Simply put, as more information was acquired about the New World, it became less myth and more reality, and the epic portrayal of Columbus was therefore no longer appropriate. Eventually, Columbus became less relevant as Spain's empire in the Indies grew. A second reason Martyr stopped characterizing Columbus in the mode of Aeneas was that it became clear to everyone that Columbus's career and reputation had been irreparably damaged by allegations that he abused his power and misgoverned Hispaniola. No one, and certainly not Martyr as a foreigner, even if he were favored by the queen, "would have been interested in defending [Columbus's] position."⁴⁴ Columbus could no longer be deemed a hero in the Spanish court, and his playing the role of heroic founder of empire in Martyr's narrative would have been too far-fetched.

Hence, if books 2 and 3 portray Columbus as a colonizer who builds cities and brings the culture of the metropolis to foreign lands, book 4 instead portrays Columbus as a victim of evil enemies who disparaged the imperial ideal. He remains an Aeneas, but his contributions to Spain's empire are not appreciated as such by the Spaniards in the story. (We are reminded of Columbus's own self-portrayal as a martyr for the Spanish Empire.) The contrast could not be more apparent between books 2 and 3 on the one hand and book 4 on the other (book 4 begins with Columbus's return from the second voyage and then covers what occurs on Hispaniola while Columbus is in Spain). Although book 4 briefly mentions that Columbus built the Fortress of

Concepción, this is the only instance in this book when Martyr refers to Columbus's role as builder. Although he does not construe Columbus as a city-building colonist in book 4, Martyr does depict him as a man worthy of sympathy because his career and status at court are in jeopardy. Book 4 begins with Columbus's discovery that Friar Bernardo Buil and Pedro de Margarit have returned to Spain "with wicked intentions"—Columbus's intentions, the text predictably implies, were good.

Martyr says in book 4 that he is writing in the year 1501. This would have been after Columbus had returned to Spain against his will, arrested by Francisco de Bobadilla, who was sent by the sovereigns to Hispaniola to investigate charges against Columbus. This event was the nadir of Columbus's career in Spain. The sovereigns nominally continued to support Columbus, but after this, he was in fact a marginal figure in Spain's activities in the Indies. It became clear to everyone not only that the exploration, conquest, and colonization of the New World was a project larger than initially anticipated, but also that Columbus had indeed abused his power. Martyr could no longer characterize Columbus as a legendary civilization builder. In 1516, when Martyr wrote *Decade* 3.4, which recounts Columbus's disastrous fourth voyage, he used a different Virgilian character to describe Columbus: Achaemenides, the character whom Odysseus abandoned on the Cyclops's island and whom Aeneas later rescued in the *Aeneid* (3.613). Martyr writes that Columbus and his crew, shipwrecked on the island of Jamaica, "lived for ten months a life of the Virgilian Achaemenides."[45] Martyr continues to establish classical analogies in his narrative, but never again does his Columbus resemble Aeneas. Columbus is no longer even central to his narrative, as is evident in Martyr's references to "them" (not Columbus) when he describes the shipwrecked victims. And lest there be any doubt that Columbus is no longer Martyr's protagonist, we have Martyr's declaration that he is ignorant about Columbus's fate after his rescue: "Thus, all of them returned to Hispaniola sick and exhausted from lack of food. I do not know what happened to them after that."⁴⁶ When Martyr writes this statement, Columbus has been dead for ten years.

My point in emphasizing the change in Martyr's portrayals of Columbus as Spain's involvement in the Indies grew is twofold. First, I wish to illustrate the constructed nature of those portrayals and the manner in which Martyr inserted Columbus within the Virgilian narrative of imperial conquest. This was Martyr's short-lived characterization that would have come easily to an Italian schooled in the humanist tradition in the first heady moments of Spain's imperial expansion. Second, I seek to emphasize the great influence of Martyr's characterization of Columbus *despite* its being so short-lived. The fact that his initial Aeneas characterization quickly gained currency and continued with such vigor through the centuries suggests that Martyr touched a fundamental chord in Western culture. He was telling the victor's side of the history of the modern world.

THE COLUMBIAN ARCHETYPE

Although Martyr did not sustain his characterization of Columbus as the protagonist in the classic Western narrative of *translatio imperii*, his earliest characterizations of Columbus were, it is worth repeating, read by many other writers who themselves then wrote about Columbus and the New World. In this sense, Martyr helped establish an interpretive tradition about Columbus as a protagonist in the *translatio imperii* that was perpetuated in Europe and was eventually taken up in the Americas. But there is more at play here than mere intertextuality and authorial influence with regard to Martyr's legacy. We would do well to remember that Columbus himself appropriated the discourse of empire that circulated at the Spanish court at the end of the fifteenth century. In doing so, he unwittingly inserted himself into a greater discourse of Western dominance and territorial expansion. Martyr merely continued the characterization of Columbus as a figure of empire and incorporated him within the humanist tradition and, within that, the story of the *translatio imperii*. It was entirely logical to do so. Columbus became a synecdoche that signified the European conquest of the New World. His story is inextricable from the establishment of European empires in the New World—and empire in general.

Martyr's response to Columbus and Spain's activities in the New World reflects the dominance of the Virgilian frame in Western thought, according to which territorial expansion and colonization was often interpreted as a contemporary reenactment of the *Aeneid* plot. As Craig Kallendorf maintains, "The story told [in the *Aeneid*] was widely interpreted as the archetypal pattern for the very establishment and diffusion of [Western] culture. Aeneas left his homeland and traveled westward, taking possession of a new land and bringing civilization to it as he merged his countrymen with the indigenous inhabitants."[47] We should not be surprised that Columbus, the "discoverer" who first claimed a New World for Spain, has often been portrayed in Western historiographic and literary discourse as a figure of empire comparable to Aeneas.

Scholars have diligently traced Columbus's appearances in a great variety of European texts since the sixteenth century.[48] It is no coincidence that many of the literary works in which Columbus appears are epics. As David Quint has eloquently shown, the epic—an extended poem composed in an elevated style that tells the story of a hero (traditionally male) and his nation's triumph over others—is the paradigmatic literary form of empire.[49] Columbus's story, as told over and over through the centuries, is an epic story.

In the discussion that follows, I focus on a few exemplary literary texts, all of them epics, in which Columbus is represented as a figure of empire and a conqueror of the savage New World, city-builder and culture-bringer from Europe.

I begin with Lorenzo Gambara's *De navigatione Christophori Columbi libri quattuor* (Rome 1581). The plot of this Latin epic poem closely follows that of Martyr's *Decades*, which Gambara credits in his *ad lectorum* as one of his primary sources. Gambara's Columbus even more closely resembles Aeneas than Martyr's did. As Manuel Yruela Guerrero notes, Gambara set out to write an epic about Columbus with the *Aeneid* as his model, which is clear from the first verse: "Perrenot, I will speak here of the man who first touched / the shores of vast Cuba," which echoes the famous first lines of the *Aeneid*, "Wars and a man I sing—an exile driven on by Fate, / he was the first to flee the coast of Troy."[50] Gambara goes as far as employing the same narrative convention seen in books 2 and 3 of the *Aeneid* (and, incidentally, in books 9–12 of the *Odyssey*) so that his Columbus narrates in first person after being prompted by his banquet host to recount his adventures. Heinz Hofmann painstakingly analyzes this and other details in Gambara's poem that remind the reader of the *Aeneid* and cast Columbus as an Aeneas.[51] We note in particular Gambara's description of Columbus, who has just finished recounting his story at the banquet:

> Sic Ligur inventos intentis omnibus a se
> Oceanique sinus, nostrisque incognita nautis
> sidera narrabat, positas et per mare terras,
> cum tandem tacuit, mediaque in nocte quievit.

> (Thus, with everyone hanging on his words, the Ligurian was describing people he found, the regions of the Ocean, constellations unknown to our sailors, and lands situated across the seas until, well into the night, he at last ended and fell silent.)[52]

Hofmann compares this passage with the following passage from book 3 of the *Aeneid*, where Aeneas is described after telling his story in Dido's palace:

> Sic pater Aeneas intentis omnibus unus
> Fata renarrabat divom cursusque docebat.
> Conticuit tandem factoque hic fine quievit.

> (So Aeneas,
> With all eyes fixed on him alone, the founder of his people
> recalled his wanderings now, the fates the gods had sent.
> He fell hushed at last, his tale complete, at rest.)[53]

As Hofmann observes, the phrases in this description evoke the *Aeneid* and "stress the fact that Columbus is alter Aeneas."[54] We also note Gambara's reference to Columbus as "Sic Ligur," likely an allusion to (and repetition of) Martyr's own subtle characterization of Columbus as a descendant of the virtuous race who defends the Roman Empire in Virgil's *Georgics*.

Giulio Cesare Stella's epic poem, *Colombeidos libri priores duo* (London 1585, Rome 1589) also portrays Columbus as an empire builder. Both Hofmann and Juan Gil have compared Stella's Columbus with Aeneas.[55] Hofmann, for example, compares the task set before each protagonist:

> It is the aim and destiny of Aeneas to reach the land in the West, to settle there and found a new domicile for his *penates* and to lay the foundation for an empire that one day will dominate the whole world. The same task is *mutatis mutandis* set for Columbus; he, too, is in search of a land in the West; he looks for places where his countrymen can settle and found a city (he himself founds a first fortification, and the historical Columbus founded two cities on Hispaniola: Isabella and San Domingo); he will give the Christian religion (the Christian *penates*) a place in the New World and his discoveries will lead to Spanish domination in the West that in the days of Stella forms a worldwide empire in which the sun does not set.[56]

More than one hundred years later, European epics written during the eighteenth century were still casting Columbus in the role of empire-builder Aeneas. Among them is *Columbus Carmen epicum* (Rome 1715) by Italian humanist Ubertino Carrara, which Francisca Torres Martínez calls "the great epic of Spain's expansion." Torres Martínez and José Sánchez Marín discuss the poem's representations of Columbus as a later-day Aeneas.[57]

Another epic about Columbus, *La Colombiade, ou la foi portée au nouveau monde* by Madame du Boccage, was published in Paris in 1756. Dedicated to Pope Benedict XIV, this poem in effect equates Columbus with the most important figures in the *translatio imperii* tradition: Odysseus (or Ulysses in the Latin appropriation), Jason, and Aeneas.[58] In the mythology of empire, all of these protagonists are charged with founding empires and imposing their cultures on foreign ones deemed inferior; and all three of these figures appear as symbols of Western empire in the *translatio imperii* tradition. In characterizing Columbus, Du Boccage refers to all of these stock characters. The poem's opening lines pay homage to both Homer and Virgil, establishing the parallel between their epic heroes and her own:

> Je chante ce Génois, conduit par Uranie,
> Combattu par l'Enfer, attaqué par l'envie,
> Ce nocher qui, du Tage abandonnant les ports,
> De l'Inde le premier découvrit les trésors;
> De l'aurore au couchant, son art vainqueur de l'onde,
> Pour y porter la foi, conquit un nouveau Monde.
>
> (I sing of this Genovese, led by Urania,
> Fought by Hades, attacked by greed,
> This oarsman who, abandoning the ports of the Tagus,
> First discovered the treasures of India;
> From dawn until sunset, his mastery of the sea,
> To bring the faith there, conquered a new World.)[59]

The poem's second stanza establishes the comparison between Columbus and his crew and Jason and the Argonauts. Columbus tells his men that they are "Argonaut rivals of the vanquishers of the Bosphorus" and that "a nobler prize" awaits them than the

Golden Fleece that awaited the Argonauts. After Columbus's speech, his crew responds by reiterating the claim that they will outdo the Argonauts: "Our warriors, in the ardor that this speech inspires, / Resolve to bring empire to a new universe, / And already see another Colchis."[60]

One of the most obvious parallels Du Boccage establishes between her Columbus and Aeneas involves Zama, the daughter of an indigenous chief. As Dido falls in love with Aeneas, Zama falls for the admiral after hearing him speak. Du Boccage makes the analogy explicit:

> A ces tendres accents, Zama versant des pleurs,
> D'un père qui l'adore enchante les douleurs;
> Mais la voix du Génois, pour son âme étonnée,
> A l'attrait que Didon trouve aux récits d'Enée.
> Jeune Indienne, hélas! un feu secret et doux
> Déjà dans vos esprits, s'allume malgré vous.
>
> (At these tender words, Zama shedding tears,
> Adds to the pain of a father who adores her;
> But the voice of the Genovese, for her surprised soul,
> Has the allure that Dido finds for Aeneas' tales.
> Young Indian, alas! A sweet and secret fire
> Already in your spirit, lights against your will.)[61]

Like Aeneas, in Du Boccage's epic Columbus must eventually break the spell of a god (Cupid) and reject the ardent love of a woman in order to fulfill his duty and establish his empire. That empire is first and foremost in *La Colombiade* a Christian empire, and Columbus is the crusader who brings his God to the New World in order to civilize it, much like Aeneas brings his penates to Latium.

La Colombiade is just one of many texts in which Columbus is portrayed as a figure of empire. I have argued that early on, even starting with the admiral himself, Columbus was interpreted as a figure of empire. His story is inseparable from the story of the rise of the Spanish Empire, which came to encompass more territory and inhabitants than the Roman Empire. It is not surprising that Columbus would be compared to Aeneas, founder of that Roman Empire. It is also not surprising that European settlers and their descendants in the Americas eagerly read these European texts that perpetuated this interpretive tradition. It is the American appropriation of that tradition to which we now turn.

~ 3 ~
Columbus and the Republican Empire of the United States

By the eighteenth century, Columbus was commonly represented in Europe according to an interpretive tradition that had enveloped him as a protagonist in the classic Western story of imperial conquest and domination. Many of the texts that formed this interpretive tradition were read either in the original or in translation by European settlers in the Americas. For example, Peter Martyr's *Decades de orbe novo* and Richard Eden's translation of Martyr's text were read by American colonists, as I discuss later in this chapter. Given the colonial projects of the European powers in the Americas, Columbus's role as the first representative of those powers, and his traditional association as a figure of empire, made him highly relevant to the American colonial experience. One might think that Americans supporting political independence from their respective European metropolises would discard the figure of Columbus as a relic of the Old World, as a symbol of the monarchical political system they sought to end in their land. But instead they adopted Columbus as a symbol of their newly independent nations. How and why this occurred in colonial British America and then the United States is the subject of this chapter.

In the myth of national origins that was popular in the United States in the eighteenth century, if not before, Columbus was commonly portrayed as the seed of individualism and liberty that left Europe, arrived in the New World in the fifteenth century, and then flowered in 1776 with the Declaration of Independence and the rise of the republic. In this manner, Columbus has long been represented as a founder of the nation, alongside George Washington. The nation's capital was named in honor of both men in 1791.[1] Beginning in the 1770s with the poetry of Phillis Wheatley, Philip Freneau, Timothy Dwight, and Joel Barlow, British American and US writers helped construct Columbus as a national symbol. Washington Irving's biography, *A History of the Life and Voyages of Christopher Columbus*, was also integral to that construction. When the 1492 quadricentennial was celebrated in Chicago at the World's Columbian Exposition of 1893, Columbus's prominence as a national symbol was at an all-time high.

Scholars addressing portrayals of Columbus in the British American colonies and then the United States have adeptly analyzed how Columbus has been employed to represent republicanism, liberty, entrepreneurship, and scientific progress. They have also considered how he has symbolized religious and ethnic identity in the United States. I do not disagree with these analyses, but I do seek to add another dimension to the figure of Columbus in the United States. Previous scholarship has focused mostly on his appearances in American contexts, divorcing those appearances from the international tradition through which Columbus was interpreted for centuries. This study seeks to broaden our approach to the American Columbus in terms of both geography and chronology. It considers the figure of Columbus as a mutable cultural product of a conversation that began in the late fifteenth century about the issues at the crux of the West's encounter with the New World: the justification of the economic, political, and cultural domination of a people who considered themselves civilized over a people they deemed savage. In a word, that conversation is about empire, which had different meanings in different contexts and which is certainly relevant, as I illustrate in this chapter, in the case of the United States. Some representations of Columbus in the United States, I acknowledge, do not tap into this conversation. The majority of them do.

Sources of the American Columbus

British Americans in the seventeenth and eighteenth centuries learned about Columbus from European sources. As discussed in the previous chapter, one of the most influential of those was Peter Martyr's *Decades de Orbe Novo*, in which Martyr characterizes Columbus as a new Aeneas who founds the Spanish overseas empire. Many British colonials read Martyr's text,[2] either in Latin or in Richard Eden's 1555 English translation of the first three books of the *Decades* (which is exactly the portion dealing with the admiral), whereby they were introduced to Columbus as a stock character in the Western narrative of colonization and empire building. Eden's preface certainly frames Martyr's narrative in a way that assures that the essence of Martyr's Columbus, the paradigmatic founder of Western empire, comes across unaltered. The preface, for example, contends that the establishment of Spain's "large Empire" is more worthy of glory than the exploits of Jason and the Argonauts, Alexander the Great, and the Romans.[3] An augmented English translation of Martyr's *Decades* was published, along with other accounts of New-World discoveries, in 1589, and again in 1598–1600 by Richard Hakluyt, perhaps the greatest champion of English colonization. We know that copies of that work, entitled *The Principal Navigations, Voyages, Traffiques and Discoveries of the English Nation* were carried on the ships of the East India Company to the British colonies.[4] In compiling the *Navigations*, Hakluyt was attempting to lay the moral groundwork for England's expansion overseas.[5] As one scholar notes, Hakluyt "implicitly compare[d] his own project to Virgil's *Aeneid*," seeing his promotion of the British Empire as analogous to Virgil's promotion of the Roman Empire.[6]

Martyr's *Decades* are important in the textual genealogy with regard to Columbus not because British colonials simply reproduced Martyr's characterizations of Columbus. Specifying a particular textual influence, except in certain cases (some of which I discussed in the previous chapter), is a hazardous exercise, and while I do believe such references are relevant, they are not as important as acknowledging that Columbus continues to be a stock character in the same old story about the transfer of empire and the domination of one people over another. That narrative, which is underwritten by and reinforces the definition of civilization as "requiring transportation from somewhere else, as incapable of being homegrown, as necessitating exile, invasion, reachievement, and refoundation,"[7] was an important part of British American discourse, beginning with the first English settlers. According to the logic of that discourse, it made sense that Columbus would continue to be interpreted in America as an imperial figure.

The first treatment of Columbus published in the American colonies, "The History of the Northern Continent of *America*," written by Samuel Nevill under the penname "Sylvanus Americus," appeared in Nevill's *New American Magazine* in 1758 and was republished that same year in two newspapers, the *New York Mercury* and the *New York Gazette*. The piece relied heavily on Martyr, Hakluyt and Samuel Purchas, who continued Hakluyt's publication efforts in England after Hakluyt's death. As Claudia Bushman notes, Nevill repeats elements of the Black Legend in portraying Spain's colonization of the New World as a vicious conquest, in contrast to that of the English, which was justifiable.[8] In Nevill's account, however, Columbus is ultimately a sympathetic character in contrast to the greedy and cruel Spaniards, much like he is in both Martyr's and Columbus's own account.

Two of the most influential authors to write about Columbus in English, Washington Irving and Scottish historian William Robertson, acknowledged using Martyr as a source. Robertson's *The History of America* (1777) was one of the primary sources from which Americans in the eighteenth century learned about Columbus. The biographical information about Columbus that Joel Barlow presented to readers in *The Vision of Columbus* (1787), for example, was taken from Robertson's book, excerpts of which had been republished in American newspapers in the early to mid-1780s.[9] We are familiar with Robertson's Columbus: he is the model European colonizer. This squares with Robertson's statement in his introduction that his work illustrates "the principles and maxims of the Spaniards in planting colonies, which have been adopted in some measure by every nation."[10] By telling the story of the Spanish Empire's "discovery" and colonization, he was providing what he deemed "a proper introduction to the history of all the European establishments in America."[11] While the trope of empire is not at the forefront of Robertson's text, it lies beneath its consistent allusions to the Old World conquering the New. Just as we saw in texts that predate Robertson's, Columbus imposes European order on America, conquering the savage and civilizing through the construction of cities and churches.

EMPIRE AND EIGHTEENTH-CENTURY POETRY

The notion that the British territory in the Americas would be an empire, at least in the sense that an empire denoted a territory of great size, was not new at the time of the War of Independence. Many of the original settlers of the eastern seaboard had claimed a divine right to the interior as well, and these claims were supported by several of the first colonial charters, which held that the western boundary of the colonies was the Pacific Ocean (the "South Sea"). In *The Rising American Empire*, historian Richard Van Alstyne argues that "the attitude, predetermined in Elizabethan England, that the 'New World' belonged exclusively to the English as the people capable of colonizing and exploiting it was germinal in the formation of the American idea of empire."[12] The settlers' belief in their "right to colonize" into the interior of the continent underwrites the formation of the United States as an empire and its imperial foreign policy throughout the course of its existence:

This concept of the right to colonize, premised upon an assumed ability to implement the right, thus begins to be part of the American mentality in the eighteenth century. John Quincy Adams and James Monroe, employing the same reasoning, gave the doctrine classic expression in 1823; and the Monroe Doctrine became the chosen ideological weapon of the United States in the nineteenth century for warning intruders away from the continent. Manifest destiny, the intriguing phrase utilized by historians to label the expansion of the United States in the nineteenth century, is merely the other side of the coin. It was characteristic of the nineteenth as well as the eighteenth century, moreover, to assert the right before the actual work of colonization had begun. . . . Looked at from the standpoint of the sum total of its history, the abstract formulae and principles being disregarded or at least discounted, the United States thus becomes by its very essence an expanding imperial power. It was conceived as an empire; and its evolution from a group of small, disunited English colonies strung out on a long coastline to a world power with commitments on every sea and in every continent, has been a characteristically imperial type of growth.[13]

In America, British Americans who had surely read European sources about Columbus commonly portrayed him as a symbol of empire. British American literature of the last third of the eighteenth century reflects a growing contemporary interest in Columbus. Before the mid-1770s the empire with which Columbus was associated was most often British. After that time, the empire with which Columbus was associated by British Americas was, as we would predict, that of an independent American state. Within that conception, British Americans sought to differentiate empire in America from its European counterpart. Most important, in America the empire for which Columbus stood was headed by a republic where science, commerce, and individual liberty were prized, unlike in the British

Empire, which was ultimately unsuccessful in the attempt to join *imperium* and *libertas* because of its monarchist constitution.[14]

Philip Freneau's poem "Columbus to Ferdinand," likely written in 1770 (but not published until 1779), is one of the earliest works written in England's American colonies to take Columbus as its subject. Its fifteen stanzas recount the arguments that Columbus, guided first and foremost by reason, purportedly presented to King Ferdinand in the former's effort to garner royal support for his enterprise. The poem quotes the same lines of Seneca's *Medea* to which Columbus himself alluded in suggesting he fulfilled prophesy by transgressing the known limits of the ocean and discovering new worlds.[15] The allusion to empire here is subtle but unmistakable. This passage from the *Medea*, as we have seen in the European context, suggests that Columbus is successor to Jason and Aeneas, founder of the Roman Empire.

The association of Columbus with empire, and a specifically American empire, is stronger in Freneau's later work. In 1771 he collaborated with Hugh Henry Brackenridge in writing *A Poem, On the Rising Glory of America*, which the latter delivered at their graduation from the College of New Jersey (later Princeton University).[16] The same quote from the *Medea* was reprinted in both the graduation program and the title page of Freneau's publication of the poem in 1772. In this case, the *Medea* epigraph works together with the poem's use of the *translatio imperii* trope—which had so often been used by Europeans in telling Columbus's story—to construct Columbus as a symbol of empire. *On the Rising Glory* begins by referring to the string of past empires that now cede their place to America:

> No more of Memphis and her mighty kings,
> Or Alexandria, where the Ptolomies
> Taught golden commerce to unfurl her sails,
> And bid fair science smile: No more of Greece
> Where learning next her early visit paid,
> And spread her glories to illume the world,

> No more of Athens, where she flourished,
> And saw her sons of mighty genius rise
> Smooth flowing Plato, Socrates and him
> Who with resistless eloquence reviv'd
> The Spir't of LIBERTY, and shook the thrones
> Of Macedon and Persia's haughty king.
> No more of Rome, enlighten'd by her beams,
> Fresh kindling there the fire and eloquence,
> And poesy divine; imperial Rome!
> Whose wide dominion reach'd o'er half the globe;
> Whose eagle flew o'er Ganges to the East
> And in the West far to the British isles.
> No more of Britain, and her kings renown'd,
> Edward's and Henry's thunderbolts of war;
> Her chiefs victorious o'er the Gallic foe;
> Illustrious senators, immortal bards,
> And wise philosophers, of these no more.
> A Theme more new, tho' not less noble, claims
> Our ev'ry thought on this auspicious day;
> The rising glory of this western world.[17]

In this passage we note what Eric Wertheimer has called "the poem's thematic obsession with imperial beginnings."[18] It lists a series of old empires in order to introduce a "Theme more new, tho' not less noble / . . . / The rising glory of this western world." In this context, the reader understands the "western world" as an empire, as it concludes the poem's queue of previous empires. It is a "nobler" empire than the empires of Europe (especially the Spanish Empire) for two reasons. First, its main activity is not war but agriculture ("But agriculture crowns our happy land"[19]), which in the West has always been deemed necessary to sustain cities and "civilization." Second, it is grounded in commerce, which in turn depends on science, which in turn depends on liberty.[20] According to the poem, the fertile ground for commerce, science, and liberty is uniquely American.

On the Rising Glory identifies the moment "when first Columbus touch'd / [t]he shores so long unknown" as the origin of "this western world." While the poem does not focus on Columbus, it identifies him as being responsible for bringing empire to the New World, as the epigraphic frame quoting Seneca also suggests. The prosperous future of empire in America is expressed by the character of Acasto, who sees numerous peoples, a great territorial expanse, and nations that will compete with the fame of Greece and Rome:

> I see, I see
> A thousand kingdoms rais'd, cities and men
> Num'rous as sand upon the ocean shore;
> Th' Ohio then shall glide by many a town
> Of note: and where the Missis[s]ippi stream
> By forests shaded now runs weeping on
> Nations shall grow and states not less in fame
> Than Greece and Rome of old: we too shall boast
> Our Alexanders, Pompeys, heroes, kings
> That in the womb of time yet dormant lye
> Waiting the joyful hour for life and light.[21]

The importance of the city as the site of civilization is clear in Acasto's vision of a "thousand kingdoms rais'd." That he sees "cities and men" as "num'rous as sand" underscores the great expanse of this western territory, as do the references to the "many a town" and the "nations" that will grace the lengths of the Ohio and Mississippi rivers. Acasto explicitly compares his vision with Greece and Rome, stating that these "states" will rival the fame of antiquity.

In the final stanza, Acasto declares that this land, like all great empires, will be a fertile home for the arts and sciences:

> This is thy praise America thy pow'r
> Thou best of climes by science visited
> By freedom blest and richly stor'd with all

> The luxuries of life. Hail happy land
> The seat of empire the abode of kings,
> The final stage where time shall introduce
> Renowned characters, and glorious works
> Of high invention and of wond'rous art.[22]

Here, in the reference to the "seat of empire," the poem draws on the notion, based on the biblical book of Daniel, that there would be five empires in human history, the fifth being a utopia or, in the alternative, an apocalypse.[23]

Freneau also represents Columbus as a figure of empire in his poem entitled "Pictures of Columbus, the Genoese," written in 1774 and published in 1788. This poem recounts "the shameful story" of Ferdinand's ungratefulness toward Columbus. It ends with Columbus alone on his deathbed, having none of the honors he merits, his only comfort being the promise of a future "when empires rise where lonely forests grew."[24] The poem suggests that Columbus is responsible for this future, as these "empires" are the reward of his toils.

In 1771, at almost the same time that Brackenridge and Freneau composed their *On the Rising Glory*, nineteen-year-old Timothy Dwight wrote *America: Or, A Poem on the Settlement of the British Colonies*. Like Freneau and Brackenridge, Dwight first portrays Columbus as responsible for introducing the Old World to the New. Near the poem's end, when Freedom triumphantly addresses America as an empire destined to expand, the poet invokes Columbus's name:

> Hail Land of light and joy! thy power shall grow
> Far as the seas, which round thy regions flow;
> Through earth's wide realms thy glory shall extend,
> And savage nations at thy scepter bend.
> Around the frozen shores thy sons shall sail,
> Or stretch their canvas to the ASIAN gale,
> Or, like COLUMBUS, steer their course unknown,

> Beyond the regions of the flaming zone,
> To worlds unfound beneath the southern pole,
> Whose native hears Antarctic oceans roll;
> Where artless Nature rules with peaceful sway,
> And where no ship e'er stemm'd the untry'd way.[25]

The poet envisions a great empire that conquers other peoples ("savage nations at thy scepter bend"). Eventually, the empire itself will be "like Columbus," expanding its domain to new regions ("through earth's wide realms thy glory shall extend"). The poem continues with a reference to the Roman Empire:

> Earth's richest realms their treasures shall unfold,
> And op'ning mountains yield the flaming gold;
> Round thy broad fields more glorious ROMES arise,
> With pomp and splendour bright'ning all the skies;
> EUROPE and ASIA with surprise behold
> Thy temples starr'd with gems and roof'd with gold.
> From realm to realm broad APPIAN ways shall wind,
> And distant shores by long canals be join'd,
> The ocean hear thy voice, the waves obey,
> And through green vallies trace their wat'ry way.[26]

The Appian Way was the most famous of the Roman Empire's many roadways that facilitated its territorial expansion. Dwight's reference here to "Romes" connected by "Appian ways" that "shall wind" "from realm to realm" further characterizes America as the heir to Western (Roman) empire. Like the empire described in *On the Rising Glory* by Freneau and Brackenridge, Dwight's empire in America is unlike its European counterpart. Dwight's vision of empire is different because it is based on "freedom, and science, and virtue," instead of war, as in Europe.

A similar casting of Columbus as agent of *translatio imperii* is seen in Joel Barlow's *The Columbiad*, published in 1807. This poem is a reworking of Barlow's *The Vision of Columbus*, published in

1787 but composed between 1778 and 1787. Barlow appears to have relied on Sylvanus Americus's (Nevill's) "History of the Northern Continent of America" as well as Robertson's *History of America*. Although in his preface Barlow criticizes the classical epics of Homer and Virgil—he disdains, for example, the "moral tendency" of the *Aeneid*, saying that Virgil "wrote and felt like a subject, not a citizen"—he begins his poem by declaring its subject to be Columbus, echoing the first lines of the *Aeneid:*

> I sing the Mariner who first unfurl'd
> An eastern banner o'er the western world,
> And taught mankind where future empires lay
> In these fair confines of descending day.[27]

Barlow's language recalls Virgil's "Arma virumque cano, Troiae qui primus ab oris / Italiam, fato profugus Laviniaque venit / Litora." (I sing of arms and the man who first from the coasts of Troy, exiled by fate, came to Italy and Lavine shores.)[28] Barlow's appropriation of Virgil's epic formula is charged with imperial connotations. Steven Blakemore argues that Barlow's republican critique of the ancient epics shows a measure of "ideological schizophreni[a]."[29] The description of Columbus spreading "an eastern banner o'er the western world" echoes Columbus's own description of his most important imperial act: his taking possession of the New World for Spain with "the royal standard extended." In Barlow's poem, Columbus's pointing out "where future empires lay" serves as the first step in the nation's journey to fulfilling its future imperial destiny.

Freneau, Brackenridge, Dwight, and Barlow all drew upon current ideas circulating in the British Atlantic world about the changing British Empire and its colonies. In particular, they tapped into the *translatio imperii* tradition, which was commonly found in poetic and political discourse about the American continent.[30] The model of that expression is George Berkeley's "Verses on the Prospect of Planting Arts and Learning in America," written in 1725 and published in 1752.³¹ In the words of Kenneth Silverman, "virtually every large colonial newspaper and many books and magazines reprinted [Berkeley's poem] in its entirety at some time during the third quarter of the eighteenth century. Berkeley's metaphors of Translation—a growing plant, a genial rising sun, the final act of a drama—seeped into colonial speech, so that diaries, orations, poems, and conversation everywhere in the period register a prophetic awareness of growth."³²

An important part of the *translatio imperii* narrative as Berkeley and others applied it to America was the belief that the British Empire was in decline.³³ This widespread belief was based largely on Sallust's analysis of Roman history and his contention that empires have a natural life span—they rise and fall according to cycles of expansion, glory, corruption, overextension, and decay. This narrative is evident in the criticisms of the Cromwellian Protectorate that surfaced in the 1650s and denounced the Protectorate's unsuccessful Western Design in the Spanish Caribbean and, more generally, its failed attempt to balance *imperium* and *libertas*.³⁴ Berkeley himself discussed the degeneration of England in "An Essay towards Preventing the Ruin of Great Britain," published anonymously in 1721. The opening sentence first refers to the recent financial disaster caused by the South Sea Bubble and then concludes, "we are actually undone, and lost to all sense of our true interest." The rest of the essay elaborates on the corruption of English values and predicts England's inevitable demise: "we are doomed to be undone," he bemoans.³⁵

In the context of this decline, Berkeley brought attention to the role of the American colonies. His remedy for the doomed British Empire, articulated in *A Proposal for the Better Supplying of Churches in Our Foreign Plantations and for Converting the Savage Americans to Christianity by a College in the Summer Islands* (1725), was to establish a missionary seminary on the island of Bermuda which would serve as an isolated, pristine, incorruptible base from which to launch an English imperial advance on the American continent.³⁶ America, in Berkeley's view, was a clean slate upon which could be written the virtues of England's empire, the civic virtues that were encoded in the Bill of Rights but were now corrupt in Britain. Hence, while Berkeley portrays Europe in "Verses" as "decay[ed]" and "barren" to the point that "the Muse" who dwells there is "disgusted," he presents America as the site of the last of the five great empires:

> Westward the course of empire takes its way,
> The four first acts already past
> A fifth shall close the drama with the day;
> Time's noblest offspring is the last.[37]

It is important to recognize that Berkeley's prediction of the future glorious America is fully British. His poem "explain[s] and justif[ies] the expansion of British imperial power."[38] In fact, Berkeley's "Verses" about the westward movement of the empire to America was composed during the Parliamentary debate about his Bermuda project. Its subject deals with the very beginnings of the idea of the British Empire.[39] It was believed that English political liberties, the sciences, and the arts would flee to the colonies. (The original title of Berkeley's "Verses" emphasized this migration: "America; or The Muse's Refuge: A Prophecy in Six Verses.") This *translatio libertatis et studii* would make England's North American colonies the new "seat of empire," that is, "the British Empire *in* America" or "the British Empire *of* America."[40] Anglo-Americans who shared this line of thinking often saw themselves as more British than their corrupt counterparts in England. But they still saw themselves as part of England's political framework. It was not until the 1770s, when the political crisis between England and its colonies became acute, that colonists began to advocate political separation in order to maintain their Britishness.[41]

The Britishness of empire is evident in some of the texts that were discussed earlier in this chapter. Consider, for example, Freneau and Brackenridge's *On the Rising Glory*. The *translatio imperii et studii* to America is clearly described—"Dominion" leaves the empires of the east, then Britain, and now "hastens onward to th' American shores"—yet the poets who composed the poem in 1771 identify themselves as "we the sons of Britain." They employ Columbus in this poem to sing the story of England's renovated empire in America, which will be "the seat of empire the abode of kings."[42] The empire described in Timothy Dwight's *America* is similarly British. He prefaces the description of that empire, whose sons will be "like Columbus" and whose glory and territorial expanse will be like Rome's, with a section praising the British victory in the French and Indian War: "At length these realms the British scepter own, / And bow submissive at great GEORGE'S throne."[43] Dwight's version of America's "rising glory" was, in the words of one scholar, "a glory conceived as an extension of Britannia's Protestant sway and submissiveness 'at great GEORGE'S throne.'"[44] Dwight had yet to declare his support for independence, which according to his own account he did in 1775. After that, in 1777, while he was a chaplain in the Connecticut Continental Brigade, Dwight composed his ode "Columbia," whose title takes on the feminized form of Columbus's name, which I discuss later and which continues the "rising glory" theme but refers to an independent American empire:

> COLUMBIA! Columbia! to glory arise,
> The queen of the world and the child of the skies!
> Thy genius commands thee, with raptures behold,
> While ages on ages thy splendor unfold.
> Thy reign is the last and the noblest of time,
> Most fruitful thy soil, most inviting thy clime;
> Let the crimes of the east ne'er encrimson thy name,
> Be freedom, and science, and virtue thy fame.[45]

Again we note here that empire in America, while still British, is distinct from European empire because its fame is rooted in "freedom," "science," and "virtue."

The flurry of cultural production related to Columbus from the 1770s on in British America and then the United States has been well documented.⁴⁶ After independence, Columbus became a symbol of the new nation that safeguarded what were considered English liberties by replacing the monarchical system with a republic. American revolutionaries sought to purge the English empire of its faults, to replicate that empire without the weaknesses inherent in a monarchical system that doomed the attempt to secure both imperial grandeur and liberty. In the late eighteenth century, representations of Columbus continued British Americans' identification not only with empire and the imperial ideal but also with a republican system. Herein lies what was unique in American representations of Columbus: his ties to empire, discursively constructed through the centuries, remained intact, yet he was now also held up as a democratic, anti-monarchical symbol.

The coexistence of republican liberty and empire, which is at the heart of the American Columbus, is also at the center of the discourse of the American Revolution, and its origins lie in the ideology of the British Empire itself. As David Armitage has deftly illustrated, "British republicans . . . attempted to reconcile the convergent, but antagonistic, claims of empire and liberty in the century between the Elizabethan *fin-de-siècle* and the Glorious Revolution, and beyond." However, that attempt, according to contemporary critics like James Harrington, failed when the Cromwellian Protectorate did not safeguard liberties while expanding its *imperium*.⁴⁷ British Americans, who had inherited the republican notion of empire embraced by the English, believed that they alone could reconcile *imperium* and *libertas* because they were free of the flaws of monarchy. Jefferson's "empire for liberty," which was at the foundation of the political experiment embraced by the framers of the new nation, was, in the words of Jefferson scholar Peter Onuf, "an empire without a metropolis, a regime of consent, not coercion."⁴⁸

One of the rhetorical moves that made possible the combination of the imperial and the republican in the figure of Columbus in the British American context had already been performed in the Columbian interpretive tradition. This is the characterization of Columbus as a victim of the Spanish monarchs, or at least of Ferdinand. We see this portrayal in Columbus's own writings, in Peter Martyr's *Decades*, and in Ferdinand Columbus's biography of his father. All of these texts were widely used as sources by historiographers like Eden, Hakluyt, and Robertson. Their works were in turn read by generations that followed. In British America, a notable early expression of this characterization of Columbus is Freneau's "Pictures of Columbus."

The popularity of the *translatio imperii* trope and the adoption of Columbus in the *translatio* narrative in British America reflect the centrality of empire in contemporary political thought in British America. The impulse to expand westward into the interior of the continent, already evident in seven colonial charters and expressed throughout the eighteenth century before independence was declared—most notably in the wars involving territorial disputes with the French and native populations—, was popularly understood as a movement toward empire. Since the Romans, the term "empire" has been associated with great swaths of territory.[49] One of the primary definitions of "empire" in the Oxford English Dictionary, first appearing in the year 1297, is: "An extensive territory (*esp.* an aggregate of many separate states) under the sway of an emperor or supreme ruler; also, an aggregate of subject territories ruled over by a sovereign state."[50] British Americans' desire to conquer more territory is famously expressed in Benjamin Franklin's pamphlet entitled *Observations Concerning the Increase of Mankind*, which was published in 1751, twenty years before Freneau and Brackenridge's *A Poem, On the Rising Glory of America*. In this piece Franklin predicts that the English population in the colonies will double every twenty years and that, although it would take "many ages," the English would eventually colonize the entire continent.[51] The important point here is that the drive to acquire more territory, to acquire what was imagined as an empire of extensive territory, was present long before independence was declared in 1776. The acquisition of the trans-Appalachian territory, so skillfully negotiated by American representatives in the 1783 Treaty of Paris, set the new nation's territorial boundaries far beyond the settled cities of the eastern seaboard and was the legal expression of this drive to empire. In *Habits of Empire: A History of American Expansion*, historian Walter Nugent argues that this territorial acquisition was "an absolutely essential platform for America's further expansion." Moreover, he writes, it was an early expression of "manifest destiny," this notion that America had a God-given mission to rule the continent as a great empire:

> American assumptions that Transappalachia was indivisibly part of their territory went far back in time to the colonial charters. They also rested on cultural attitudes about English Protestant civilization's superiority to Catholic French and Spanish pretensions and, more to the day-to-day point, to Indian "savagery." . . . The American romance with Transappalachia included land-grabbing and moneymaking, but it was hardly just that. It involved patriotism, and even more, many thought, the fulfillment of the plans of God and Nature for America. Diverse American voices—religious, cultural, and economic—converged in the assumption that Transappalachia was and had to be American.[52]

While the term "manifest destiny" was coined much later, in 1845, the sense that British Americans had a right to the continent that would become home to an extensive American empire was present at the beginning of the nation and, indeed, long before then when a British Empire was envisioned. This sense nourished policies of Indian removal and fed into the ideologies that underwrote the War of 1812, the Monroe Doctrine, and the long list of attempts to take over foreign territory during the nineteenth and twentieth centuries. It is no wonder that Columbus, who had always been interpreted as a figure of empire, became so popular in British America during the last third of the eighteenth century.

Washington Irving

One of the most influential nineteenth-century texts that helped make the Columbus legend part of the United States' national story was Washington Irving's *Life and Voyages of Christopher Columbus*. Irving was already a recognized author—his *Sketch Book of Geoffrey Crayon, Gent.* (which includes his famous "Rip Van Winkle") was published in 1819—when he was invited in 1826 by the American Minister to Spain to translate into English Martín Fernández de Navarrete's recently published collection of documents about Columbus and Spain's early explorations in the New World. Irving's sojourn to Spain lasted three years, until 1829, and included three months spent writing at the Alhambra. Upon his arrival, he almost immediately decided to write a biography of Columbus instead of translating Navarrete's volume, and he composed the work in less than two years.

Published in 1828, Irving's biography was the first extended study of Columbus written in English. It was immensely popular, going through 116 editions and reprints in its first eight decades. Its influence was much increased by the 1829 issue of Irving's abridged edition, which was frequently used in schools and universities. Irving's most important sources were Ferdinand Columbus's biography and Bartolomé de las Casas's *Historia de las Indias*, both of which draw from Martyr's *Decades*. The Columbus described in Irving's account represents the values of the new republic: he is a self-made man who became successful, despite many obstacles in his path, by virtue of his goodness, genius, hard work, and faith in science and the benefits of commerce.[53] Take, for example, the following passage from the end of chapter 1, which describes Columbus's general character:

He was one of those men of strong natural genius, who from having to contend at their very outset with privations and impediments, acquire an intrepidity in encountering and a facility in vanquishing difficulties, throughout their career. Such men learn to effect great purposes with small means, supplying this deficiency by the resources of their own energy and invention. This, from his earliest commencement, throughout the whole of his life, was one of the remarkable features in the history of Columbus. In every undertaking, the scantiness and apparent insufficiency of his means enhance the grandeur of his achievements.[54]

Irving's Columbus, including his association with empire, conformed to the values of the new nation. Only five years before the biography's publication in 1828, President James Monroe openly articulated the nation's imperialist agenda in what became known as the "Monroe Doctrine," which warned Europe that "the American continents . . . are henceforth not to be considered as subjects for future colonization by any European powers." Irving's Columbus-turned-American-hero was very much an imperial figure. Following the model whereby Columbus is portrayed as a new Aeneas, Irving quotes the famous passage from Seneca's *Medea* in his epigraph, setting up the characterization of Columbus as founder of empire. We note the manner in which Irving follows Las Casas's description of Columbus's entry into Barcelona as a Roman conqueror who has just won more territory for the Empire: "His entrance into this noble city has been compared to one of those triumphs which the Romans were accustomed to decree to conquerors."[55] Shortly after this description, Irving repeats Las Casas's description of Columbus as he meets Ferdinand and Isabel: "At length Columbus entered the hall, surrounded by a brilliant crowd of cavaliers, among whom, says Las Casas, he was conspicuous for his stately and commanding person, which with his countenance rendered venerable by his gray hairs, gave him the august appearance of a senator of Rome."⁵⁶ Irving again portrays Columbus as a founder of empire in his last chapter, "Observations on the Character of Columbus":

> His conduct as a discoverer was characterized by the grandeur of his views, and the magnanimity of his spirit. Instead of scouring the newly found countries, like a grasping adventurer eager only for immediate gain, as was too generally the case with contemporary discoverers, he sought to ascertain their soil and productions, their rivers and harbours. He was desirous of colonizing and cultivating them, of conciliating and civilizing the natives, of building cities, introducing the useful arts, subjecting every thing to the control of law, order and religion, and thus of founding regular and prosperous empires.⁵⁷

This passage is consistent with the Black Legend in distinguishing Columbus from other "contemporary discoverers" who are here described as "eager only for immediate gain." Irving's Columbus, in contrast, has superior motives. Most importantly, he is an empire builder: a new Aeneas who is "colonizing and cultivating," "civilizing the natives" by imposing his "law, order and religion," "building cities," and "thus . . . founding . . . empires."

Irving's Columbus also provides a lesson on the faults of monarchical government. His message is clear: because societies based on hereditary kingship and nobility do not value individual liberty and enterprise, the ingenious, hard-working Columbus is scorned by "the cold and calculating Ferdinand," "a sovereign who was so ungratefully neglecting him."⁵⁸ At the end of his life, Columbus is infirm, destitute, and offered no assistance from the Crown, whose empire he increased. "We can scarcely believe," Irving declares, "that this is the discoverer of the New World, broken down by infirmities and impoverished in his old age, by his very discoveries; that the man who had added such vast and wealthy regions to the crown who is the individual thus wearily and vainly applying to the court of Spain for his dues, and pleading almost like a culprit, in cases wherein he had been so flagrantly injured."[59] As he describes Columbus on his deathbed, Irving reminds the reader that the admiral is the son of a republic (Genoa), subtly suggesting that his origins explain not only his values and his character but also his aptness as a symbol of the United States.[60]

Nineteenth-Century Painting

After Irving, there was an explosion of cultural production with Columbus as its subject. Much of the artwork installed during the nineteenth century at the nation's capital, for example, threw into sharp relief Columbus's status as a national symbol of empire. Take, for example, John Vanderlyn's well-known painting, *Landing of Columbus at the Island of Guanahani, West Indies, October 12th, 1492* (see Figure 1). Prominently displayed on the east wall of the Capitol Rotunda, Vanderlyn's painting shows Columbus taking possession of the New World for Spain. In one hand he brandishes a sword, and in the other he plants the royal flag of Ferdinand and Isabel. Natives, in awe or fear, hide behind a nearby tree. The painting portrays a paradigmatic moment of imperial conquest of the savage other. "The Italian navigator," in the words of Vivien Green Fryd, "has invaded the Arawack's [sic] territory, the darkened area [of the painting], bringing Old World civilization, represented by the highlighted shore and ocean. Not only are the Indians smaller than the dominant arrivals, but they are also painted with thinly applied pigment with loose edges, unlike the more hardened contours of the sculpturally defined central figures."[61] It is telling that this painting was commissioned for the Capitol in 1837, fourteen years after the Monroe Doctrine and seven years after the Indian Removal Act of the Jackson administration. As Fryd notes, "the subject matter and iconography of much of the art in the Capitol" is consistent with the messages of Vanderlyn's painting, promoting

Figure 1. John Vanderlyn, *Landing of Columbus at the Island of Guanahani, West Indies, October 12th, 1492*. Courtesy of the Architect of the Capitol.

a "remarkably coherent program of the early course of North American empire, from the [European] discovery and settlement to the national development and westward expansion that necessitated [or, more appropriately, resulted in] the subjugation of the indigenous peoples."[62] We should not be surprised to see much of Columbus in this artwork, including the *Columbus Doors*, designed by Randolph Rogers and installed in 1863 and 1871.

Like Vanderlyn's painting, which is hanging nearby, the first panel of Constantino Brumidi's frieze depicting the course of American history also illustrates Columbus's taking possession of the New World for Spain (see Figure 2). The frieze was commissioned by the supervising engineer of the Capitol extension (1853–59), Montgomery C. Meigs, who described the design of the frieze's historical episodes to Secretary of War Jefferson Davis:

Figure 2. Constantino Brumidi, et al. *Frieze of American History, Landing of Columbus*. Courtesy of the Architect of the Capitol.

> The gradual progress of a continent from the depths of barbarism to the height of civilization; the rude and barbarous civilization of some of the Ante-Columbian tribes; the contests of the Aztecs with their less civilized predecessors; their own conquest by the Spanish race; the wilder state of the hunter tribes of our own regions; the discovery, settlement, wars, treaties, the gradual advance of the white, and retreat of the red races; our own revolutionary and other struggles, with the illustration of the higher achievements of our present civilization.[63]

Within this narrative as expressed by Meigs, Columbus plays a role we are familiar with: the bringer of "civilization," which was understood as European and white and imposed by imperial conquest. This is also the narrative told by Brumidi's lunette, *Columbus and the Indian Maiden* (c. 1875), painted above the chamber doors of the Senate Committee on Indian Affairs (see Figure 3). In this fresco, a patriarchal Columbus stands above a seated Indian woman. In his hand is a rolled parchment, likely the record of his having taken possession of the new territory he "discovered." He lifts her veil, and she leans away from him as if his advance is unwanted. The scene, regardless of Brumidi's intent, alludes to the white man's

Figure 3. Constantino Brumidi, *Columbus and the Indian Maiden*. Courtesy of the Architect of the Capitol.

disrobing and rape of the indigenous female and is symbolic of the policies of "removal" advocated by the senate committee whose members passed under Brumidi's fresco.

In the nineteenth century, the allegorical, female figure of Columbia became popular. As discussed in the Introduction, the term "Columbia" has a long history. In an effort to honor Amerigo Vespucci and following in the tradition of designating continents with feminine Latin nouns (e.g., Europa, Asia, Africa), Martin Waldseemüller was the first to employ the name "America" on a map he made in 1507. Shortly thereafter, and for centuries to come, the term "Columbia" and its many variants

Figure 4. John Gast, *American Progress*. Courtesy of the Autry National Center of the American West.

were proposed as alternative names for the continent that many believed should honor Columbus instead of Vespucci. The term "Columbia" became a synonym in English of "America" well before the Revolution. I disagree with those who argue that the name "Columbia" became so common that it lost all association with Christopher Columbus.[64] Rather, we should keep in mind Columbus's role as stock character in the dominant Western narrative of conquest and empire building.

To substantiate this observation, let us consider the 1872 painting by John Gast entitled *American Progress* (see Figure 4). This painting was commissioned by publisher George A. Crofutt, whose magazine *Crofutt's Western World* and guidebooks about the West were integral in marketing the western territories to the nation. Crofutt, who produced chromolithographs of the painting to include in his magazine and guidebooks, instructed Gast on the elements to include in the painting and even what it should be titled.[65] The work features the feminine Columbia, representing the United States, with the "Star of Empire" on her forehead, flying effortlessly westward (toward the left of the painting) as she leads the white settlers in the conquest of territory held by now-fleeing natives. The right side of the painting, the east, where the light of civilization shines, contrasts with the darkness of the left side, the west, where there are "savages" yet to be conquered. Columbia, an emblem for the United States' westward-advancing empire, holds a book, symbolic of the *translatio studii*, and she brings technology with her, stringing telegraph wires and leading trains in her wake. The scene captures the meaning of Columbus as a symbol of empire in the nineteenth-century United States.

World's Columbian Exposition, Chicago 1893

The United States' insatiable appetite for foreign territory since its inception has been well documented.[66] By the end of the nineteenth century, the United States already had more than a century of experience with "empire building," to use Nugent's term. First was the acquisition of Trans-Appalachia, realized in the peace treaties of 1782 and 1783 that ended the Revolutionary War. This was followed by constant acquisitions, the territories of Louisiana, Florida, Texas, Oregon, and Alaska among them. By the last decade of the nineteenth century, the United States had expanded across the continent and was eyeing Hawaii. The last major battle of the "Indian wars" at Wounded Knee occurred in 1890. According to data collected in the census of that year, the frontier had closed. Looking at this scenario in his famous essay "The Significance of the Frontier in American History," Frederick Jackson Turner declared that continued expansion, now abroad instead of "domestic" expansion, was necessary to guarantee the prosperous future of the nation. Turner presented his essay at a fitting venue: the World's Columbian Exposition of 1893, a world's fair celebrating Columbus and marking the apogee of his popularity in the United States.

This event was initially planned for 1892 to celebrate the quadricentennial of Columbus's "discovery" of America, but its ambitious size and scope required that it be postponed one year. Approximately twenty-seven million people attended the fair, which contained over 250 thousand displays. It was one in a series of world's fairs, beginning with London's 1851 Crystal Palace Exhibition, that became increasingly popular as industrialized nations sought to expand their economic activities and influence overseas. World's fairs articulated especially well nationalist discourses of imperialism and were particularly important before the advent of mass communication media because of their capacity to expose large numbers of people to a coherent interpretation of the nation and its role in the world. Organized and promoted by the socio-economic elites of economically advanced nations of the West, fairs were, as Robert Rydell explains with regard to these fairs in the United States, both "symbolic edifices" and "triumphs of hegemony." Rydell, citing Antonio Gramsci, defines the term "hegemony" as "the exercise of economic and political power in cultural terms by the established leaders of American society and the 'spontaneous' consent given by the great masses of the population to the general direction imposed on social life by the dominant fundamental group; this content is 'historically' caused by the prestige (and consequent confidence) which the dominant group enjoys because of its position and function in the world of production." Rydell concludes that "world's fairs performed a hegemonic function precisely because they propagated the ideas and values of the country's political, financial, corporate, and intellectual leaders and offered these ideas as the proper interpretation of social and political reality."[67]

The elites who organized and promoted the Chicago World's Exposition propagated their hegemonic views about what was "civilized" and "barbaric," what was "history" and what was "knowledge." According to one contemporary history of the Exposition, "Among monuments marking the progress of civilization throughout the ages, the World's Columbian Exposition of 1893 will ever stand conspicuous. Gathered here are the forces which move humanity and make history, the ever-shifting powers that fit new thoughts to new conditions, and shape the destinies of mankind."[68] The emphasis in this statement on "the progress of civilization" reminds us of the *translatio imperii* narrative that is now told by the United States citizen "victor," using the term as David Quint does, and imperial subject. That subject benefited from and promoted the expansion of Western capitalism and Western epistemology. The figure of Columbus, I have argued here, has always found a comfortable home within the discourses of imperialism. He himself, after all, played an important role in the expansion of the European economic system across the Atlantic and the beginnings of the modern capitalist system.

The figure of Columbus at the Chicago Exposition was an especially apt conduit for the imperialist discourse of the day. Although the tradition by which Columbus had been interpreted for centuries had changed in the United States, where he had become a symbol of the republic, his status as conqueror and his association with empire—as a stock protagonist in the narrative of the *translatio imperii*—remained. Many of the poems and speeches presented at the Exposition's October 1892 opening ceremonies characterized Columbus as the agent responsible for the westward transfer of empire. We are familiar with this Columbus from our survey of earlier portrayals of him in US literature. One example is *The Columbian Oration*, delivered by Chauncey M. Depew, an unsuccessful candidate for the 1888 Republican Party presidential nomination. After first crediting the explorer with "the planting, the nurture and the expansion of civil and religious liberty" in America, Depew soon turned his attention to the *translatio imperii* trope, addressing history's record of empires that had been conquered and replaced by new ones to the west.[69]

"Ancient history," Depew asserted, "is a dreary record of unstable civilizations. Each reached its zenith of material splendor, and perished. The Assyrian, Persian, Egyptian, Grecian and Roman Empires were proofs of the possibilities and limitations of man for conquest and intellectual development." These empires operated by force, and "their destruction involved a sum of misery and relapse which made their creation rather a curse than a blessing." In contrast, Depew claimed, the empire in the United States was superior to those of the past largely because of the influence of Christianity. Most importantly for our purposes, it was made possible by Columbus: "The spirit of equality of all men before God and the law, moved westward from Calvary with its revolutionary influence upon old institutions, to the Atlantic Ocean. *Columbus carried it westward across the seas.*"[70]

In the course of Depew's speech, a contradiction arises between his negative portrayal of empire and his subsequent characterization of the United States as both empire and home of republican liberty. Depew attempts to negotiate this contradiction by characterizing Columbus, the imperial agent, as the unknowing transporter of the spirit of democracy. The seed of democracy is a stowaway on Columbus' ship: "Individual intelligence and independent conscience . . . were the passengers upon the caravels of Columbus, and he was unconsciously making for the port of civil and religious liberty."[71] Columbus's ignorance allows him to be the symbol of both empire and the *res publica*. Depew can thus compare Columbus not only to the imperial rulers Caesar, Charlemagne, and William the Conqueror, but also to the national heroes Washington and Lincoln. Columbus, in Depew's rendition, serves as a hinge connecting the nation with both empire and Europe.

At the Exposition's second opening ceremonies, held in May of 1893, Columbus was yet again portrayed as playing a key role in the *translatio imperii* and the rise of the nation as empire. This time it was Thomas Brower Peacock who interpreted Columbus in this manner in *The Columbian Ode*, which won first prize in an international poetry contest sponsored by the Exposition's Board of Managers. At the end of this poem—the main thematic concern of which is the United States as the fifth and final empire of world history—the "Star of Empire" unambiguously alights in America after moving west through Asia, Greece, Rome, and Germany.[72] The primary role of Columbus in the transfer of empire to America is alluded to by the poem's title as well as by the portrayal of Columbus as the national hero who caused nothing less than the rebirth of man and the redefinition of empire itself. *The Columbian Ode* begins by alluding to the Exposition's benevolent imperial mission "to all nations" to which it "extend[s] . . . the hand of fellowship":

> Here Peace her olive branch now brings,
> An offering to all nations,
> And from the tips of her white wings
> Fall Love's own sweet ovations.
> By power of song, we here extend, impearled,
> The hand of fellowship to all the world.[73]

These lines echo the Exposition's interpretation of the imposition of US power abroad as the generous gift of civilization. The imperialist message, which the Exposition articulates in part through its manipulations of the figure of Columbus, is first supported in the poem by Peacock's naming of his audience as a "congress of imperial minds." After characterizing the nation as the benevolent friend "to all the world," the first stanza establishes the importance of "westward movement" ("Westward the pilgrim millions go / From out the shadows of the throne—/ Far from the lands of legends old they teem, / To bathe and live in Hope's immortal dream"). This movement to the west is associated in the poem with escape from tyranny ("From out of the shadows of the throne") and progress, a *sine qua non* of the *translatio imperii* narrative, according to which each empire conquers and improves upon the previous one. The language of power in the first stanza ("power," "to all the world," "throne," "imperial," "kings") underscores the message in the following stanzas that the United States is an empire, yet one unlike those that preceded it.[74]

The poem then traces the history of empire before it reached America's shores. It is a history of war and death, and the situation improves only with the appearance of Columbus, who enters the poem at its midpoint. Peacock insinuates that in bringing empire to America, Columbus is responsible for the rebirth of the individual and his ultimate rise to power: "Not till Columbus crossed the watery main, / Did man, renascent, his true dominion gain."[75] The poet's message is supported by the imperial resonances of the word "dominion": not only was the Latin variant of the term used in the legal code of the Roman Empire to denote ownership, but it was also used in the British Empire to refer to overseas territories under the Crown's control.

Like the contradictions in Depew's speech, the contradiction in Peacock's poem regarding the idea of the nation as an "empire of liberty" requires a slight modification of the *translatio imperii* narrative in which Columbus is the protagonist. Early in the poem, Peacock portrays emperors as tyrants, clearly indicting imperial power itself with the crimes of war and murder. This creates difficulties later in the poem when the empire of the United States is extolled. Peacock's solution is to position this empire "above the dust of empires and the crash of worlds." He thus reconceptualizes empire in the United States, casting it as an empire *sui generis*. Affirming its essentially democratic nature, he writes: "Here all are crowned—no potentate alone—/ Each separate altar-fire itself a peerless throne."[76] In Peacock's version of American antimonarchical republicanism, the *imperium* of the sovereign is granted to the people. The sovereign is thus severed from the concept of empire, but the sovereign's *imperium* is preserved in the people, all of whom are now "kings." Columbus makes possible this vision in Peacock's poem of the United States as an imperial nation-state.

The Exposition's geographical layout and architecture also conveyed the notion that Columbus, imperial conqueror, was an apt symbol for the contemporary United States. The centralized cluster of buildings that housed the major exhibits of the Exposition was dubbed the "White City," because the buildings were covered in white plaster of paris. Its neoclassical buildings and Greek and Roman statutes reminded fairgoers of the *translatio imperii* narrative: while the seat of empire had once been Greece and then Rome, Columbus had brought it westward to the United States. The focal point of the White City was the Court of Honor. Here, in the middle of the Exposition's central lake, on a forty-foot-high base, stood the colossal sixty-five-foot-high Statue of the Republic, a gilded, robed woman who symbolically controlled the world as she grasped the globe in one hand and the staff of power in the other. Behind her towered *The Columbus Quadriga*, an impressive statue featuring Columbus arriving at the Exposition as a triumphant Roman emperor in a horse-drawn chariot (see Figure 5). Lastly, the central basin displayed *The Columbian Fountain*, which featured the allegorical figure of "Columbia" seated on the "Barge of State," a ship pulled by the "Sea horses of Commerce" and oared by the Industries and the Arts (see Figure 6). These statues, together with the neoclassical architecture and classical allusions of the Court of Honor, contributed to the Exposition's construction of Columbus as a symbol of republican empire.

Outside the confines of the White City, the symbolic heart of "civilization" where Columbus was on display in a multitude of venues and forms, was the twelve-block-long Midway. Here the inhabitants of barbarous non-industrialized nations were isolated and on display in several "ethnological villages." The foreigners on display at the Chicago Exposition functioned as the flip side of the "civilized" world (read: capitalist, white, Western/European) touted in the White City. By their difference, these foreigners defined what it meant to be civilized, and their lack of civilization rendered them objects to be both feared and dominated (see Figure 7).

Figure 5. Daniel C. French and E. C. Potter, *The Columbus Quadriga*. Courtesy of the Paul V. Galvin Library at the Illinois Institute of Technology.

The practice of exhibiting foreigners at world's fairs, all of which were hosted by colonial powers, did not originate with the Chicago Exposition. Burton Benedict writes that "almost without exception the major international exhibitions were sponsored by nations with colonial dependencies. Each displayed its colonies, or its internally colonized peoples, to its home population, to its rivals and to the world at large."[77] At the Paris Exposition of 1889, Otis Mason, the US delegate from the Smithsonian who was later involved in planning the Chicago Exposition, was impressed with the display of France's colonized subjects.[78] The decision to imitate these exhibits in Chicago by installing a series

Figure 6. Frederick MacMonnies, *The Columbian Fountain*. Courtesy of the Paul V. Galvin Library at the Illinois Institute of Technology.

of "ethnological villages" reveals the extent to which Mason and other planners identified, whether consciously or not, the United States with imperial France: like France, America was an empire.

Many fairgoers had never before seen the different peoples on display at the Exposition. In this, they were like those who witnessed Columbus's return to Spain in 1493, when he paraded through the streets with a sampling of the booty he had found in the New World, including Amerindians, parrots, stuffed animals, and plants. If we consider the fairgoer's experience in viewing these displays as an introduction to the world's "barbarous" others, we can see how these exhibits worked together with the

Figure 7. *The South Sea Islanders*. Courtesy of the Paul V. Galvin Library at the Illinois Institute of Technology.

Exposition's discourse about Columbus to construct the United States as an empire and the fairgoer as imperial subject. Like European "cabinets of curiosities," which displayed items collected from the uncivilized world, the collections of foreigners at the Exposition revealed the nation's dominance over a microcosmic reflection of the diversity of the world. The acts of collecting, categorizing as "other," and displaying these peoples articulated the dominance of the United States, which set the terms of what was civilized and what was not. The Exposition deemed these peoples "ethnological" and worthy of exhibition because they were the foreign others who fell within the sphere of the nation's dominance.

Organized by the Exposition's Department of Ethnography, the "ethnological villages" were placed on the entertainment-oriented

Midway, which contributed to the interpretation of the foreigners as abnormal and uncivilized "curiosities" that existed outside the framework of the "civilized" world. The Midway offered an array of entertainment and exotic shows. Visitors could amuse themselves by riding the world's first Ferris wheel, viewing belly dancers and sword fights, or riding camels. *Cosmopolitan* magazine editor John Brisben Walker emphasized the contrast between the "playground" of the Midway and the White City, which he termed a "university" because it educated the fairgoer:

> But is it [the Exposition] all work and no play? On the contrary, after his morning at the university has been spent in study, the student wends his way to the playground, the Plaisance. . . . Hither have come the nations of the earth to minister to his enjoyment: the Arab, on his splendid steed with nostrils dilated and champing at the bit, spurs, blunted lance in hand, gallops after his fellow. And we may see the sports of the desert and take part in the applause which comes up from the encampment of Arab women and children on the other side of the enclosure, when one spearman has planted his blunted lance fairly in the back of the man he is pursuing.[79]

In this citation, the words associated with the White City, "university" and "study," are opposed to the "playground" of the Midway. The comprehensive scope of the collection of foreigners ("Hither have come the nations of the earth") again reminds the reader that a microcosm of the world is assembled and controlled by the imperial collector. Only one foreign other, "the Arab," is required as an example after the colon prompts the reader to expect a list of "the nations of the earth." The Arab's difference is effectively conflated with and deemed equivalent to the differences of other foreigners. What is most important is not the unique identity of the Arab, but his status—like the status of all foreigners—as a subservient other that "minister[s] to" the "enjoyment" of the American fairgoer (and, on a parallel level, US foreign policy). Again we see that the foreigner is to be feared: he must be kept in an "enclosure," and he carries a "lance," which he "has planted . . . fairly in the back of the man he is pursuing." And while his difference is to be feared, it also makes him a legitimate object of domination, a status which appears justified by the ease with which he can be dominated: that his lance is "blunted" suggests that his otherness is manageable.

Native Americans were displayed next to the Midway's collections of foreigners in separate exhibits. Because Native Americans were both popularly viewed and legally treated as colonized subjects, these displays helped to further legitimize the fairgoer's identification as imperial subject. The nation's history of internal colonization, of course, provided imperialists at the end of the nineteenth century with important rhetorical weaponry in their arguments for international expansion. They reasoned that the colonization of Native Americans had established a precedent for colonialism abroad.[80] The juxtaposition of the nation's internally colonized peoples and other not-yet-colonized (or, in fact, financially colonized) foreigners on the Midway suggested that the nation was capable of and justified in imposing its power on both groups.

The Midway's messages regarding colonized Native Americans were reinforced by "Buffalo Bill's Wild West," the privately owned spectacle that operated a short distance from the Midway. The Wild West show featured historical protagonists and actors who reenacted important scenes from US history, beginning with the colonial period and ending with "Custer's Last Fight." The Wild West program claimed that it presented "the story of the gradual civilization of a vast continent," an assertion that the public surely interpreted in light of the Massacre of Wounded Knee, which had occurred only three years earlier and marked for many the end of the conflict between Native Americans and European Americans, as well as the closing of the domestic frontier.[81] Columbus's usefulness in the narrative of western expansion presented at the Exposition was not lost on the promoters of the Wild West show. John Burke, Buffalo Bill Cody's publicist, made the following analogy: "As Columbus was the pilot across the seas to discover a new world, such heroes as Boone, Fremont, Crockett, Kit Carson, and last, but by no means least, Cody, were the guides to the New World of the mighty West, and their names will go down in history as 'Among the few, the immortal names / That were not born to die.'"[82] Portraits of Buffalo Bill and Columbus were even featured on Wild West stationery during its 1893 season. The portraits' captions reveal the deliberate comparison constructed between Cody and Columbus: "Pilot of the Ocean, 15th Century—the First Pioneer" and "Guide of the Prairie, 19th Century—the Last Pioneer." The Wild West show itself was framed at the beginning and end with a procession of "the Congress of Rough Riders of the World": skilled horsemen, including US cavalrymen and Native Americans, led by Cody himself, who was described in the program as "Prince of the Border Men," "King of the Scouts," and even "King of all the Rough Riders of the World." The staging of this procession declared the final victory of the white man over the savage Native American and, just as importantly, the latter's submission to the expanding nation of the United States. Cody's position of command at the head of the parade, Richard Slotkin notes, "was not merely personal but national, signifying the American assumption of a leading role in world affairs."[83]

By opening the field of inquiry and going beyond the Anglo-American tradition, we find that the significance of Columbus in the United States had long been constructed by a transatlantic discourse that was originally created by Columbus himself, later perpetuated by historiographers and literati, and eventually taken up by writers in British America and then the United States. Through this discourse, British Americans and later United States citizens constructed Columbus as an archetype of a republican empire, and this rendered him uniquely suited to convey their imperial designs. As we have seen in this chapter, in the US literary tradition and at the 1893 World's Columbian Exposition, Columbus was the protagonist in the centuries-old narrative of the westward transfer of empire. This portrayal squared ideologically with the fact that "manifest destiny" and imperial ambition have always had a central place in US public discourse.

~ 4 ~
Colombia: Discourses of Empire in Spanish America

Before Colombia was declared an independent state in 1819, the terms "Colombia" and "Colombiano" were used by many Spanish American patriots to mean "America" and "American," just as the corresponding terms in English were used in the North. In Spanish America, however, these terms were used less frequently than they were in the United States, where they denoted everything from rivers, mountains, and buildings to books, journals, symphonies, and universities. Although numerous cities in nearly every part of Spanish America adopted Columbus's name, in the United States there were many more such places.[1] The different roles that Columbus played in the rhetoric of the independence and early national periods in Spanish and British America are explained not only by Columbus's place in the historiographical traditions of the two regions but also, as I will demonstrate in the following chapter, by the different meanings of the term "empire" in the North and the South.

In Spanish American history, Columbus was traditionally seen as the first representative of the Spanish Crown to arrive in the Americas. In the nineteenth century, when Spanish American Creoles sought political independence from Spain, these political actors viewed Columbus primarily as a character very similar to the Columbus portrayed by Bartolomé de las Casas. He was not seen as an evil colonizer who started three centuries of political domination (this characterization would require that Creoles renounce their own Spanish ancestors and, indeed, many of their own claims to power). Instead, he was viewed as a hero who devoted himself to Spain, brought Christianity to the New World under its aegis, and then was neglected by its kings. There was no need, as in the United States, to construct an elaborate myth in order to incorporate Columbus into the story of the independent nations of Spanish America. He was already present—indeed he was the protagonist—at the crucial, founding moment of Creole Spanish American history (which denies the importance of pre-Columbian history). His role in that moment was well known by Spanish American elites of the eighteenth and nineteenth centuries, most of whom had access to the same histories of Spain's colonization of the New World that were popular in Spain itself, including those written by Peter Martyr, Bartolomé de las Casas, Ferdinand Columbus, and Antonio de Herrera. In addition, as did their counterparts to the north, Spanish Americans read William Robertson's *History of America* even though, as David Brading writes, "Robertson's narrative of the discovery of America and conquest of Mexico and Peru is little more than a paraphrase of Antonio Herrera's *Décadas*."[2]

Francisco de Miranda

Much of the credit for the employment of the figure of Columbus in Spanish American discourses in favor of political independence goes to one person: the colorful Venezuelan Francisco de Miranda (1750–1816). Known as the "precursor" of the Spanish American independence movements, Miranda was a privileged Venezuelan Creole who fully participated in the transatlantic republic of letters and spent much of his life abroad advocating for Spanish American independence. Through Miranda, we can begin to trace the ways in which Columbus was employed in Spanish American discourse during the late colonial and early national periods.

Like most Creole young men in Spanish America, Miranda was educated in the Greek and Roman classics, as well as in

European history and literature, including the Spanish peninsular tradition. Among the materials Miranda studied at the Universidad Real y Pontificia de Caracas were Antonio de Nebrija's *Gramática de la Lengua Castellana* (1492) and the rhetoric of Cicero and Virgil. Throughout his life, he was an avid reader of texts in Spanish, French, English, Greek, and Latin. When he traveled he brought with him an extensive collection of books, to which he was always adding. Early in his life, Miranda predicted that his would be "a famous library."[3] According to his will, he intended to bequeath his collection to the University of Caracas. Some of the most important figures of the Spanish American independence movements, including Simón Bolívar, Andrés Bello, and José de San Martín, consulted the library at his London home. A catalog of its contents lists several books from which Miranda likely learned about Columbus: Peter Martyr's *De orbe novo* (Miranda owned the English translations of both Eden [published in 1555] and Hakluyt [published in 1598]), Ferdinand Columbus's biography of his father (*Historie del F. Colombo e de fatti dell'Ammiraglio Colombo*, Venice 1676), William Robertson's *History of America* (1777), and Antonio de Herrera's *Historia general de los hechos de los castellanos en las islas y tierra firme del mar océano* (also known as *Historia de las Indias occidentales*) (1728), which incorporates Bartolomé de las Casas's account of Columbus from the *Historia de las Indias*.[4] It is likely that Miranda also read Las Casas's biography of Columbus in a manuscript version of the *Historia de las Indias*, which was not published until 1875 but which was commonly circulated in Spanish America during the eighteenth century.

At the age of twenty, Miranda left Caracas to finish his education in Europe. After almost two years, his father purchased the office of Capitan in Spain's army for him, and Miranda served in North Africa and the peninsula until 1780 when, at the age of thirty, he was transferred to the Caribbean. There, he encountered firsthand the American Revolution. He witnessed the Battle of

Pensacola and acted as translator during negotiations with the British regarding the terms of the Spanish surrender. Miranda was later falsely accused of spying for the British, and he fled into exile, traveling through the United States in 1783 and 1784 before returning to Europe. As Karen Racine notes in her probing biography, Miranda often "managed to be at the center of events when a historic moment occurred."[5] He became the confidant of Catherine the Great, witnessed the French Revolution, and was commissioned as a general in the French army. All the while he never relented in his attempt to persuade those he met—many of the famous intellectual and political figures of the Age of Revolution—of the righteousness of Spanish American independence.

Miranda lived in the London home of Joel Barlow, author of *The Vision of Columbus* (published in 1787), from June 1789 through September 1791. While the catalog of Miranda's library does not list *The Vision of Columbus* (the only work of Barlow's listed is *Advice to Privileged Orders*), it is likely that Miranda read Barlow's poem during this time. However, there is no evidence to suggest that Barlow's poem inspired Miranda to use the term "Columbia" and its variants. In fact, as I discuss below, the first appearance of "Columbia" that I could find in Miranda's writings is dated 1788, before he lived with Barlow. Nevertheless, we note this connection between two men who both considered themselves American revolutionaries and who both invoked the name of Columbus.

Given Miranda's familiarity with the Atlantic world's print culture, his cosmopolitan background, and especially his eighteen-month sojourn in the United States, where the figure of Columbus and the term "Columbia" were already popular, it is not surprising that he is probably the first person who used the word "Colombia" in Spanish to refer to an independent Spanish America. He was almost surely familiar with the argument, especially common in sixteenth-century texts, that America had been unjustly named in honor of Amerigo Vespucci and that some form of Columbus's name would be more appropriate. That argument is presented, for example, in Juan de Solórzano Pereira's *Política Indiana* (1647), a copy of which Miranda owned, and in Cotton Mather's *Magnalia Christi Americana* (1702), which Miranda read during his travels through the United States in 1784.[6]

Miranda was undoubtedly exposed to the term "Columbia" during his tour of the United States in 1783–84, when it was commonly used to refer to the newly independent nation. A survey of newspapers published during the time Miranda was in the country confirms the popularity of the word "Columbia." Eleven days after Miranda arrived in North Carolina on 10 June 1783, for example, the *South Carolina Weekly Gazette* featured a poem, entitled "Peace," in which "Columbia" figures prominently. This poem opens with the image of Columbia, "tir'd with the labours of an eight years war," welcoming the goddess of Peace.[7] As was common in the literature of the day, this poem counterposes "Columbia" to "Britannia," described here as finally foregoing "her haughty claims" to possessing North America.[8] Many similar references to "Columbia" can be found in newspapers published when Miranda was in the country, making it difficult to believe that this traveler, so interested in learning all he could about his surroundings, would not have taken note of the term and what it represented. While Miranda was in New York in 1784, the previously named King's College, which had closed during the Revolution, reopened with the new name Columbia College. He also may have seen excerpts of William Robertson's *The History of America* reprinted in two Massachusetts newspapers from January 1784 to June 1785.[9] The second book of Robertson's *History*, which was serially reprinted in Worcester's *Massachusetts Spy* and Boston's *Continental Journal*, beginning in October 1783, is a biography of Columbus. If Miranda did not come across Robertson's study of Columbus while he was in the United States, he was nevertheless likely familiar with it given that the catalog of his library lists two copies of the *History of America*.[10]

Not a systematic thinker, Miranda neither explained his use of the term "Colombia" nor recorded at length his impressions of Christopher Columbus. As mentioned earlier, Miranda appears to have first employed the term "Colombia" in 1788, in French, in a letter to the German Prince Charles of Hesse, where Miranda refers to "disgraced Columbia" (la malheureuse Colombia).[11] His next use of the term appears in 1790, when he labeled a map of the American continent that accompanied materials he submitted to English Prime Minister William Pitt and Home Secretary William Wyndham, Lord Grenville in hopes of convincing them to sponsor an invasion to liberate his *patria*.[12] Although the map is labeled with the term "Columbia," Miranda's proposal itself does not refer to "Colombia," nor does it mention Columbus. The Spanish version of the proposal employs the term "la América" five times and "la América española" twice. The English translation of the document, prepared for Miranda's British audience, uses the term "South America" seven times.

In 1801, Nicholas Vansittart, the British joint secretary of the treasury and member of Parliament, requested that Miranda submit a new emancipation plan to the government of Prime Minister Henry Addington. Miranda's proposal, his "Esquisse de Gouvernement Federal" (Draft of [a] Federal Government) dated 2 May 1801, was a revised version of his previous plan of 1790. One of the most notable changes in this new plan is its reference to a much larger territory: whereas before Miranda concentrated especially on Venezuela, in this document he suggests liberating all of Spanish America, advocating that the capital of the newly independent state be located at "the most central point (perhaps on the Isthmus [of Panama])." This capital was to bear "the august name of Colombo to whom the world owes the discovery of that beautiful part of the earth."[13] In the margins of his copy of the document, Miranda scrawled: "If one adopts the name Colombia to designate the new republic, the inhabitants ought to be called Colombianos; this name is more sonorous and majestic than Colombinos."[14] The aesthetic element—and the lack of anything else of substance—in these references to Columbus is striking. In the first, Miranda gives Columbus credit for discovering "that beautiful part of the earth." In the second, Miranda illustrates his preference for the term "Colombianos" because of its aesthetic superiority over the term "Colombinos." Miranda invoked Columbus in an effort to sell his plan; his version of Columbus often did not appeal to reason but to the emotions and the aesthetic sensibilities of his audience.

Angel Rosenblat argues that the moment marking Miranda's definitive adoption of the term "Colombia" as an integral part of his independence project was when he wrote the first version of his *Proclamación a los Pueblos del Continente Colombiano, alias Hispanoamérica* (*Proclamation to the Peoples of the Colombian Continent, alias Hispano-America*). This document is undated, but Arturo Ardao believes it was produced in 1800 or 1801, at the same time or perhaps before Miranda wrote the "Esquisse de Gouvernement Federal" (2 May 1801). On the draft of this document, Miranda purportedly first wrote "to the peoples of the Hispano-American Continent." However, according to Rosenblat, "he at once crosses it out and corrects it with: 'To the peoples of the Colombian (a.k.a., Hispano-American) Continent.'" According to Ardao, "This correction offers documentary proof: it records the decisive moment in which Miranda attempts to definitively baptize Hispano-America with the name that had been engendered in his mind by the spirit of Revolution."[15]

Although Miranda's references to Columbus and his use of the term "Colombia" (or "Columbia," as he wrote in French and English, as well as in Spanish) do not conform to any rigorous pattern, they are best understood as part of his greater propagandistic effort to promote Spanish American independence. A skilled rhetorician, Miranda refers to "Colombia" most frequently when he addresses an American, as opposed to a European, audience. In his 1791 letter to William Pitt, Miranda identifies his "own country" not as "Colombia" but as "South-America."[16]

Fifteen years later, Miranda is still using the term "South America" with his British audience. In a 1804 memorandum about a meeting with British officials, for example, Miranda refers to "that great Continent of South America," adding in parentheses: "if I may be allowed to call all the Spanish possessions South America, because in a geographical division the line between North and South is drawn I believe across the Isthmus of Darien."[17] In addition to the terms "South America," "Spanish America," and the simpler "America," Miranda frequently uses the phrase "the Spanish colonies of the American continent."[18] Even the 1797 Act of Paris, which defined for European political actors Miranda's mission to liberate Spanish America, contains no mention of "Columbia" or Columbus.[19]

Miranda's references to Columbia, and his few references to Columbus, appear when he addresses an American (hemispheric) audience that he senses will be receptive to his revolutionary message. One of the few instances in his writings when Miranda mentions Columbus by name is in his letter dated 10 October 1800 to Manuel Gual, who was working to agitate for independence in Trinidad. Miranda holds up Columbus's hard work as an example for all supporters of independence to follow: "If we consider Columbus's great effort in the discovery of the New World, his perseverance, the risks he ran, his generosity of spirit, we will see, my friend, how very little the sons of America have done to grant the New World the glory and happiness that Nature appears to have destined to her. Let us work with determination and upright intentions in this noble enterprise, leaving the rest to Divine Providence, Supreme Arbiter in human affairs!"[20]

In Miranda's letters to Alexander Hamilton, General Henry Knox, and Thomas Jefferson, all of whom he met during his 1783–84 sojourn in the United States, Miranda consistently refers to "Columbia." In his 1792 letter to Hamilton, for example, Miranda writes: "The affairs and success of France take a happy turn in our favour . . . I mean in favour of our dear country America, from the

North to the South ... things are grown ripe and into maturity for the Execution of those grand and beneficial projects we had in Contemplation, when in our Conversation at New Yorck the love of our Country exalted our minds with those Ideas, for the sake of unfortunate Columbia."[21] Playing to Hamilton's sympathies, but also appropriating an American tradition that counterposed the New World against the Old, Miranda here—as in another letter he wrote to Hamilton several years later[22]—portrays "America" as one single country ("from the North to the South") that both he and Hamilton share ("our Country"). The term "unfortunate Columbia" in this excerpt refers only to Spanish America, but Miranda relies on Hamilton's experience with the term "Columbia" and its implication regarding independence from a colonial regime. The "grand and beneficial projects" that Miranda purports to have previously discussed with Hamilton in New York are designed to benefit this "unfortunate" half of the country that the two men share. In his 1795 letter to Knox, Miranda—although just released from a Parisian prison and now pessimistic about the political situation in France—uses the same kind of inclusive language when he talks about "Colombia": "I take up the pen only to tell you that I live, and that my sentiments for our dear Colombia as well as for all my friends in that part of the world have not changed in the least in spite of the events which are bound to ruin France."[23]

In 1806, after years of planning and petitioning the British government for assistance in freeing Spanish America from imperial domination, Miranda finally crossed the threshold into action by leading the *Leander* expedition in an attempt to liberate Venezuela (if not the whole South American continent).[24] Miranda proclaimed himself the "Comandante-General del Exercito colombiano," a title of his own invention, as there was no such "Columbian army." While on tierra firme, Miranda appears to have distributed to the local population handkerchiefs manufactured in England that featured a portrait of Columbus. According to Robertson:

On this handkerchief were portraits of Sir Home Popham, General Beresford, Washington, and Miranda, associated, as it were, to obtain the same end, or because of the similarity of their undertakings, with many sketches of naval battles and bordered with these four inscriptions: "It is not commerce but union; Let arts, industry and commerce flourish; Religion and its holy ministers be protected; Persons, conscience and commerce be at liberty." The apotheosis of Christopher Columbus filled the center and English colors adorned the sides. England was depicted as goddess of the seas, the lion of Spain at her feet. A youth was pictured rolling up the French colors, and poking the lion with the hilt of his sword. On the handkerchief was this inscription: "The dawn of day in South America."[25]

The design of these handkerchiefs suggests Columbus's significance in Miranda's propaganda effort. With little regard for historical fact, Columbus occupies the center of this scene, which depicts the new trade-based empire of England as victorious over Spain's old-style empire of conquest. Columbus is surrounded by four phrases, three of which contain the word "commerce." This alludes to Miranda's argument to entice Britain to support Spanish American emancipation: in exchange for Britain's military and financial help, it would receive privileged access to Spanish American markets. Free trade was, of course, one of the values of the Enlightenment and one that Spanish American Creoles shared. Columbus's "apotheosis" suggests, if not his deification, certainly his (re)arrival on the scene—this time of Spanish America's rebirth as an independent entity. While I have found no corroborating evidence, it is likely that Miranda directed the manufacture and printing of the handkerchiefs. This would have been consistent with Miranda's general strategy, which was beginning to rely more heavily on propaganda. As Karen Racine argues, this was one of several "carefully constructed images" that Miranda hoped would inspire the populace to support independence.[26]

The "proclamation" dated 2 August 1806 that Miranda issued to the inhabitants of the region where he landed also alludes to Columbus. The adjective "colombiano" appears twice in the proclamation's heading: "Don Francisco de Miranda, Comandante-General del Exercito colombiano, á los Pueblos habitantes del Continente Americano-Colombino" (Don Francisco de Miranda, Commander-General of the Columbian Army, to the People Inhabiting the Columbian-American Continent.) The unusual phrase that describes the continent, "americano-colombino," is reminiscent of what we saw much earlier in Miranda's 1792 letter to Hamilton—that is, the designation of the "Columbian" part of the Americas to be Spanish America. A similar distinction from Anglo-America is suggested by the term "our America" (*nuestra América*) in the phrase "the day has arrived when, recovering the sovereign independence of our America, its sons will be able to freely show their generous souls to the universe." Similarly, when Miranda refers to "the recovery of our rights as citizens and our glory as Columbian American," he designates Hispanic Americans as different from other Americans.[27]

Miranda's Columbus rhetoric appears in both the handkerchiefs and his "proclamation," both of which were designed for the local audience that he sought to revolutionize. It is perhaps significant that there are no references to Columbus in Miranda's letters to the clergy and the local town council, two groups he may have deemed more resistant to his revolutionary message. In his 3 August 1806 letter to the town council, for example, Miranda merely urges them as "members of the Hispanic American Public" to agree on reasonable measures to protect public order.[28] Compare this to the language in Miranda's second proclamation to the people of Coro, issued on 7 August 1806, upon his leaving, where he states that he wishes "to combat . . . the oppressors of the Columbian people."[29]

After returning to London in December 1807, Miranda launched a propaganda blast to promote the independence of Spanish America in both the English- and Spanish-speaking

Atlantic worlds. In 1810, Miranda began directing the publication of a short-lived serial entitled *El Colombiano*, which promoted emancipation and was explicitly addressed to "the Columbian continent." Nowhere in the five issues of *El Colombiano* does Miranda discuss the figure of Columbus. Although financial problems caused it to cease publication in short order, the newspaper's reach, and hence the diffusion of the term "Colombiano" in Spanish America, was greater than it might seem. Several of its articles were reprinted in the *Gazeta de Caracas* and the *Gazeta de Buenos Aires*.[30]

In the summer of 1810, after working in London on his own for years in an effort to pressure British diplomats to support Spanish American independence, Miranda welcomed three representatives of the junta of the government of Caracas—Luis López Méndez, Simón Bolívar, and the delegation's secretary, Andrés Bello—, who had been sent to talk to the British government about emancipation. The delegation members stayed in Miranda's Grafton Street home during the six weeks they spent in London. Miranda was instrumental in introducing them to the elite of London society and the Spanish Americans who supported independence who frequently met at Miranda's home. The Caracas junta gave explicit instructions to López Méndez and Bolívar, who left England in September, not to bring Miranda back with them, as its members did not trust his political ambition and believed him to be too volatile. Undeterred, Miranda followed on his own a month later. He arrived in Caracas in December 1810, and he quickly began promoting independence and liberal political ideals, publishing the works of Jeremy Bentham and James Mill in the *Gazeta de Caracas* and forming the Patriotic Club, which began to issue its own serial, *El Patriota de Venezuela*. Still distrusting him in April 1811, the younger generation designated Miranda as the representative in the National Congress of the small providence of Pao, a post that Miranda likely viewed as beneath him. Although Miranda did not write the constitution issued on 14 July 1811, its multiple references to "the Columbian continent," as well as its provision that the phrase "of the Columbian Era" ("de la Era Colombiana") be used to distinguish post- from pre-independence time, is likely a sign of Miranda's influence.[31] According to Ardao, the period during and after independence was declared in Venezuela marked "the apogee of... the idea of Magna Colombia, by means of the crowning in the official lexicon and in the political press—from the *Gaceta de Caracas* to *El Patriota de Venezuela*—of the term Colombia and its derivatives, always as a name for the totality of Hispanic America."[32]

Miranda's influence is surely evident in the first Venezuelan republic's flag, which he and two other members of the congress were assigned to create. The new flag, which bore the same colors as the flag Miranda devised for the *Leander* expedition, mixed European and American references. It featured an Amerindian sitting on a seaside rock next to a crocodile and holding a staff, on top of which was perched a liberty cap. The words "free Venezuela" (Venezuela libre) appear in the top left corner, and the word "Colombia" is featured on a banner that anchors the bottom center of the scene.[33]

Miranda's early adoption of the term "Colombia" and its variants should be considered not only in light of his experience in the United States, but also in relation to three other factors. The first is Miranda's understanding of the special meaning in Spanish America and in the Hispanic tradition of Columbus as the first conquistador in the New World. I discuss this below, in my observations about Juan Pablo Viscardo y Guzmán's *Letter to the Spanish Americans*, which Miranda espoused so heartily. Suffice it to say here that Miranda surely understood the figure of Columbus to be the first of the conquistadors whose contract with the king and queen had been broken by the Crown.

The second issue we should consider regarding Miranda's references to Columbus, while a conjecture, merits consideration: the possibility that Miranda personally identified with Columbus as the emblematic victim of the Spanish.[34] Miranda perhaps felt a certain affinity with the underappreciated Genoese. Miranda had never felt justly compensated by Spain for his loyal service in the military, just as Columbus felt that he was not fairly compensated by Spain for his discoveries. The Venezuelan often recorded his belief that his talents were not sufficiently valued by others. Since 1783 he had been on the run from the Spanish authorities, who had kept track of his movements in the United States and in Europe. As the years passed, he developed an ever-increasing sense of being persecuted. Karen Racine explains that "in [Miranda's] mind, he was always the victim, the idealistic hero who had been condemned to lead a wandering, rootless life because of the threat that his greatness posed to nervous authorities."[35] Could this sense of being persecuted have drawn Miranda to the figure of Columbus, whom he likely viewed as another man whose greatness was not acknowledged during his time? It is indeed odd that the sad trajectory of the end of Miranda's professional life is reminiscent of Columbus's. His 1806 *Leander* expedition was a resounding failure. In 1810 when he returned to Venezuela to aid in the independence effort, the Spanish Americans whom Miranda believed he served attempted to marginalize the elder man. Not only did his younger peers feel that Miranda was out of touch with current realities, but they also did not trust him. Therefore, they first attempted to keep Miranda busy with important but limited responsibilities, like restructuring the financial system. Eventually, in the tumultuous post-independence environment, exacerbated by a devastating earthquake on 26 March 1812, they turned briefly to Miranda to lead them, granting him the title of *generalissimo*. This was the moment Miranda had been waiting for. His short reign, however, ended in disaster. After Miranda failed to provide the reinforcements Bolívar had requested in the fight against royalist forces at Puerto Cabello, Bolívar lost that battle, and the royalists took Caracas, ending the first Venezuelan republic. Before Miranda could flee, he was arrested by the royalists and shipped off to prison, first in Spain and then in North Africa, where he died in captivity.

The third and most important issue with regard to his allusions to Columbus is Miranda's affinity for empire. Miranda was likely drawn to Columbus not only because he appeared in similar anticolonial discourses of British America but also because the figure of Columbus had so long been intimately tied to empire via a centuries-long discursive tradition with which Miranda was very familiar. With regard to Miranda's preference for empire, I refer to two things. First, his inherent distrust of democracy. Miranda wanted independence from Spain, yet he had been daunted by the excesses of the Haitian and French Revolutions. While he styled himself a revolutionary, at heart he was more of an aristocrat, like many Spanish American Creoles. "I confess," he wrote in 1798, "that much though I desire the independence and liberty of the New World, I fear anarchy and revolution even more."[36] And like many Spanish Americans, Miranda believed that after three centuries of imperial rule, his fellow citizens were unprepared to govern themselves. In Miranda's view, a constitutional monarchy like England's could best allow for a virtuous republic for the politically unprepared Spanish Americans.

Also relevant to Miranda's imperial leanings is his never quite clarified vision of the *grandezza* of his future country, both in terms of its territorial expanse (although he makes no reference to the active expansion of borders) and its glory. Hence, the government that he proposed to William Pitt in 1790 covered a huge expanse of territory, from Mexico to Tierra del Fuego. At its head was to be a hereditary executive called "the Inca"—a term obviously borrowed from the region's indigenous imperial history—, who would appoint "caciques" (or local chiefs) for life. As Racine writes, "All told, [Miranda's proposed government] was a strange hybrid of ideas from Britain, ancient Rome, indigenous America, and the United States."[37] This was not, as William Spence Robertson observed, "what may be called a pure republic, but an empire or an imperial republic."³⁸ Indeed, Miranda envisioned "rising upon the ruins of the Spanish Empire in the New World a congeries of states or more likely a huge imperial state. That state he evidently intended to designate Colombia: its capital should be on the Isthmus of Panama."³⁹ The figure of Columbus, with its historical ties to empire and imperial discourse, was emblematic of the importance of the idea of empire, however indeterminate, in Miranda's project.

Juan Pablo Viscardo y Guzmán

At the age of nineteen, Juan Pablo Viscardo y Guzmán (1748–98) had come to Cuzco, Peru from his hometown of Pampacolca to study for the priesthood with his older brother. He had only just made his first vows in the priesthood when King Charles III exiled all Jesuits from his American realms in 1767. Viscardo was first removed to Spain and then to Italy, where he lived for years in poverty. The Crown forbade him from returning to his homeland to claim an inheritance left by his uncle in 1776. In 1781 Viscardo sent two letters to the British consul in Livorno, arguing that Spanish America was ripe for political independence and offering to help the British plan an invasion to liberate the region. In 1782 Viscardo moved to London, where he lived supported by a government pension until his death in 1798, his plans and petitions largely having been ignored. Among the documents Viscardo produced during his years in London is the *Letter to the Spanish Americans*, a document that has been called "the Declaration of Independence of Spanish America"⁴⁰ and has often been compared to Thomas Paine's *Common Sense*.⁴¹ Viscardo completed the *Letter* in Spanish in 1791, but it was not printed until 1799, after Viscardo's death, when Miranda was responsible for translating it into French and publishing it in London.⁴² Such was Miranda's enthusiasm for the *Letter*'s argument for political independence from Spain that, in Karen Racine's words, it became his "mission statement."⁴³ During his 1806 *Leander* expedition, after he landed in Venezuela, Miranda not only distributed copies of the *Letter* to the local population, the majority of whom were illiterate Afro-Venezuelan slaves, but he also mandated that the *Letter* be read aloud once a day to the local inhabitants. Miranda likely never met Viscardo, although they both lived in London at the same time and were separately attempting to persuade William Pitt to support Spanish American independence before the Jesuit's death.

Viscardo was the first to invoke Columbus in the Creole argument, alluded to above, that the Crown had not met its obligations to the conquistadors and their descendants, who had alleged since the sixteenth century that they had been denied the privileges to which they were entitled by virtue of their families' service to the Crown. These claims to privileges were based on practices established during the reconquest and the colonization of the Canaries by which those who served the Crown were rewarded *encomiendas*, or grants of land and native laborers.[44] Ovando in Hispaniola, Cortés in Mexico, and Pizarro in Peru all adhered to this tradition, awarding their followers these grants. Seeking to satisfy the demands of the conquistadors, the Crown ratified this practice but became worried about reports of mistreatment of the natives and the rapid decline in their populations. The Crown was also reluctant to duplicate the kind of aristocracy that was the cause of so many political problems at home. These concerns led to the creation of the New Laws of 1542, which, among other things, prohibited the creation of new *encomiendas* and mandated that the title to existing *encomiendas* revert to the Crown upon the death of the current holder. This change was viewed by Spaniards in the Indies as an attack on their well-earned rights. In New Spain, the viceroy reacted to these new provisions in the New Laws by "obeying but not complying," a strategy that became standard practice in the Indies; in Peru a force of angry conquistadors led by Gonzalo Pizarro killed the viceroy who was sent to Lima to enforce the New Laws. As David Brading has shown, Spanish American "Creole patriotism" developed in part out of the injustice felt by conquistadors and their descendants in similar circumstances.⁴⁵ The sense of umbrage that Creoles felt in the sixteenth century continued throughout the colonial period and erupted in some of the revolts of the late eighteenth century. At that time, Creoles like Viscardo y Guzmán saw Columbus as the first victim of the Crown's neglect. Just as the Crown failed to meet its contractual obligations to Columbus as set out in the *Capitulaciones de Santa Fe*, it had failed to meet its obligations to the conquistadors and their descendants.

The opening sentence of Viscardo's *Letter* alludes to Columbus's famous landing in 1492: "Our proximity to the fourth century since the establishment of our ancestors in the New World is an occurrence too remarkable to not more seriously attract our attention."⁴⁶ Viscardo finished writing his *Letter* in 1791, one year before the tercentennial of Columbus's first voyage to the New World. In Viscardo's view, 1492 is important because it marks "the establishment of our ancestors in the New World." This date serves as the touchstone for Viscardo's discussion. Its importance is underlined by the *Letter's* repetition four times of the phrase "three centuries." The thrice-repeated possessive pronoun in the first sentence ("our near approach," "our ancestors," "our attention") reveals the Creole Viscardo's self-identification as a descendant of the Spanish. From this subject position, he declares: "The New World is our country; its history is ours," thereby erasing native peoples, mestizos, and those of African descent who populated Spanish America at the end of the eighteenth century. Viscardo's continued use of possessive pronouns in the first section of his *Letter* further emphasizes the Spanish descent of American Creoles.

The *Letter's* allusion to Columbus's landfall in 1492 and its definition of that event not as the year modern Europeans encountered the New World but when Viscardo's ancestors arrived there also reveal Viscardo's genealogical claim to Columbus, whom he viewed as a stand-in for those ancestors. This same claim is seen in newspapers printed later during the fight for independence, when rebels are described as "sons of Columbus." We note that there is a genealogical meaning here that was lacking in the phrase's use in Anglo-American revolutionary rhetoric. In Spanish America, as Viscardo's *Letter* illustrates, Columbus's status as first ancestor in the Americas of the Creoles was woven into the argument about the neglect of the rights of conquistadors and their descendants: Spain's breach of contract with the first conquistador, Columbus, became metonymic of Spain's neglect of its obligations to the Creole descendants of the conquistadors.

Viscardo carefully constructs his argument about the unfair treatment of the conquistadors and their descendants. First, in the section most frequently quoted by modern scholars, he condemns the entire history of Spanish colonization since Columbus, saying, "Our history for three centuries . . . might [be] abridge[d] . . . into these four words—**ingratitude, injustice, slavery, and desolation**" (emphasis in original).[47] The remainder of the letter elaborates on these grievances, laying the groundwork for Viscardo's justification for political independence. In this manner, the *Letter's* framework mirrors that of the US Declaration of Independence with its list of "injuries and usurpations" suffered by the colonists.[48]

The first grievance Viscardo addresses is Spain's ingratitude regarding the accomplishments of the conquistadors, who served loyally at great personal cost in order to expand the realm. "Our ancestors," he states, conquered the Indies "by the most excessive exertion, with the greatest dangers, and at their own expense." Their "natural affection for their native country led them to make her the most generous homage of their immense acquisitions, having no reason to doubt that such an important and freely offered service would be worth a proportionate recompense for them according to the Spanish custom of recompensing those who had contributed to extending the dominion of the nation." Viscardo laments that although their service "gave them a right . . . to appropriate to themselves the fruit of their valour,"[49] the conquistadors were denied this right: "all that we have lavished upon Spain has been taken, contrary to all reason, from ourselves and from our children."[50]

Viscardo rhetorically equates the Crown's refusal to fulfill the "legitimate hopes" (las legítimas esperanzas) of the conquistadors with its subsequent mistreatment of the Creoles.[51] This linkage is in part achieved by the subtle switch in the narrative voice from the third person plural (used to describe the conquistadors) to the first person plural (used to describe the Creoles):

> These legitimate hopes having been frustrated, *their descendants* and those of other Spaniards who continued to arrive in America, and despite that *we* only recognize her as our Patria, and despite that our subsistence and that of *our descendants* is based in her, *we* have respected, preserved, and sincerely venerated the attachment of *our ancestors* to their former country: it is for her that *we* have sacrificed infinite riches of every kind: only for her have *we* resisted until now, and it is for her that *we* have shed our blood with enthusiasm.[52]

The principal clause above, beginning with "their descendants," is narrated in the third person. The disinterested narrative voice here focuses on the conquistadors and their descendants. As the sentence progresses, however, the subject position of the narrative voice changes so that it now issues from the position of a Creole who speaks about "our ancestors." The rest of the sentence lists the sacrifices made by Creoles, thus mirroring the sacrifices of the conquistadors. The analogy established here is that just as the Crown was ungrateful for the sacrifices made by the conquistadors, it has been ungrateful for the sacrifices made by "us," the Creoles, whose "foolishness (necedad) has been forging chains for us."[53] The Creoles portrayed in Viscardo's *Letter* feel duped by Spain. Viscardo paints an image of the victimized Creole in chains that resembles the image of Columbus in chains after his arrest in 1500, suggesting the aptness of the Creole identification with Columbus.

Viscardo continues with the theme of Spain's ingratitude while introducing the topic of injustice. This time the narrative voice is that of an ambiguous first person plural that combines the perspective of the conquistador and the Creole:

> An immense empire, treasures greater than could be imagined in other times, glory and power superior to all that was known to antiquity: these are our titles to the gratitude of Spain and her government, and to their most distinguished protection and benevolence. Yet our recompense has been that which the most rigid justice could have dictated if we had been guilty of the opposite crimes: she exiles us from the Old World, and cuts us off from the society to which we are so closely connected.[54]

It is at this point that Viscardo directly references Columbus in his argument, implying that Spain's ingratitude began with its dealings with Columbus. Such ingratitude is, in Viscardo's eyes, despicable, fundamentally unjust, and constitutes treason: "Let us consult our annals for three centuries. After the Spanish Court's ingratitude, injustice, and its breach of contract, first with the great Columbus and then with the other conquistadors who gave to it the empire of the New World according to conditions solemnly stipulated, we find in its descendants only the effects of the scorn and hatred with which they were slandered, persecuted, and ruined."[55]

Viscardo's rhetoric here pits the Creole descendants of the conquistadors, represented by Columbus, against the Spanish Court. Columbus and "the other conquerors" are portrayed as great men, imperial conquerors, whose actions are summed up in the past tense of the verb "to give" and the phrase "solemnly stipulated." Columbus and the conquistadors respected the rules and behaved in a righteous manner when they "gave to [Spain] the empire of the New World." The Spanish Court, on the other hand, broke the rules. Its actions are summed up with the nouns "ingratitude," "injustice," and "breach of contract," and it is the agent that caused the Creoles to be "slandered, persecuted, and ruined."

An important part of Viscardo's argument is the portrayal of Spain as once having been just. He points to the creation of the

Cortes after the destruction of the last Gothic kings, when "our ancestors, during the re-establishment of their kingdom and its government, thought of nothing as carefully as they did about guarding against absolute power to which our kings have always aspired."[56] Viscardo suggests, however, that all of these good intentions turned sour around 1492, when after the consolidation of the kingdoms of Castile and Aragon, together with their acquisition of so many territories, including the great wealth of the Indies, "the crown acquired such an unforeseen preponderance that in a very short time it overthrew all barriers raised by the prudence of our forefathers who sought to safeguard the liberty of their descendants; the royal authority, like the sea overflowing its boundaries, inundated the whole monarchy, and the will of the king and his ministers became the only universal law."[57]

This narrative of Spain's rise and fall is one of the keys to Viscardo's underlying argument for independence. It also points to the primacy of Columbus in the Creole narrative justifying independence. Viscardo implies that the conquistadors, his ancestors, brought with them to the New World the "noble spirit of liberty"[58] that was embodied in the institution of the *Cortes* and the Aragonese office of *El Justicia*. According to Viscardo, that spirit, once at the core of Spanish governance, was snuffed out in Spain in approximately 1492 but lives on in the Creoles of the New World, who value liberty and natural rights by virtue of their Spanish descent, which remains uncorrupted by contemporary developments on the peninsula. It is in this sense that Viscardo speaks of "the prudence of our forefathers" and argues for independence in order to safeguard that prudence. It is this authentic spirit of Spain—embodied in the Creoles' actions and their genes—that Viscardo's Columbus represents.

Simón Bolívar

As mentioned earlier, Simón Bolívar (1783–1830) spent time with Francisco de Miranda in the summer of 1810 during his visit to London as part of the delegation sent by the Caracas junta to discuss prospects for emancipation with the British government. Known as the great liberator and the father of Spanish American independence, Bolívar has become a nationalist myth in his own right.[59] He grew up in a wealthy Caracas family and, like most young elite Creole men, he finished his education in Europe. On his way home from Europe in late 1806 and early 1807, he visited New York, Washington, Boston, and Philadelphia. Bolívar was extremely well read, in both the classics and the European and Spanish traditions; he surely would have read most of the same texts about Columbus that Francisco de Miranda read.

Likely influenced by Miranda during his visit to London in 1810, Bolívar also used the term "Colombia" in reference to an independent Spanish America as one political entity. Ardao traces Bolívar's use of the term, showing that early on, in the *Cartagena Manifesto* (1812), Bolívar refers to the destroyed First Venezuelan Republic as the "birthplace of Columbian independence," suggesting that Venezuela was the touchstone for the independence of the rest of Spanish America.[60] Similarly, Bolívar refers in 1814 to Caracas as "that immortal city, the first to give the example of liberty in the hemisphere of Colombia."[61] After September 1815, Bolívar stops using the term "Colombia" to refer to all of Spanish America as Miranda did. In his *Jamaica Letter*, he admits that while forming one political entity out of the former Spanish American colonies is desirable, doing so is impossible: "Forming of the New World a single nation with one tie that connects its parts to each other and to the whole is a grandiose idea. Since it has one origin, one language, similar customs, and one religion, it should have one government that would form a confederation of the different states that will be created; but this is not possible, because America is divided by remote climates, diverse situations, opposing interests, and dissimilar characteristics!"[62]

If the formation of one large nation composed of Spain's former colonies was no longer feasible in Bolívar's mind, now he suggested in the *Jamaica Letter* that Venezuela and New Granada should unite and be called "Colombia."[63] Simon Collier characterizes Bolívar's "Columbian experiment" (the unification of New Granada and Venezuela) as the practical application of his more idealistic desire to unify the independent republics of Spanish America in some kind of political relationship. Regarding the name for his practical project, Bolívar states, "This nation would be called Colombia as a tribute of justice and gratitude to the creator of our hemisphere."[64] It is not surprising that Bolívar viewed Columbus as the "creator of our hemisphere." This was the typical Creole, Eurocentric perspective that denied the existence of indigenous peoples and their civilizations before 1492.

The only other item in the historical record that enlightens us as to Bolívar's ideas about Columbus is written by Bolívar's aide de camp, Daniel Florencio O'Leary, who recorded Bolívar's belief, purportedly expressed in 1819, that Columbus had been a victim of the Spaniards. According to O'Leary, Bolívar felt that by honoring Columbus as Spain failed to do, Spanish Americans would show themselves to be worthy of independence:

> The plan [to create Colombia] in itself is great and magnificent; but, in addition to its utility, I wish to see it realized because it gives us the opportunity to rectify, in part, the injustice that has been done to a great man and to whom in this way we erect a monument that justifies our gratitude. Calling our republic Colombia, naming its capital Las Casas, we will prove to the world that not only do we have the right to be free but also to be considered sufficiently just to know to honor to the friends and benefactors of humanity: Columbus and Las Casas belong to America. Let us honor them by perpetuating their glories.[65]

Bolívar's language here (in the words of O'Leary) is typical of the way Columbus was appealed to in New-World nationalist discourse. First, he is portrayed as a victim, as a loyal servant, who (as in Viscardo's *Letter to the Spanish Americans*) is rebuffed by the imperial mother. Bolívar suggests that this crime can be remedied by adopting Columbus's name, as Bolívar surely knew many commentators through the centuries had advocated. We note how Bolívar pairs Columbus with Las Casas, the so-called "Defender of the Indians," and how both are disassociated from the aggressor's side of the history of conquest and three hundred years of colonial domination.[66] The strongest part of this passage is the statement that "Columbus and Las Casas belong to America," purportedly because its inhabitants alone know how to honor them, but also because both, in the typical Creole view, sought to create a peaceful empire for Christendom in the New World. Indeed, the last phrase of the above quote suggests that in honoring them, Spanish Americans will perpetuate "their glories." I would argue that this refers to their fame, as well as their impulse to build an empire.[67]

Empire and *Translatio imperii* in Spanish America

In the collective imagination of the early United States, as I discussed in Chapter 3, the notion of empire building and of constructing the nation in the image of empire was a commonplace. George Washington, for example, characterized his country several times as "a rising empire."[68] The founders sought to perfect the British attempt to marry empire and republic—to achieve *grandezza* (a great territorial expanse) and to guarantee liberty. From its birth, the republic was set on a path for territorial expansion and was commonly thought of as an empire.

But what about empire and the story of its westward movement (the *translatio imperii*) in the construction of the nation-states in post-independence Spanish America? The pattern of conquest and settlement in Spain's colonies was characterized by a gradual process of constructing urban settlements throughout the vast region and then filling in the empty spaces between settlements. Therefore, unlike in the early United States, where a "line of settlement" divided the British from the natives, in early independent Spanish America there generally was less of a concerted push to expand borders and incorporate new territory.[69] Nevertheless, the rhetoric of empire building was an important part of early nationalist discourses in Spanish America. While the *translatio imperii* narrative was employed to help justify political independence and undergird the construction of new nation-states, just as it had been employed in the North, in Spanish America early nationalists did not employ the *translatio imperii* story to justify systematic territorial expansion.

In Spanish America there was, in general, less of an emphasis on empire as a large and continually expanding territory. Although both Miranda and Bolívar were fond of expressions describing the great size of independent Spanish America, their notions of empire were not underwritten and realized by law, as was the case in the United States. There were no policies of continual expansion, no systematic invasion of foreign territories, no policies that as a matter of course sought the destruction of native populations, no filibustering by land-hungry individuals tacitly underwritten by governments, and no multiple attempts to buy other countries from foreign governments, as in the United States. Rather, Spanish American patriots employed the term "empire" to denote a political entity that would outdo the glory of the classical empires of Greece and Rome. This entity was often referred to, both practically and poetically, as "Colombia."

To recognize the ethereal quality of empire as it was employed in nationalist discourse in Spanish America, I consider a speech given in 1819 by Venezuelan Francisco Antonio Zea. Although Zea does not refer to Columbus or use the term "Colombia" in his address, he compares his country with the empires of antiquity, using the language of ancient empires to incite his compatriots to imagine the future of their new nation. After having been selected as president of the new second national congress, Zea addressed the assembly as follows:

> All nations and all empires were in their infancy feeble and little, like man himself, to whom they owe their origin. Those

great cities which still inflame the imagination, Memphis, Palmyra, Thebes, Alexandria, Tyre, the capital even of Belus and Semiramis, and thou also, proud Rome, mistress of the universe, were nothing more at their commencement than diminutive and miserable hamlets. It was not in the Capitol, nor in the palace of Agrippa nor of Trajan, but it was in a lowly hut, under a thatched roof, that Romulus, rudely clad, traced the capital of the world, and laid the foundations of his mighty empire. . . . It is not by the luster nor by the magnificence of our installation, but by the immense means bestowed on us by nature, and by the immense plans which you will form for availing ourselves of them, that the future grandeur and power of our republic should be measured. The artless splendor of the noble act of patriotism which General Bolivar has just given so illustrious and so memorable an example, stamps on this solemnity a character of antiquity, and is a presage of the lofty destinies of our country. Neither Rome nor Athens, nor even Sparta, in the purest days of heroism and public virtue, ever presented so sublime and so interesting a scene. The imagination rises in contemplating it, ages and distances disappear, and we think ourselves contemporary with the Aristides, the Phocions, the Camillus, and the Epaminondas of other days.[70]

That Zea compared Venezuela with the empires of antiquity, especially the Roman Empire, on the inauguration of the first congress at Angostura, suggests the seductiveness of this kind of comparison for Creole patriots who believed that it was their turn to develop into the world's new dominant society. The poetic nature of Zea's language is illustrative of the utopian and lyrical quality of the discourse of Spanish American nationalists who referred to the greatness of Rome and its Empire, especially in comparison to their counterparts in the United States.

Several texts that are now considered foundational in the Spanish American canon reveal the complicity of empire and nation building in the region. Among these is Juan Pablo

Viscardo y Guzmán's *Letter to the Spanish Americans*. I have already discussed the *Letter*'s employment of Columbus in the Creole argument for independence. A corollary of this employment is the *Letter*'s vision of the future American empire. Indeed, it is likely that one of the reasons Viscardo's *Letter* resonated to such an extent with Miranda was its articulation of a new empire that would arise after independence. Viscardo writes that in the future "the national glory [will] be reborn in an immense empire [and] become the secret asylum of all Spaniards."[71] The pure, uncorrupt spirit of Spain would be at the heart of this "immense empire," which would abide by Enlightenment values of reason and justice and free trade. Viscardo ends the essay, and his vision of empire, with a marked universalism: "Thus the extremities of the earth would be united by America, and her inhabitants would be united by the common interests of one great family of brothers!"[72] In this essay we see the same pan-American emphasis that Miranda advocates and that Bolívar later attempts to bring into fruition with the 1826 Panama Congress. But there is more to Viscardo's poetic vision: his America, an independent Spanish America, would not only be "an immense empire," it "would . . . unite the extremities of the earth," much like Rome and Columbus himself were credited for doing.

Simón Bolívar penned several foundational texts that reveal how the nation was thought of in terms of empire. Bolívar consistently articulated his vision of a united Spanish America using the language of empire and an intensely lyrical style; however, like Miranda, he was not a systematic thinker, and he never explained precisely how he understood the relationship of empire and the modern nation-state. Rather, in his writings Bolívar describes his envisioned nation using consistent rhetorical flourishes that employ the language and images of empire.

Simon Collier hints at this kind of rhetoric when he parenthetically states, "The reader of Bolívar's writings can hardly fail to be struck by how often he summoned up images of power, vastness, and grandeur—there is something deep in his psychology here."⁷³ These images that Collier refers to, I would argue, go beyond mere expressions of sovereignty. Rather, they are an appeal to the collective imaginary of empire, which Bolívar employed to great effect in his discourse about Spanish American nation building. Notable characteristics of this discourse include an emphasis on unity, the exercise of power, and the New World outdoing the Old World in terms of greatness and glory.

First, let us look at the importance of unity in Bolívar's discourse. Despite the pragmatic moment in the *Jamaica Letter* where he recognizes the impossibility of "forming the entire New World into one single nation with one single tie that connects its parts together and gives them cohesion," soon after this quote, Bolívar continues to wax poetic about a future united league of Spanish American nations: "How beautiful it would be if the Isthmus of Panama were for us what Corinth was for the Greeks! I hope that one day we have the good fortune to establish there an august congress of representatives of republics, kingdoms and empires in order to address and discuss the lofty themes of peace and war with nations from other parts of the world!"⁷⁴

Not long after he wrote the *Jamaica Letter*, in 1818 Bolívar invited the inhabitants of the River Plate to form "one single society." "Americans should have a single *patria*," he wrote to Juan Martín de Pueyrredón that same year, referring to an "American pact" to "[form] a single body of all our republics." Similarly, in 1822 Bolívar wrote to Bernardo O'Higgins about "the social pact which must form, in this hemisphere, a nation of republics."⁷⁵ "Such words," concludes Collier, "can hardly be taken as implying anything other than some kind of vision of ultimate Spanish American unity."⁷⁶ Historian John Lynch concurs: "Whatever he meant by a 'nation of republics,' he advocated supranational unity of some kind."⁷⁷

Collier believes that Bolívar was "obsessed, certainly by the 1820s, with devising schemes to link the new republics, sundered from the Spanish Empire and from each other, in some kind of collaborative arrangement that might, in the fullness of time, lead to a united Spanish America."⁷⁸ This obsession led not only to the formation of the new state of Colombia and his plans for an Andean Federation, but also to his design for the Panama Congress of 1826, which grew in part out of Bolívar's desire to unify the region in the face of threats from the Holy Alliance to help Spain regain its American possessions. In the 1824 invitation to attend the Congress, which he extended to the leaders of Colombia, Mexico, Río de la Plata, Chile, and Guatemala, Bolívar reasoned that "it is time that the interests and relations that unite the American republics, which were previously Spanish colonies, be granted a fundamental base that immortalizes, if possible, the duration of these governments."⁷⁹ The formation of a confederation of states, Bolívar felt, would bind the republics together in this way and allow for their common defense in the face of the continuing European threat.

While the Panama Congress was largely a flop, it reveals the importance of unity for Bolívar as well as his long-lasting desire for a continental-wide political union. Collier's analysis of Bolívar's ideals for the Congress and the language he used to describe them are worth quoting here. Bolívar, he says,

> clearly envisioned it as something a good deal more substantial than a simple league, as a kind of supranational organization that could (among other things) intervene to restore order in countries in turmoil. As he told Santander, he would like to see the powers of the Panama Congress "amplified almost infinitely, to give it strength and a truly sovereign authority." The eloquent phrase shows that Bolívar was not really interested in setting up a loose consultative association of states. In his correspondence, in fact, Bolívar gives the game away completely by his evident preference for the term *federation* as a descriptive scheme.⁸⁰

Bolívar's own description of the power that such a Spanish American federation would exert is illuminating. It would "form the most vast, or most extraordinary or most strong league that has appeared to date on the earth."[81] He clearly desired his united political entity to exercise extensive dominion, very much in the Roman sense of the term *imperium*. Bolívar admired both the Roman and the British Empires. Both, he said in the Angostura Address, "were born to rule and be free."[82] Their constitutions, he argued, were the most fitting political models for Spanish America, not those of France or the relatively new United States. He particularly admired the imperial stature of Great Britain, which he called "Señora of nations," before whom the nations of "the Holy Alliance all tremble." Great Britain, Bolívar stated, "is the Roman Empire at the end of the republic and at the beginning of the empire. England finds herself in an ascendant progression, unhappy all those who oppose her."[83] In his "Thought on the Congress of Panama" (1826), Bolívar suggested making Great Britain a "Constituent Member" of the Congress, and he alluded to the possibility of "the union of the new states with the British Empire." Such an alliance, he went so far to suggest, "could, perhaps, find itself, in the fullness of time, one single nation covering the universe."[84]

In a similar vein, Bolívar finished his speech to the Angostura Congress with a lofty vision in which he saw his Colombia (the newly united New Granada and Venezuela) someday ruling the world:

> On contemplating the unification of this immense region, my soul soars to the heights demanded by such a colossal vista, such an astonishing scene. Flying from age to age, my imagination reflects on the centuries to come, and as I look down from such a vantage point, amazed at the prosperity, splendor, and vitality of this vast region, I feel a kind of rapture, as if this land stood at the very heart of the universe, spread out from coast to coast between oceans separated by nature and which it is our task to reunite with long, broad canals. I see her as unifier, center, emporium for the human family, sending out to the entire earth the

treasures of silver and gold hidden in her mountains, extracting health and vitality from her lush vegetation for the suffering men of the old world, communicating her previous secrets to the wise men still unaware of the vast stores of knowledge and wealth so bountifully provided by nature. I see her seated on the throne of liberty, grasping the scepter of justice, crowned by glory, and revealing to the old world the majesty of the modern world.[85]

Bolívar paints this image of a ruling Colombia using the words of empire: she sits on a throne, holds a scepter, and wears a crown.

Bolívar's use of the rhetoric of empire to describe the new Spanish American nation-states is also seen in his *Jamaica Letter*. At the end of this *Letter*, Bolívar focuses on the *translatio studii*, the transfer from east to west of the culture of the victorious in the subjugation of foreign others, a transfer which is concomitant with the *translatio imperii:* "When we are at last strong," he writes, " . . . then we will cultivate in harmony the virtues and talents that lead to glory; then we will follow the majestic path toward abundant prosperity marked out by destiny for South America; then the arts and sciences that were born in the Orient and that brought enlightenment to Europe will fly to free Colombia, which will [invite them by offering asylum]."[86]

Here Bolívar uses the term "Colombia" in the continental sense, in the same way that Miranda used it, to refer to Spanish America. His direct reference to the westward flight of "the arts and sciences that were born in the Orient," then landed in Europe, and now move to America, implicitly suggests that "Colombia" will also be home to Western empire.

Two other foundational texts in the Spanish American tradition are worthy of note. While only the second invokes the figure of Columbus, both are relevant with regard to how Bolívar thought of the nation-state in terms of empire. The first is Bolívar's "Oath in Rome," in which he swears to liberate Spanish America from Spain. He supposedly made this oath in 1805 atop the Mons Sacer, one of Rome's seven hills. The end of the oath is most often quoted:

> The civilization that has blown from the East has shown all its faces here, all its parts. But with regard to resolving the great problem of man in liberty, it seems that the matter has been unknown and that clearing up this mysterious unknown can only be verified in the New World. I swear before you, I swear by the God of my fathers, I swear on their graves, I swear on my Country that I will not rest body or soul until I have broken the chains that bind us by the will of Spanish power![87]

These words were recorded years later by Simón Rodríguez, Bolívar's teacher, with whom he traveled through Europe and climbed the Mons Sacer. Rodríguez recalled the event in his memoirs, and some have speculated that they are Rodríguez's invention or at least the product of his embellishment. (We note, however, that there is likely at least a kernel of truth to the story, as Bolívar himself in a letter to Rodríguez dated 1824 remembers "when we went to the Mons Sacer in Rome to swear to free our country on that holy ground."[88]) Historian Gerhard Masur opined in 1948 that "a reconstruction of what Bolívar actually said is hardly possible. Forty-five years after the event took place S. Rodríguez gave a novelistic description of the famous vow which is quite obviously an imaginative invention; its historical value is nil."[89] Today, most critics would probably disagree with Masur's evaluation. Regardless of the authenticity of the "Oath," it merits our attention because it has become part of the Venezuelan nationalist narrative. Susan Rotker's judgment is exemplary: "It does not matter how many footnotes refute its content since it has the element of an icon; as such, the category of Truth becomes completely secondary." Rotker goes further, concluding, "If this did not happen, it does not matter: *it should have happened.*"[90] Christopher Conway adds, "Indeed, as an emblem of Bolívar, and of his iconicity as a national and Pan-American symbol, the 'Oath of Rome' faithfully represents a foundational scene of Latin American identity."[91] Indeed, today the "Oath" is still important in Venezuela's self-image: it is memorized by Venezuelan school children and quoted by politicians.

O'Leary's account of the scene of the "Oath" is typical in the historiography of Spanish American independence: "On Monte Sacro the sufferings of his own country overwhelmed his mind, and he knelt down and made that vow whose faithful fulfillment the emancipation of South America is the glorious witness."[92] In 1950, Venezuelan painter Tito Salas captured the scene of the "Oath," with Bolívar overlooking the ruins of the Roman forum, in a painting that hangs in the National Pantheon in Caracas (see Figure 8).

On the surface, the "Oath" appears to be a simple statement against the tyranny of empire. Before modern historiographers clarified the geography of Rome, the Mons Sacer on which Bolívar purportedly stood was often confused with the Aventine; both places were sites to which the plebian lower class seceded in its struggle to end debt-slavery and win official recognition for its representatives, its own assembly, and access to magistracies.[93] This struggle is recorded in Livy's *History of Rome*, which both Bolívar and Rodríguez likely read. Livy's narrative notes how the plebs of the Republic withdrew to the Aventine in order to pressure the patricians (who resided on the Palatine hill) into political negotiations. And it is at the site of the plebs' struggle with the perceived tyranny of the patricians that Bolívar declares he will set Spanish America free from the tyranny of the Spanish Empire. Yet, Bolívar's stance regarding empire is not so clear-cut in the "Oath." The republican and imperial phases of Roman history are lumped together, and both are declared failures. The first part of the "Oath," where, in Lynch's words, "the pen of Rodríguez may well have prevailed,"[94] reads as follows:

Figure 8. Tito Salas, *El juramento en el Monte Sacro*. Courtesy of Alberto Borrego.

So then, this is the nation of Romulus and Numa, of the Gracchi and the Horaces, of Augustus and Nero, of Caesar and Brutus, of Tiberius and Trajan? Here every manner of grandeur has had its type, all miseries their cradle. Octavian masks himself in the cloak of public piety to conceal his untrusting character and his bloody outbursts; Brutus thrusts his dagger into the heart of his patron so as to replace Caesar's tyranny with his own; Antony renounces his claim to glory to set sail on the galleys of a whore; with no projects of reform, Sulla beheads his fellow countrymen and Tiberius, dark as night and depraved as crime itself, divides his time between lust and slaughter. For every Cinncinatus there were a hundred Caracallas, a hundred Caligulas for every Trajan, a hundred Claudiuses for every Vespasian. This nation has examples of everything: severity for former times, austerity for republics, depravity for emperors, catacombs for Christians, courage for conquering the entire world, ambition for turning every nation on earth into a fertile field for tribute; women capable of driving the sacrilegious wheels of their carriages over the decapitated bodies of their parents; orators, like Cicero capable of stirring crowds to action; poets, like Virgil, for seducing with their song; satirists, like Juvenal and Lucretius; weak minded philosophers, like Seneca; complete citizens, like Cato.[95]

This text collapses the Roman Republic and Empire, a collapse that points to the porous line between the categories of empire and republic in much of the political discourse of the Americas during the Age of Revolution. The "Oath" refers indiscriminately to figures of Roman history, moving from the Roman kings Romulus and Numa to the republican figures of the Gracchi brothers, and then to the emperors Augustus and Nero, among others. Bolívar's point is that both the Roman Republic and the Roman Empire failed in the "emancipation of the spirit" and in the "final perfectibility of reason," despite their greatness: "This nation has examples for everything, except for the cause of humanity: corrupt Messalinas, gutless Agrippas, great historians, distinguished naturalists, heroic warriors, rapacious consuls, unrestrained sybarites, golden virtues, and foul crimes; but for the emancipation of the spirit, the elimination of cares, the exaltation of man, and the final perfectibility of reason, little or nothing."[96] It is only in the New World, Bolívar then posits, that the unfulfilled grandeur of Rome, both Republic and Empire, will be realized.

For Bolívar both the Roman Republic and the Roman Empire were useful models to be superseded. Here Leopoldo Zea's observation about the meaning of Rome in Bolívar's thought is helpful:

> Before it transformed into Empire, Rome had been the creator of the republican archetype for free men. Bolívar would attempt to do something more than Rome did, not extend dominium, but create other republics, not [engage in] imperial expansion, but in the reproduction of the republic throughout the America that Bolívar would go about liberating. That is, [he sought] to create multiple republics and, with all of them, form a Confederation of Republics. Not an Empire but rather a great community of free republics equally formed by free men. Both the Republic and the Empire of Rome supplied models for attaining what could seem an impossible libertarian dream.[97]

It is within this context of a murky employment of political typologies reflecting his understanding of Rome that Bolívar suggests that the post-independence nation-state be named after Columbus, a figure associated for centuries with empire.

The second foundational text, also probably apocryphal, which some attribute to Simón Bolívar, is "My Delirium on Chimborazo," published for the first time in 1833, after Bolívar's death. Most experts find some reason to doubt the authenticity of this document, the original of which has never been located.[98] Lynch writes that "the lack of collaborative evidence and contemporary reference invites an agnostic response."[99] Narrated in first person, the piece relates Bolívar's supposed trek to the summit of Chimborazo, which at an altitude of 20,565 feet above sea level was thought at the beginning of the nineteenth century to be the highest mountain in the world. After surpassing the tracks of Humboldt, who climbed partway up the mountain in 1802, Bolívar finally reaches the top, when, the text reads, "a feverish delirium suspends my mental faculties. I feel as if I were aflame with a strange, higher fire. It was the God of Colombia taking possession of me." He then converses with Time about the past and the future, and he is finally revived by "the tremendous voice of Colombia": "Absorbed, frozen in time, so to speak, I lay lifeless for a long time, stretched out on that immense diamond serving as my bed. Finally, the tremendous voice of Colombia cries out to me. I come back to life, sit up, open my heavy eyelids with my own hands. I become a man again, and write down my delirium."[100]

Regardless of this text's authenticity, its status in the Spanish American cultural tradition merits our consideration. Angel Grisanti, writing in 1964, called it "the most profoundly lyrical of Bolívar's writings and one of the most beautiful pieces of literature in the Spanish language."[101] Grisanti contended that Bolívar climbed the mountain on 5 July 1822, inspired by the eleventh anniversary of the Declaration of Independence of Venezuela. According to Grisanti, "The Liberator is euphoric, beside himself, impassioned, burning with the glow of so many glorious memories. Along the route, Venezuela is on the hearts and minds of everyone. . . . And it is Bolívar, as protagonist of the epic, who becomes most delirious."[102] Given the complicity between epic and empire, the epic being the story of domination told by the dominators, it is apt that Grisanti refers to Bolívar as the protagonist of the epic of Venezuelan (and Spanish American) independence. It is also fitting that the "God of Colombia tak[es] possession" of Bolívar during the spiritual experience described in the "Delirium," for Columbus has always been an archetype of empire.

~ Conclusion ~

The Meaning of Empire in Nationalist Discourses of the United States and Spanish America

As discussed in detail in the Introduction, in the last decade or so an increasing number of scholars have critiqued the dominance of the nation-state as a unit of analysis. In doing so, they have challenged exceptionalist views of US history, according to which empire and the nation-state are viewed as oppositional, empire being replaced by the nation-state at the moment it is born from the ashes of the colonial experience. Scholarship critical of this view takes its impetus from the so-called "global turn" and is sometimes called post-national American studies or "New Americanist Studies."[1]

Although this recent scholarship has created a better understanding of the nation as empire, it has yet to consider the significance of Columbus as he was represented in the Americas in the eighteenth and nineteenth centuries. Instead, our view of Columbus has remained impeded by nation-centric methodologies that exclude the supranational contexts in which the meanings of Columbus were constructed. This book attempts to rectify this situation.

Understanding the figure of Columbus in the Americas requires a comparative approach. The American nationalists of the eighteenth and nineteenth centuries who were responsible for appropriating Columbus as a nationalistic symbol of empire did not live in isolated linguistic bubbles. Instead, they were citizens of the Atlantic "republic of letters": they read widely and were familiar with the textual conversations in different languages and through the centuries about Columbus, and indeed about empire and conquest in the Western world, with which he became so closely associated. If we seek to understand the meaning of the word "Colombia" as it appears on the flag of the first Venezuelan republic, we must consider Francisco de Miranda's own experience with the term. This entails our investigation of how it was employed in the United States during Miranda's travels there as well as Miranda's encounters with Columbus and his legacy throughout his diverse readings of the canonical texts, both historiographic and literary, in the various languages used in the Atlantic republic of letters and in the Hispanic tradition.

By opening the field of inquiry and going beyond nation-centered traditions, I have argued that the meaning of Columbus in the Americas is constructed by a transatlantic discourse that was originally created by Columbus himself, later perpetuated by historiographers and literati, and eventually taken up by writers in the Americas, both North and South. Through this discourse, the figure of Columbus was constructed as an archetype of empire that was uniquely suited to convey not only the imperial designs for real territorial expansion in the United States during the eighteenth and nineteenth centuries, but also the desire of Spanish Americans for imperial grandeur.

The embracing of Columbus as a figure of empire by New-World republics breaking free from Old-World empires shows the imperial underpinnings of the nation-state. Discourses about Columbus in the Americas reveal the desire of nationalists to set the New World apart from the Old. Yet these discourses simultaneously illustrate an aspiration to these same old imperial ideals via the consistent employment of the classic narrative of the *translatio imperii*, the westward transfer of empire.

The meaning of the figure of Columbus, however, was not set in stone as soon as Columbus portrayed himself as a representative of empire. While I do believe that Columbus, as a sign, has generally been interpreted as a figure associated with empire, conquest, and colonization, and although I have focused on this argument, there are clearly other interpretations of him. For Italian Americans in the United States, for example, the figure of Columbus has been a symbol of Catholicism and ethnic and cultural identity. For some commentators in Spanish America, Columbus is a racial link to Europe and *limpieza de sangre* (purity of blood), or a cultural link to Spain and Hispanidad. The different meanings of Columbus constructed by various groups that uphold him as their hero or symbol have been thoroughly discussed by various scholars. I seek to add to the scholarship about Columbus by taking the long view of the transatlantic history of Columbus representations, whereby it becomes apparent that a great many of the contexts in which these representations have been produced are thematically related to empire, in a variety of meanings. Indeed, I would argue that it was the West's obsession with empire, its history and its future, that gave life to the symbol of Columbus in the Americas.

THE MEANING OF EMPIRE IN NATIONALIST DISCOURSES OF THE UNITED STATES AND SPANISH AMERICA

A critical study of the articulations of Columbus in the Americas reveals that empire was very much at the heart of the ideological foundations of the modern nation-states in the New World. It helped supply the language with which the new nations were rhetorically constructed. But what did empire mean in British America and in Spanish America?

In both his 1991 essay and his 2008 book, *The Language of Empire: Rome and the Idea of Empire from the Third Century BC to the Second Century AD,* John Richardson examines the "extension of meaning" of the term *imperium* during the growth of the Roman

Empire, from the third century BCE, when *imperium* referred simply to the power granted to a magistrate, to the early decades of the first century ACE, when the term also came to mean something more: "The earlier significance, the right of command within the Roman state ... was never lost, but in addition the meaning 'empire,' in an increasingly concrete, territorial sense came to be a normal usage, so that, at least from the second half of the first century AD, *imperium Romanum* is used as we would use 'Roman Empire.'" Richardson encourages us to think of this "extension of meaning" as having created a continuum: "It is apparent that we are not dealing with two alternative and incompatible meanings [of the term *imperium*], but with the co-existence of a pair of meanings, of which in any particular case one is likely to be more dominant than the other."[2] The second meaning of the term *imperium* (the territory over which power is exercised) developed as the Roman Empire grew, and it soon subsumed the first meaning of the term (the power of a magistrate).

This notion of a semantic continuum whereby *imperium* is defined is helpful when we consider the meaning of empire in the Americas during the period covered in this book. As discussed in the Introduction, references to empire in nationalist discourses were often nothing more than vague allusions to power or to the grandeur that was popularly associated with Rome. But sometimes they were particular references to the kind of territorial expansion that had become part and parcel of what Rome meant in the Western imagination. In British America and later the United States, then, we can think of empire as meaning both power and territory. There, the term "empire" was employed with territorial expansion in mind much more frequently than in it was in Spanish America. This jibed with the political realities of the day. In the early United States there was consistent pressure to acquire territory and influence abroad that was absent in the early independent republics of Spanish America. Bolívar recognized that his project to create a politically unified state was impossible, and the issue of territorial expansion was never a dominant theme in nationalist discourses, except perhaps for short periods of time in the cases of border disputes and later in the nineteenth century. But even in these cases, only a limited amount of territory believed to belong to the nation was desired, and the issue at hand was not territorial expansion per se, as it was in many instances in the United States. In Spanish America, therefore, the meaning of the term "empire" tends to remain closer to the first side of the continuum—that is, it refers to power and authority, or the ethos of empire, and only very infrequently does it refer to territory. Even in the case of Iturbide's Mexican Empire (1821–23), when the language of empire was employed to great effect and the imperial trappings of the royal courts of Europe were imitated, territorial expansion was not an issue.

In considering further the meaning of empire in post-independence Spanish America, I return to Richardson's essay and, in particular, to his reminder that even in Rome there was a certain obscurity to the term *imperium*, as the authority granted to a consul or praetor in part came from the gods. "Even in the period of the late republic and early empire," he writes, "at least a certain element of the mysterious is to be expected: in part *imperium* belongs not to the precise complexities of constitutional law but to the proper obscurities of religion."[3]

This brings to mind the mystical tenor of the Spanish American foundational texts that I analyzed in Chapter 4. In those texts, the language of empire is used to describe the new nations in a highly lyrical mode. That intense lyrical quality is lacking in similar foundational texts of the United States. This is not to say that texts produced in British America and the United States did not wax poetic when they used the language of empire; rather, I wish to point out that the lyricism of the Spanish American texts is more pronounced, more profound, often even venturing on the mystical. Surely part of this aesthetic difference is explained by the different influences and characteristics of the literary traditions in the North and South.

But I would suggest, too, that another explanation is found in the different natures of the Spanish and English colonial experiences. Spain's colonial system was more hierarchical and controlled by the metropolis than England's for multiple reasons: the different timing of the Spanish and the British colonial projects in the Americas (the British beginning theirs roughly a century after the Spanish), the differences in national traditions and previous histories of conquest, and the differences among the American landscapes and peoples the Spanish and the British encountered.[4] The daily lives of British colonists were generally less restricted by colonial government than were the lives of their Spanish counterparts, but this depended on where both sets of colonists lived and how they made their living. The Spanish Empire in the Americas also lasted more than three hundred years, much longer than Britain's empire. My point is that the long shadow of the colonial experience rendered the possibility of thinking about territorial expansion largely irrelevant for the early Spanish American nationalists of the nineteenth century. Conquering new territory in order to incorporate it into the new nations was simply not on their agenda. How different was the situation in the early United States.

While post-independence Spanish American Creoles conjured up visions of their new nation-states as greater than Rome, and while they used the language of empire to describe them, the manner in which they did so took on a poetic air. It was almost as if telling the story of their becoming an empire, becoming all-powerful, after years of colonial subjugation, required a highly charged lyricism. Again, I do not wish to imply that US texts that deal with empire and Columbus are not lyrical. Joel Barlow's *Columbiad* and Thomas Brower Peacock's *Columbian Ode*, for example, are certainly lyrical and surely contain elements of fantasy, but I would not venture to say they are as ethereal as the passages in Spanish American foundational texts such as "The Oath Taken in Rome" and "My Delirum on Chimborazo," both of which are discussed in Chapter 4.

Echoing Richardson's description of the religious authority signified by the Roman word *imperium*, we may effectively characterize the language of empire in Spanish American national discourses as consistently containing "a certain element of the mysterious."

~ Notes ~

INTRODUCTION

1. Enrique Dussel, for one, argues that modernity is a discursive construct that emerged out of the dialectic initiated by the European encounter with America, whereby Europe defined itself as the center in relation to the "other" of the periphery. "Eurocentrism and Modernity," 65–76.
2. Jefferson, *Memoir, Correspondence and Miscellanies*, 1:433.
3. The most thorough study of the *translatio imperii* trope I have read is Breuninger, "Morals, the Market, and History," chs. 8 and 9.
4. Anthony Pagden explains, "The modern term 'empire' and the related words 'emperor,' 'imperialism,' etc., all derive, significantly, from the Latin word *imperium*, which in ancient Rome indicated supreme power involving both command in war and the magistrate's right to execute law. The term has therefore linked the history of European imperialism very closely to the legacy of the Roman Empire. Originally, it meant little more than 'sovereignty,' a sense it retained until at least the eighteenth century. Ever since the days of the Roman Republic, however, 'empire' has also been a word used to describe government over vast territories." Pagden, *Peoples and Empires*, xxi–xxii. For more on the primacy of the *Aeneid* in this regard, see Waswo, *The Founding Legend of Western Civilization*.
5. Virgil, *Aeneid* 1.278–79. Livy's *History of Rome* also incorporates the view that Rome was destined for world domination. Specifically, in his story about the founding of Rome he writes that the god of boundaries, Terminus, was the only god absent: "This was interpreted as an omen and augury: the fact that the seat of Terminus was not moved and that he alone of all the gods was not summoned from his consecrated boundaries portended that everything would be stable and secure. After this auspice of permanence had been received, another prodigy portending the greatness of empire ensued. It is said that a human head, its features intact, was found by the men who were digging the foundations of the temple. This phenomenon undoubtedly foretold that this was to be the citadel of empire and the head or capital of the world." Livy, *History of Rome*, 1:55, 76.

6. Bolton, "The Epic of Greater America," 448. Bolton delivered this address to the American Historical Association on 28 December 1932, and it was subsequently published in the *American Historical Review* in April 1933.
7. See Rowe, *Literary Culture and US Imperialism*; Rowe, *The New American Studies*; Rowe, *Post-Nationalist American Studies*; Gillman, "The New, Newest Thing: Have American Studies Gone Imperial?"; Brückner, "The Critical Place of Empire in Early American Studies"; and Kaplan and Pease, *Cultures of United States Imperialism*. In that volume, see, in particular, Kaplan, "'Left Alone With America': The Absence of Empire in the Study of American Culture," 3–21. See also Kaplan, *The Anarchy of Empire in the Making of US Culture*.
8. Burton, "Introduction: On the Inadequacy and the Indispensability of the Nation," 4.
9. For a discussion on the different perspective of "early Americanists" and what she calls "US-Americanists," see Sandra Gustafson, "Histories of Democracy and Empire." Regarding Latin America, postcoloniality has been thoroughly theorized in the work of Enrique Dussel, Aníbal Quijano, and Walter Mignolo. See also Moraña, Dussel, and Jauregui, *Coloniality at Large: Latin America and the Postcolonial Debate*.
10. The bibliography is too extensive to list here. Among the works I have found helpful are the following: Bellini and Martini, *Colombo e la scoperta nelle grandi opere letterarie*; Bushman, *America Discovers Columbus*; Cock Hincapié, *Historia del nombre de Colombia*; Hart, *Columbus, Shakespeare, and the Interpretation of the New World*; Larner, "North American Hero?"; Regazzoni, *Cristoforo Colombo nella letteratura spagnola dell'Ottocento*; Sale, *The Conquest of Paradise*; Schlereth, "Columbia, Columbus, and Columbianism"; Spengemann, *A New World of Words*; Spina, *Cristoforo Colombo e la poesia*; Stavans, *Imagining Columbus*; and Steiner, *Cristoforo Colombo nella poesia epica italiana*.
11. Spengemann, *A New World of Words*, 118.
12. Ibid., 122.
13. Ibid., 171.
14. Limerick, *The Legacy of Conquest*. See also, for example, Walter Nugent's discussion of the issue of territorial boundaries in the charters of the colonies and the US peace treaties of 1782–83 in *Habits of Empire*, ch. 1.
15. Las Casas's detailed account of Columbus and his life appears in his *Historia de las Indias*, which although not published until 1875–76 was well known to Atlantic intellectuals before then in manuscript form. See Las Casas, *Historia de las Indias*, 2:35–40, 91, 114–19, 132–34, 140–41.

16. Las Casas, *Las Casas on Columbus*, 24–25.
17. Arias, *Retórica, historia y polémica*, 49.
18. Cock Hincapié, *Historia del nombre de Colombia*, 43.
19. See Larner, "North American Hero?" 48.
20. "The Speech of his Grace . . ."
21. See, for example, Samuel Sewall, *Phaenoomena quaedam apocalyptica*, 49–50; Cotton Mather, *Magnalia Christi Americana*, 1:581; and William Douglass, *A Summary, Historical and Political*, 1:65.
22. This is the argument proposed in Dennis, "The Eighteenth-Century Discovery of Columbus," 209.

CHAPTER I

1. Cartagena, *Poesía*, 126.
2. Frances Yates (*Astraea*), Marie Tanner (*The Last Descendant of Aeneas*), and Anthony Pagden (*Lords of all the World*) have all written about the meaning of empire and the imperial legacy in Spain during the reign of the Hapsburgs, especially when Charles V claimed the title to the Holy Roman Empire from 1519 to 1556. Peggy Liss ("Isabel of Castile") analyzes the long and vibrant tradition of empire in Spain before the Hapsburgs.
3. For more on this topic, see Milhou, *Colón y su mentalidad mesiánica*, ch. 3.
4. Liss, *Isabel the Queen*, 43.
5. Muldoon, *Empire and Order*.
6. Milhou, *Colón y su mentalidad mesiánica*, 438.
7. Liss, "Isabel of Castile," 128. See also Fraker, *The Scope of History*, 5.
8. Liss, "Isabel of Castile," 127–28.
9. Ibid., 144.
10. Ibid., 144n71.
11. "Bula *Inter caetera* de 3 de mayo," 14–17.
12. López de Gómara, *Historia general de las Indias*, 8. My translation. López de Gómara's history was written in the early 1540s but not published until 1552. The original reads: "Comenzaron las conquistas de los indios acabadas la de moros, por que siempre guerreasen españoles contra infieles."
13. Elliott, *Imperial Spain*, 49.
14. See Muldoon, *Empire and Order*, and Weckmann, *The Medieval Heritage of Mexico*.
15. Elliott, *Imperial Spain*, 33.
16. Ibid., 50.
17. Some of this discussion draws on Bartosik-Vélez, "The First Interpretations of the Columbian Enterprise."

18. We should note that one pre-discovery document, a "Salvoconducto" (or Letter of Safe Conduct) given to Columbus and signed by the royal secretary on behalf of the king and queen, refers to a religious purpose of the voyage. Written in Latin, the letter is addressed to the sovereigns Columbus might encounter and reads in part: "Mittimus in presenciarum nobilem virum Christoforum Colon cun tribus caravelis armatis per maria Oceania ad partes Indie, pro alquibus causis et negociis, servicium Dei ac fidei ortodoxe augmentum, necnon benefficium et utilitatem nostram, concernentibus." "Salvoconducto," 23. (By these presents we sent the noble Christopher Columbus with three caravels fitted out for the ocean sea toward the regions of India for certain reasons and matters regarding the diffusion of the divine faith as well as for our use and benefit.) I use the translation provided by Taviani, "Notes for the Historicogeographical Reconstruction," 77.
19. Zamora, *Reading Columbus*, 28.
20. Nader argues that Ferdinand and Isabel, in commissioning Columbus in 1492, sought to mimic the Portuguese method of building a trade empire. "The End of the Old World," 797. See also Kicza, "Patterns in Early Spanish Overseas Expansion." Morison points out the similarities of the *Capitulaciones* to the letter of donation issued in 1486 by the Portuguese King João II to the Flemish explorer Fernão Dulmo, a.k.a. Ferdinand van Olm. Morison, "The Earliest Colonial Policy," 544. Morison cites Bensaúde, *Lacunes et surprises de l'histoire des découvertes maritimes*.
21. Regarding "missionary purpose," see Weckmann, *The Medieval Heritage of Mexico*, 179; and Zunzunegui, "Los orígenes de las misiones."
22. Cf. Muldoon, *Popes, Lawyers, and Infidels*, 133.
23. Phillips, *The Medieval Expansion of Europe*, 95.
24. Columbus, *The Journal*, 1:9. The originals read: "este presente año de 1492, después de Vuestras Altezas aver dado fin a la guerra de los moros" and "después de aver echado fuera todos los judíos de todos vuestros reinos y señoríos." Colón, *Textos*, 95–96.
25. Milhou, *Colón y su mentalidad mesiánica*, 177–78.
26. Columbus, *The Journal*, 1:9. The original: "para ver los dichos prínçipes y los pueblos y las tierras y la disposiçión d'ellas y de todo. . . . para ver los dichos prínçipes y los pueblos y las tierras y la disposición d'ellas y de todo, y la manera que se pudiera tener para la conversión d'ellas a nuestra sancta fe." Colón, *Textos*, 95–96.
27. Columbus, *The Journal*, 1:9. "cathólicos cristianos y prínçipes amadores de la sancta fe cristiana y acreçentadores d'ella y enemigos de la secta de Mahoma y de todas idolatrías y heregías." Colón, *Textos*, 95.

28. Columbus, *The Journal*, 1:9. "muchas vezes él y sus anteçessores avían enbiado a Roma a pedir doctores en nuestra sancta fe porque le enseñasen en ella, y que nunca el Sancto Padre le avía proveído y se perdían tantos pueblos, cayendo en idolatrías e resçibiendo en sí sectas de perdiçión." Colón, *Textos*, 95.
29. I follow David Henige's suggestion to refer to the original record kept by Columbus, which is now lost, as the "log" in order to distinguish it from the particular version of the log created by Las Casas. Henige, *In Search of Columbus*, 8.
30. Any conclusions based on a textual analysis of the *Diario* are necessarily tentative because the original was lost, and the only extant version of it is Las Casas's summary of a copy of it. Despite Consuelo Varela's faith in the "overall integrity of Las Casas's text of the Journal," it is impossible to verify how much of the *Diario* is Las Casas's creation as opposed to Columbus's. Varela, "Notes," 55. So, while some maintain that Columbus is the author of the *Diario* (see, for example, Varela, "Notes," 55–58; Gil, Introduction to *Textos y documentos completos*, 30; and Morison, "Texts," 239), Henige and Zamora treat the document as a constructed text manipulated and mediated by Las Casas. Zamora emphasizes Las Casas's own ideological agenda, reminding us that his primary goal was the peaceful evangelization of the natives. She asserts that Las Casas's version of the *Diario* was likely designed to serve him as an "aide mémoire" in the production of his own writings as opposed to a faithful reproduction of Columbus's original log. Zamora, *Reading Columbus*, 42.
31. Columbus, *The Journal*, 1:213, 215. "Y dize qu'espera en Dios que, a la buelta que él entendía hazer de Castilla, avía de hallar un tonel de oro, que avrían resgatado los que avía de dexar, y que avrían hallado la mina del oro y la espeçería, y aquello en tanta cantidad que los Reyes antes de tres años emprendiesen y adereçasen para ir a conquistar la Casa Sancta, 'que así,' dize él, 'protesté a Vuestras Altezas que toda la ganançia d'esta mi empresa se gastase en la conquista de Hierusalem, y Vuestras Altezas se rieron y dixeron que les plazía, y que sin esto tenían aquella gana.'" Colón, *Textos*, 181.
32. I refer to these letters collectively as "the Santángel/Sánchez letter." The original Santángel and Sánchez letters are lost. Available copies share the same content but different dates (and signatures, probably due to the translators of the letters and/or their publishers). The Santángel letter is dated 15 February 1493, and the Sánchez letter is dated 14 March 1493. While both missives underwent multiple editions, the Sánchez letter was more widely distributed in Europe. See Rumeu de Armas, *Libro copiador*, 1:51. The

letter most often cited in current scholarship is that addressed to Santángel. For a discussion of the likely dates, locales, and circumstances of the letters Columbus wrote immediately after the "discovery," including the 4 March 1493 letter to the sovereigns, see Rumeu de Armas, *Libro copiador*, 1:27–51; and Davidson, *Columbus Then and Now*, 196.

Regarding the argument that Columbus's 4 March 1493 letter to the sovereigns is the product of a royal revision of the Santángel/Sanchez letter, see Ramos Pérez, *La primera noticia de América*; and Zamora, *Reading Columbus*.

33. Zamora, *Reading Columbus*, 26–27.
34. Zamora, *Reading Columbus*, 190. The original Spanish reads: "Aquel eterno Dios que a dado tantas victorias a V.Al., agora les dió la mas alta que hasta oy a dado a prínçipes." Colón, *Textos*, 227.
35. Zamora, *Reading Columbus*, 190. I have modified Zamora's translation slightly to reflect more literally the repetitive use of the first person pronoun. The original reads: "*Yo bengo* de las Yndias con el armada que V. Al. me dieron, adonde *yo pasé* en treinta y tres días después que *yo partí* de vuestros reinos." Colón, *Textos*, 227–28 (emphasis added).
36. Columbus, *Journal*, 309. "Señor: Porque sé que avréis plazer de la gran vitoria que nuestro Señor me ha dado en mi viaje vos escrivo ésta, por la cual sabréis cómo en treinta y tres días pasé a las Indias." Colón, *Textos*, 219–20.
37. Zamora, *Reading Columbus*, 194. Because Zamora does not attempt to render the damaged portions of the document, I have supplemented her translation. The damaged sections are noted by asterisk in the original: "Mas Nuestro Señor, qu'es lumbre y fuerça de todos aquellos que andan a buen fin y les da victoria de cosas que pareçen inposibles, quiso hordenar que yo hallase y oviese de hallar oro y minas d'él y espeçería y gente sin número,* ** unos dispuestos para ser christianos y otros para que los christianos * * *" Colón, *Textos*, 231.
38. Columbus, *The Journal*, 1:321. "Eterno Dios nuestro Señor, el cual da a todos aquellos que andan su camino victoria de cosas que parecen imposibles." Colón, *Textos*, 225.
39. Zamora, *Reading Columbus*, 194–95. "Concluyo aquí que, mediante la graçia divinal de Aquél qu'es comienço de todas cosas virtuosas y buenas y que da favor y victoria a todos aquellos que van en su camino, que de oy en siete años yo podré pagar a V. Al. çinco mill de cavallo y çincuenta mill de pie en la guerra e conquista de Jherusalem, sobre el cual propósito se tomó esta empresa; y dende a çinco años otros çinco mill de cavallo y cincuenta mill

de pie, que serían diez mill de cavallo y çient mill de pie, y esto con muy poca costa que faga agora V.A. en este comienço, para que se tengan todas las Yndias y lo que en ellas ay en la mano, como después diré por palabra a V.A. Y para esto tengo razón y no hablo inçierto, y no se deve dormir en ello, como se a fecho en la esecución d'esta enpresa, de que Dios perdone a quien a sido causa d'ello." Colón, *Textos*, 232.

40. See Bartosik-Vélez, "The Three Rhetorical Strategies of Christopher Columbus."
41. See Colón, *Textos*, 481.
42. Zamora, *Reading Columbus*, 20.
43. Diffie and Winius, *Foundations of the Portuguese Empire*, 171–72.
44. Ramos Pérez, *La primera noticia de América*, 66.
45. Zamora, *Reading Columbus*, 195. "Muy poderosos prínçipes, [de] toda la christianidad deve hazer muy grandísimas fiestas y en espeçial la Yglesia de Dios, por aver fallado tanta multidumbre de pueblos tan allegados, para <que> con poco trabajo se tornen a nuestra sancta fee, y de tantas tierras llenas de tantos bienes a nos muy neçesarios, en que abrán todos <los> christianos refrigerio y ganançia, donde todo estava incógnito ni se contava d'ello salvo en manera de fábulas. Grandes alegrías y fiestas en las igle(sias y mu)chas alabanças a la Sancta Trinidad deve en espeçial mandar hazer V. Al. (en todos) sus reinos y señoríos por el gran amor que les a amostrado, más que a otro prínçipe." Colón, *Textos*, 232–33.
46. Columbus, *The Journal*, 1:321. The Spanish reads: "Así que, pues nuestro Redemtor dio esta victoria a nuestros illustrísimos Rey e Reina e a sus reinos famosos de tan alta cosa, adonde toda la christianidad deve tomar alegría y fazer grandes fiestas y dar gracias solemnes a la Sancta Trinidad con muchas oraciones solemnes, por el tanto enxalçamiento que havrán en tornándose tantos pueblos a nuestra sancta fe, y después por los bienes temporales que no solamente a la España, mas a todos los christianos ternán aquí refrigerio y ganancia." Colón, *Textos*, 226.
47. Morison provides this English translation in *Journals and Other Documents*, 203–4. The original reads: "Primeramente, pues á Dios nuestro Señor plugo por su alta misericordia descobrir las dichas islas, é tierra-firme al Rey é á la Reina nuestros Señores por industria del dicho D. Cristóbal Colon, su Almirante, Visorey, é Gobernador dellas, el cual ha fecho relacion á sus Altezas, que las gentes que en ellas falló pobladas, conoció dellas ser gentes muy aparejadas para se convertir á nuestra Santa Fe Católica, porque no tienen ninguna ley ni seta; de lo cual ha placido y place mucho á sus Altezas, porque en todo es razon que se tenga principalmente respeto

al servicio de Dios nuestro Señor, é ensalzamiento de nuestra Santa Fe Católica: por ende sus Altezas deseando que nuestra Santa Fe Católica sea aumentada é acrescentada, mandan é encargan al dicho Almirante, Visorey, é Gobernador, que por todas las vias é maneras que pudiere procure é trabaje atraer á los moradores de las dichas islas é tierra-firme, á que se conviertan á nuestra Santa Fe Católica." Quoted in Fernández de Navarrete, *Colección de los viajes y descubrimientos*, 2:83–84.

48. Morison, *Admiral of the Ocean Sea*, 368.
49. Juan Gil's disagreement with this idea is not supported by the text. Gil says, "Columbus alludes to the conquest of land, but only at the end of the relation on the third voyage." (A la conquista de tierra alude Colón, pero sólo al fin de la relación del tercer viaje.) Gil, "Génesis y desarrollo del proyecto colombino," 83n2. My translation.
50. Wey Gómez, *Tropics of Empire*.
51. My translation. "En el cual cabo de Alfa e O puse colunas con cruz en nombre y señal de V.Al., por ser el estremo cabo de oriente de la tierra firme, ansí como tiene en poniente el cavo de Finisterre, qu'es otro cabo estremo de la tierra firme a poniente, en medio de los cuales amos <cavos> se contiene todo el poblado del mundo." Colón, *Textos*, 292.
52. Columbus, *Accounts and Letters*, 211. "Cada año mucho abremos de acreçentar en la pintura, porque <se> descubrirá continuamente." Colón, *Textos*, 240.
53. Columbus, *Accounts and Letters*, 89. "Creo qu'esta tierra que agora mandaron descubrir V. Al. sea grandísima e aya otras muchas en el austro." Colón, *Textos*, 380.
54. See, for example, Colón, *Textos*, 383.
55. My translation. "Estoy inclinado con todos los sentidos a le dar descanso y alegría y a le acresçentar su alto Señorío." Colón, *Textos*, 472.
56. On surpassing the ancients, see Lupher, *Romans in a New World*. Lupher focuses on later conquistadors, but his argument is also useful for understanding Columbus.
57. My translation. The original, from a fragment of a letter from Columbus to the sovereigns, written between September 1498 and October 1500, reads: "Digo que me respondan, quien leyó las historias de griegos y de romanos, si con toda poca cosa ensancharon su señorío tan grandemente, como agora hizo Vuestra Alteza aquel de la España con las Indias." Colón, *Textos*, 410.
58. Columbus, *Accounts and Letters*, 65. "Ni valía dezir que yo nunca avía leído que prínçipes de Castilla jamás obiesen ganado tierra fuera d'ella, y que acá es otro mundo en que se trabajaron romanos y Alexandre y griegos, para le aver, con grandes exerçiçios." Colón, *Textos*, 368.

59. My translation. In Columbus's February 1502 letter to Pope Alexander VI, he writes: "Gozara mi ánima y descansara si agora en fin pudiera venir a Vuestra Santidad con mi escriptura, la cual tengo para ello, que es en la forma de los Comentarios e uso de César, en que he proseguido desde el primero día fasta agora, que se atravesó a que yo aya de haçer en nombre de la Sancta Trinidad viaje nuevo, el cual será a su gloria y honra de la Santa Religión Cristiana." Colón, *Textos*, 480.
60. See Bartosik-Vélez, "The Three Rhetorical Strategies of Christopher Columbus."
61. Regarding Gorricio's role in the *Book of Prophecies*, see Rusconi, Introduction to *The Book of Prophecies*, 15, 26; and Rusconi, "Escatologia e conversione," 278.
62. Columbus, *The Book of Prophecies*, 317. This prophecy was erroneously attributed to Joachim of Fiore (c.1132–1202).
63. Ibid., 77. It is likely, however, that Columbus never sent the *Book of Prophecies* to the sovereigns.
64. Focusing on his status as victim and his insufficiently rewarded dedication to Spain's empire, Columbus himself, not Las Casas as is commonly argued, sowed the seed of the "Black Legend," which alleged Spain was primarily motivated by greed and cruelty in the colonization of the New World.
65. Colón, *Textos*, 218.
66. Jane, *The Four Voyages*, 2:lxxxviii. The original reads: "Ha placido así darme el galardón d'estos afanes y peligros. Veramente abalumado con esta grande vitoria, plege a Dios que se reduzgan los disfamadores de mi honra, que con tanta deshoesidad y mal<i>cia han fecho burla de mí e disfamado mi empresa sin coñoscimiento de mi dezir y del servicio e acrescentamiento de Sus Altesas." Colón, *Textos*, 218.
67. Columbus's complaints about the Spaniards who accompanied him are not without merit. The Crown had encouraged people to enlist in Columbus's first voyage by granting pardon to convicted criminals. Recognizing the need for better control, the Crown established the Casa de la Contratación in Seville in 1503 in order to administer the Indies. Among this administrative entity's responsibilities was to control who was permitted to emigrate to Spanish territories overseas. See Fisher, *The Economic Aspects of Spanish Imperialism*, 47.
68. Columbus, *Accounts and Letters*, 27. "Item: diréis a Sus Altesas e suplicaréis de mi parte cuanto más umildemente puede . . . que para las cosas del servicio de Sus Altesas escojan tales personas que non se tengan recelo d'ellas, e que miren más a lo porqué se envía que non a sus propios intereses." Colón, *Textos*, 262.

69. Columbus, *Accounts and Letters*, 13. "Me encomendaréis en sus Altezas como a Rey e Reina mis señores naturales, en cuyo servicio yo deseo fenecer mis días." Colón, *Textos*, 254.
70. Jane, *The Four Voyages*, 2:54. "Seis meses avía que yo estava despachado para venir a Sus Altezas ... y fuir de governar gente dissoluta, que no teme a Dios ni a su Rey ni Reina, llena de achaques y de malicias." Colón, *Textos*, 432.
71. Jane, *The Four Voyages*, 2:60. I have modified Jane's translation slightly to better reflect the sense of the phrase "acrecentar el señorío." The original reads: "Mas el sostener de la justiçia y acrecentar el señorío de Sus Altezas fasta agora me tiene al fondo." Colón, *Textos*, 434.
72. Jane, *The Four Voyages*, 2:50. "Si yo robara las Indias e tierra que ia[n] faze en ello, de que agora es la fabla, del altar de San Pedro y las diera a los moros, no pudieran en España amostrarme mayor enemiga. ¿Quién creyera tal adonde ovo tanta nobleza?" Colón, *Textos*, 430–31.
73. See Jane, *The Four Voyages*, 2:66, 68; Colón, *Textos*, 436.
74. Thacher, *Christopher Columbus*, 2:294 (emphasis added). The original reads: "Yo he perdido en esto mi juventud y la parte que me pertenece d'estas cosas y la honra d'ello; mas non fuera de Castilla, adonde se julgarán mis fechos y seré julgado como a capitán que fue a conquistar d'España fasta las Indias, y non a gobernar cibdad ni villa ni pueblo puesto en regimiento, salvo a poner so el señorío de Sus Altezas gente salvaje, belicosa y que biben por sierras y montes." Colón, *Textos*, 438. Varela's comment about the nature of this document ("Debe de ser el borrador de una carta a los miembros del Consejo de Castilla") is also found on p. 438.
75. The subject of Marie Tanner's *The Last Descendant of Aeneas* is the frequent manipulation throughout the sixteenth century of the Trojan and Argonautic legends in Europe.
76. Ibid., 17.
77. Ibid., 149–50.
78. Ibid., 150.
79. Seneca, *Hercules*, 377.
80. Venient annis
secula seris, quibus Occeanus
vincula rerum laxet, et ingens
pateat te<l>lus tiphisque novos
detegat orbes, nec sit terris
ultima Thule.
(Columbus, *The Book of Prophecies*, 290.)
81. Romm, "New World and 'novos orbes,'" 84.

82. Clay, "Columbus's Senecan Prophecy," 618–19.
83. Columbus, *The Book of Prophecies*, 291.
84. Columbus, *Accounts and Letters*, 143 (emphasis added).
85. Rusconi, Introduction to *The Book of Prophecies*, 34.
86. Romm, "New World and 'noves orbes,'" 84.
87. Brading, *The First America*, 23.

CHAPTER 2
1. Brinton, "The Ships of Columbus in Brant's Virgil," 86.
2. Ibid., 83.
3. Mortimer, "Vergil in the Light of the Sixteenth Century," 160.
4. Wilson-Okamura, "Virgilian Models of Colonization in Shakespeare's Tempest," 711.
5. "Civilized" and "civilization" are, of course, relative terms. I do not mean to imply that "the West" is civilized and the rest of the world is not. Rather, the West (and the North) has generally been politically and economically dominant and has imposed its civilization and values on others whom it has deemed savage by virtue of the fact that their values differ from those of the West (and North).
6. Waswo, "The Formation of Natural Law to Justify Colonialism, 1539–1689," 744.
7. Waswo, *The Founding Legend*, 27.
8. Virgil, *Aeneid* 1.279.
9. Quint, "Epic and Empire," 15.
10. Hamilton, *Virgil and* The Tempest, 65.
11. Kallendorf, "Virgil's Post-classical Legacy," 576. Kallendorf cites Tanner, *The Last Descendant of Aeneas*, another excellent source that discusses the importance of the Virgilian model and how it was appropriated by European rulers.
12. Thacher, *Christopher Columbus*, 2:294. The original text describes the natives as "gente salvaje, belicosa y que biben por sierras y montes." Colón, *Textos*, 438.
13. This discussion draws on Bartosik-Vélez, "*Translatio imperii:* Virgil and Peter Martyr's Columbus."
14. Regarding references to alternate years of his birth, see Lunardi, *The Discovery of the New World in the Writings of Peter Martyr of Anghiera*, 371.
15. López Grigera, "Iberian Peninsula," 198.
16. Martire d'Anghiera, *The Discovery*, 245. "Scipsit enim ad me Praefectus ipse marinus, cui sum intima familiaritate devinctus" (ibid., 246).

17. Although an unauthorized version of the first *Decade* was published in 1504 in Venice, the volume was not published in a complete form until 1511 in Seville. The first three *Decades* were then published at Alcalá in 1516 by the Spanish humanist Antonio de Nebrija. For a detailed publishing history of the many different editions of the *Decades*, see Brennan, "The Texts of Peter Martyr's *De orbe novo decades*." I quote the Latin-English edition published in 1992 by the Nuova Raccolta Colombiana, which collates the editions published by the following: Nebrija (1516), M. de Eguía (1530), I. Bebel (1533), and R. Hakluyt (1587). English translations are based on those provided in the Nuova Raccolta Colombiana edition and graciously modified by Christopher Francese. Martire d'Anghiera, *The Discovery of the New World in the Writings of Peter Martyr of Anghiera*.
18. Sale, *The Conquest of Paradise*, 222–26.
19. Martire d'Anghiera, *The Discovery*, 241. "Varios ibi esse reges hosque illis atque illos his potentiores inveniunt, uti fabulosum legimus Aeneam in varios divisum reperisse Latium, Latinum puta Mezentiumque ac Turnum et Tarchontem, qui angustis limitibus discriminabantur et huiuscemodi reliqua per tyrannos dispartita" (ibid., 240).
20. Ibid., 223. "Ad foetus procreandos equas, oves, iuvencas, et plura alia cum sui generis masculis, legumina, triticum, hordeum, et reliqua iis similia, non solum alimenti, verum etiam seminandi gratia Praefectus apparat" (ibid., 222).
21. Ibid., 225. "Instrumenta omnia fabrilia ac demum alia cuncta, quae ad novam civitatem in alienis regionibus condendam faciunt" (ibid., 224).
22. I use Robert Fagles's translation of the *Aeneid*, 47 (emphasis added). The original reads:
    > Arma virumque cano, Troiae qui primus ab oris
    > Italiam, fato profugus, Laviniaque venit
    > litora, multum ille et terris iactatus et alto
    > vi superum saevae memorem Iunonis ob iram;
    > multa quoque et bello passus, dum *conderet urbem*,
    > inferretque deos Latio, genus unde Latinum,
    > Albanique patres, atque altae moenia Romae.
    > (1.1–7, emphasis added)
23. Morwood, "Aeneas, Augustus, and the Theme of the City." On the importance of the word "condere" in the *Aeneid*, see James, "Establishing Rome with the Sword."
24. Quint, *Epic and Empire*, 83.
25. Waswo, *The Founding Legend*, 24.

26. Martire d'Anghiera, *The Discovery*, 247, 249. "Ipse propinquum portui cuidam editum locum ad civitatem condendam elegit ibique intra paucos dies domibus, ut brevitas temporis passa est, et sacello erectis eo die quo *Trium Regum* solennia celebramus, divina nostro ritu, in alio, potest dici, orbe, tam extero, tam ab omni cultu et religione alieno, sacra sunt decantata, terdecim sacerdotibus ministrantibus" (ibid., 246).
27. Ibid., 253. "Super edito igitur colle a septentrione civitatem erigere decrevit" (ibid., 252).
28. Ibid., 255. "Sed redeamus ad condendam urbem" (ibid., 254).
29. Ibid., 255. "Fossis et aggeribus urbe circumvallata, ut si, eo absente, praelium incolae tentarent, sese qui relinquebantur tutari possint, pridie Idus Martii cum omnibus equitibus, peditibus autem circiter quadringentis, ipsemet ad auriferam regionem recta ad meridiem proficiscitur; fluvium praeterlabitur, transgreditur planitiem, montem, qui aliud planitiei latus cingit, superat" (ibid., 254).
30. Ibid., 255. "Cum iam secundum et septuagesimum ab urbe lapidem intra regionem auriferam profectus fuisset, . . . condere arcem instituit ut interioris regionis secreta inde tuto paulatim scrutarentur" (ibid., 254).
31. Ibid., 221. "Octo et triginta viros apud eum regem . . . reliquit" (ibid., 220).
32. Ibid., 221. "De vita et salute ac tutela eorum quos ibi relinquebat, quibus potuit modis, egit" (ibid., 220).
33. Ibid., 239. "Cum autem ad castellum ligneum et casas quas sibi, aggere circunducto, nostri construxerant pervenissent." (ibid., 240).
34. See Gil, "*Decades* de Pedro Mártir de Anglería," 18–19.
35. Martire d'Anghiera, *The Discovery*, 211. "Viros, quorum industria et animi magnitudine ignotae maioribus eorum terrae panderentur" (ibid., 210).
36. Ibid., 211. "Ab ipsius . . . initio rei, ne sim cuiquam iniurius, exordiri est animus. Christophorus Colonus, quidam Ligur vir . . ." (ibid., 210).
37. Virgil, *Aeneid* 12.794–95.
38. Lunardi, *The Discovery of the New World*, 410.
39. Cicero, *Orations* 2.35, 173.
40. *Virgil's Georgics*, 189, 2.170–72. The original reads: "Et te, maxime Caesar, / qui nunc extremis Asiae iam victor in oris / imbellem avertis Romanis arcibus Indum."
41. Martire d'Anghiera, *The Discovery*, 213. The original reads: "Se deceptos fuisse ab homine Ligure, in praeceps trahi qua nunquam redire licebit" (ibid., 212).
42. Ibid., 213. "Proditione quoque taxandos esse a Regibus, si adversi quicquam in eum molirentur, si parere recusarent, praedicabat" (ibid., 212).

43. Lunardi, *The Discovery of the New World in the Writings of Peter Martyr of Anghiera*, 443.
44. Ibid., 447.
45. Martire d'Anghiera, *The Discovery*, 355. "Vitam egere mensibus decem Vergiliani Achemenidis vita" (ibid., 354).
46. Ibid., 357. "Invalidi omnes et egestate rerum extenuati veniunt ad Hispaniolam. Quid inde illis successerit non intellexi" (ibid., 356).
47. Kallendorf, "Virgil's Post-classical Legacy," 575.
48. See the Introduction, n6.
49. In *Epic and Empire* Quint refines the definition of epic, arguing that there are, in fact, two kinds: epics of winners who have successfully subjugated others and epics of the losers who have been subjugated.
50. Virgil, *Aeneid* 1.1–2. My translation of Gambara. The original Latin reads: "Perenotte, uirum referam qui littora primus / Ingentis tetigit Cubae." Yruela Guerrero, Introduction to *La navegación de Cristóbal Colón*, xlviii.
51. Hofmann, "*Adveniat tandem Typhis qui detegat orbes*," 432, 444, 446–47. See also Yruela Guerrero, ibid.
52. Gambara, *De navigatione Christophori Columbi*, 222. 4.535–38. Translation by Christopher Francese.
53. Virgil, *Aeneid* 3.716–18; Fagles's translation, 126.
54. Hofmann, "Adveniat tandem Typhis qui detegat orbes," 446.
55. Juan Gil also notes the similarities between Columbus and Aeneas in Stella's poem. See Gil, "La épica Latina quiñentista," 236.
56. Hofmann, "Adveniat tandem Typhis qui detegat orbes," 472–73.
57. Torres Martínez, Introduction to *Columbus*; Sánchez Marín and Torres Martínez, "El poema épico *Columbus* de Ubertino Carrara," 214.
58. Boccage, *La Colombiade*, 38, 115.
59. Ibid., 40. Translations of Du Boccage's text graciously provided by Kristin Beach.
60. Ibid., 41. "Nos guerriers, dans l'ardeur que ce discours inspire, / D'un nouvel univers se promettent l'empire, / Et leur espoir déjà voit une autre Colchos."
61. Ibid., 69–70.

CHAPTER 3

1. See Bushman, *America Discovers Columbus*, 53–55.
2. Nathaniel Morton and his uncle William Bradford, for example, both refer to Martyr's *Decades*. Morton, *New-England's Memorial*, 44; Bradford, *Of Plymouth Plantation*, 122.

3. Eden, *The Decades of the Newe World or West India*, 51.
4. Armitage, *The Ideological Origins of the British Empire*, 78.
5. For a discussion of how Hakluyt's work was grounded in his Christian morals, as opposed to imperial or nationalistic ambitions, as critics have often argued, see Boruchoff, "Piety, Patriotism, and Empire."
6. Sacks, "Richard Hakluyt's Navigations in Time," 34. In the dedication to Walter Ralegh of his 1587 edition of Martyr's *Decades*, Hakluyt contends that he lives in a time similar to the beginnings of the Roman Empire. Here he compares Ralegh to Achilles, Martyr to Homer, and himself to Martyr. See Sacks, ibid.
7. Waswo, *The Founding Legend*, 68.
8. Bushman, *America Discovers Columbus*, 29–30.
9. Excerpts of Robertson's *History of America*, including book 2, which focuses on Columbus, were published in 1780 in the *Pennsylvania Packet* and in 1784 and 1785 in both the *Massachusetts Spy* and the *Continental Journal*.
10. Robertson, *The History of America*, vi.
11. Ibid.
12. Van Alstyne, *The Rising American Empire*, 10.
13. Ibid., 9.
14. This notion of an empire that safeguards liberty was at the heart of British exceptionalist views of its own maritime, trade-based empire. Its commercial maritime empire, based on liberty and trade, was believed to be different in kind from the territorial universal monarchies of Europe, which were based on conquest that did not allow for personal liberties. See Armitage, *The Ideological Origins of the British Empire*, ch. 5.
15. Freneau, "Columbus to Ferdinand," 40. The first publication of "Columbus to Ferdinand" misattributes the quote to Plato. See Ronnick, "A Note on the Text of Freneau's 'Columbus to Ferdinand.'"
16. For a discussion of which of the two poets is responsible for which parts of the poem, see Smeall, "The Respective Roles of Hugh Brackenridge and Philip Freneau." I use the 1772 edition, which appears to be mostly the work of Freneau.
17. Freneau, *On the Rising Glory*, 3–4.
18. Wertheimer, "Commencement Ceremonies," 35.
19. Freneau, *On the Rising Glory*, 16.
20. The dependence of commerce on science, and science on liberty, is described by the character Leander. Ibid., 18–19.
21. Ibid., 20–21.
22. Ibid., 26–27.

23. In his study of millennialism in British America, Ernest Lee Tuveson explains the idea of five empires. In the "lunatic fringe of the central ideology of millennialism" during the English Civil War period, the "Fifth Monarchy, technically, is the name of the kingdom of righteousness, however its advent and character are understood, since it succeeds the four regimes thought to be predicted in Daniel. Even the most conservative theologians soon regarded its coming as a distinct certainty." Tuveson, *Redeemer Nation*, 31–32. See also Breuninger, "Morals, the Market, and History," chapters 8 and 9, passim.
24. Freneau, "Pictures of Columbus," 127.
25. Dwight, *America*, 11.
26. Ibid., 12.
27. Barlow, *The Columbiad*, 1.
28. Virgil, *Aeneid* 1.1–3. My translation.
29. Blakemore, *Joel Barlow's* Columbiad, 18.
30. David Shields writes that Whig poetry in particular seized on the theme of the *translatio imperii*. See Shields, *Oracles of Empire*, 32. See also Shalev, *Rome Reborn on Western Shores*, 28–35.
31. For a discussion of Berkeley's influence on Freneau, see Lubbers, "'Westward the Course of Empire.'"
32. Silverman, *A Cultural History of the American Revolution*, 10.
33. Regarding England's corruption, see Bailyn, *The Ideological Origins of the American Revolution*, 86–93.
34. Armitage, *The Ideological Origins of the British Empire*, 133–39.
35. Berkeley, "An Essay toward Preventing the Ruin of Great Britain," 185, 191.
36. For the imperialist nature of Berkeley's plan, see Lubbers, "'Westward the Course of Empire,'" 333.
37. Berkeley, "Verses on the Prospect of Planting Arts and Learning in America," 366.
38. Breuninger, "Morals, the Market, and History," 395.
39. Regarding the origins of the idea of the British Empire, see Armitage, *Ideological Origins of the British Empire*, 170–71.
40. Ibid., 175.
41. See Tennenhouse, *The Importance of Feeling English*. See also Murrin, "A Roof Without Walls."
42. Freneau, *On the Rising Glory*, 13, 20–21, 27.
43. Dwight, *America*, 7, 11.
44. Kafer, "The Making of Timothy Dwight," 205.
45. Dwight, "Columbia: An Ode," n.p.

46. The bibliography on the topic of Columbus in British America is too vast to list here. Among others, see Bushman, *America Discovers Columbus*; Larner, "North American Hero?"; Sale, *The Conquest of Paradise*; Schlereth, "Columbia, Columbus, and Columbianism"; Stavans, *Imagining Columbus*; and Trouillot, "Good Day Columbus."
47. Armitage, *The Ideological Origins of the British Empire*, 11, 132, 139.
48. Onuf, *Jefferson's Empire*, 16.
49. Pagden, *Peoples and Empires*, xxi–xxii.
50. *Oxford English Dictionary Online*, s.v. "empire," accessed May 15, 2013, www.oed.com.
51. "But not withstanding this increase, so vast is the Territory of North America, that it will require many ages to settle it fully; and till it is fully settled, labour will never be cheap here." Franklin, "Observations Concerning the Increase of Mankind, Peopling of Countries," 313.
52. Nugent, *Habits of Empire*, 22.
53. See Adorno, "Washington Irving's Romantic Hispanicism," 61.
54. Irving, *The Life and Voyages*, 1:6.
55. Ibid., 1:178.
56. Ibid., 1:179.
57. Ibid., 2:201
58. Ibid., 2:195, 189.
59. Ibid., 2:187.
60. Irving writes that Columbus bequeathed a breviary given to him by Pope Alexander IV to his native republic of Genoa. Ibid., 2:187, 196.
61. Fryd, *Art and Empire*, 55–56.
62. Ibid., 1. See also Buscaglia-Salgado, *Undoing Empire*, 16–25.
63. Quoted in Fryd, *Art and Empire*, 128–29.
64. See, for example, Larner, "North American Hero? Christopher Columbus 1702–2002," 50n22.
65. For a discussion of Crofutt's commission, see Fifer, *American Progress*, 202–4.
66. See, for example, Nugent, *Habits of Empire* and Gardner, LaFeber, and McCormick, *The Creation of the American Empire*.
67. Rydell, *All the World's a Fair*, 2–3.
68. Bancroft, *The Book of the Fair*, Preface [n.p.]
69. Depew, *The Columbian Oration*, 3.
70. Ibid., 3–4 (emphasis added).
71. Ibid., 12.
72. Peacock, *The Columbian Ode*, 8.

73. Ibid., 5.
74. Ibid.
75. Ibid., 7.
76. Ibid., 8.
77. Benedict, "International Exhibitions," 5.
78. Rydell, *All the World's a Fair*, 55–56.
79. Walker, "A World's Fair," n.p.
80. See, for example, William Appleman Williams, *Empire as a Way of Life* and Drinnon, *Facing West*.
81. Quoted in Slotkin, "Buffalo Bill's 'Wild West,'" 165.
82. Burke, "*Buffalo Bill*," 196. In her illuminating study of Buffalo Bill Cody, Joy S. Kasson argues that he made explicit "claims to the tradition of Columbus," although she does not focus on the reverberations of empire within that tradition. Kasson, *Buffalo Bill's Wild West*, 98.
83. Slotkin, "Buffalo Bill's 'Wild West,'" 173.

CHAPTER 4

1. Kirkpatrick Sale estimates that there are "65 geopolitical entities in the United States using 'Columbus,' 'Columbia,' or some variation thereof in 37 states (plus, of course, the District of Columbia)." Sale, *The Conquest of Paradise*, 360.
2. Brading, *The First America*, 433.
3. Miranda, *América espera*, 24.
4. Uslar Pietri, *Los libros de Miranda*.
5. Racine, *Francisco de Miranda*, 103.
6. See Uslar Pietri, "Catálogo de las dos Subastas, Londres, 1828 y 1833" in *Los libros de Miranda*, 41; Miranda, *Archivo del General de Miranda (AGM)*, 1:288.
7. The preliminary articles of the Treaty of Paris that ended the war had already been signed in Paris in November 1782. The treaty itself was signed later, on 3 September 1783.
8. Crito [pseud.], "Peace." *South Carolina Weekly Gazette*, June 21, 1783, vol. 1, no. 19, 4.
9. Part of book 8 of *The History of America* had been reprinted earlier in the *Pennsylvania Packet*, 1 February 1780.
10. See Uslar Pietri, "Apéndice: Lista de libros en el archivo de Miranda" in *Los libros de Miranda*, LVI, LX.
11. Miranda, *Archivo General de Miranda* (hereafter *AGM*), 7:36.
12. Racine, *Francisco de Miranda*, 108.

13. The original French reads: "*La Ville Federale* sera batie dans le point le plus central (peut-être dans l'Isthme) et portera le nom auguste de *Colombo* á qui le monde doit la decouverte de cette belle partie de la terre . . ." Miranda, *AGM*, 16:159 (ellipses in original).
14. Robertson, *The Life of Miranda*, 1:230.
15. Rosenblat, *El nombre de Venezuela*, 44–45; Ardao, *La idea de la Magna Colombia*, 11–12, 12n12.
16. Miranda, *AGM*, 15:128.
17. Ibid., 17:89
18. See, for example, Ibid., 15:357.
19. The Act of Paris, which was written in French and signed by Miranda and fellow Spanish Americans José Godoy del Pozo y Sucre and Manuel José de Salas, refers to "l'amerique Méridionale," "les Colonies hispano-américaines," and "le Continent Hispano-Americain" (South America, the Spanish American Colonies, and The Spanish American Continent). Grisanti, *Miranda: Precursor del Congreso de Panamá y del panamericanismo*, 77–85.
20. Miranda, *AGM*, 16:77–78.
21. Ibid., 15:145–46. I thank Lucile Duperron for help with the translations.
22. In his letter to Hamilton dated 6 April 1798, Miranda repeats this hemispheric appeal: "Il paroit que le moment de notre Emancipation aproche, et que l'Establissement de la Liberté sur tout le Continent du Nouveau Monde nous est Confié par la providence!" ("It seems the time of our emancipation nears, and the establishment of liberty on the entire continent of the New World is entrusted to us by providence!" Miranda, *AGM*, 16:41.
23. Quoted in Robertson, *The Life of Miranda*, 1:149.
24. In a memorandum Miranda wrote in preparation for his meeting in October 1804 with Lord Melville, he recommends that a British-aided expedition land first in the north, then at Buenos Aires, and then on the Pacific side at Chile. Miranda, *AGM*, 17:94–96. Miranda was aware that a British-sponsored invasion of Buenos Aires, led by Sir Home Popham, was carried out almost at the same time that his own attempt was made.
25. Robertson, *Francisco Miranda and the Revolutionizing of Spanish America*, 397.
26. Racine, *Francisco de Miranda*, 164.
27. The English translation of the "proclamation" is mine. The original is located in Miranda, *AGM*, 18:105–9.

28. Ibid., 18:112
29. Ibid., 18:115.
30. Racine, *Francisco de Miranda*, 199.
31. Article 223 reads: "En todos los actos públicos se usará de *la Era Colombiana* y para evitar toda confusión en los cómputos al comparar esta época con la vulgar Cristiana . . . comenzará aquella a contarse desde el día primero, del año de N. S. mil ochocientos once que será el primero de nuestra independencia" (In all public acts *the Columbian Era* will be used and to avoid confusion when comparing this era with the common Christian era . . . the former will begin on the first day of the year of our Lord 1811, which will be the first day of our Independence.) (emphasis added).
32. Ardao, *La idea de la Magna Colombia*, 15.
33. Robertson, *The Life of Miranda*, 2:116–17.
34. William Spence Robertson notes Miranda's similarity to Columbus in that he was willing to accept the support of any nation that would help him achieve his goal. Robertson, *The Life of Miranda*, 2:247.
35. Racine, *Francisco de Miranda*, 110.
36. Miranda, *AGM*, 15:207.
37. Racine, *Francisco de Miranda*, 107.
38. Robertson, *Francisco de Miranda and the Revolutionizing of Spanish America*, 420.
39. Robertson, *The Life of Miranda*, 1:242.
40. Mexican historian Carlos Pereyra characterizes Viscardo's *Letter* as "un documento que puede llamarse el Acta de la Independencia de la América Español" (a document that can be called the Declaration of Independence of Spanish America). Pereyra, *Breve historia de América*, 344.
41. Norman Fiering writes that the *Letter* "was a spur to action comparable, in some respects to Thomas Paine's 'Common Sense.'" Fiering, "Preface," vii. Timothy Anna, for one, argues that the importance of Viscardo's *Letter* has been overstated, mostly because it was not read by large numbers of people. Anna, Review of *Los escritos de Juan Pablo Viscardo y Guzmán*. Incidentally, the widespread influence of Thomas Paine's *Common Sense* has also been questioned. See Loughran, "Disseminating *Common Sense*." Regardless of the issue of its contemporary diffusion, Viscardo's *Letter* clearly struck a chord with Miranda and reflects ways in which many Creoles thought about independence.
42. For a concise and accurate discussion of the convoluted publication history of the *Letter*, see Edwards, "Bibliographical Note."
43. Racine, *Francisco de Miranda*, 147.

44. See Weckmann, *The Medieval Heritage of Mexico*, 350–66.
45. Brading, *Classical Republicanism and Creole Patriotism*; Brading, *The First America*; Brading, *The Origins of Mexican Nationalism*. See also Pagden, *Spanish Imperialism*, chs. 4–5.
46. Viscardo y Guzmán, *Obra completa* (hereafter *OC*), 205. This and subsequent translations are mine. The original: "La proximidad en que nos encontramos del cuarto siglo después de que nuestros ancestros comenzaron a establecerse en el Nuevo Mundo, es un acontecimiento demasiado notable para no atraer más seriamente nuestra atención."
47. Ibid. "A pesar que nuestra historia de tres siglos, en lo que respecta a las causas y efectos más dignos de atención, sea tan pareja y conocida que pueda ser abreviada en las cuatro palabras siguientes: **Ingratitud, Injusticia, Esclavitud y Desolación**, nos conviene leerla un poco más detenidamente" (emphasis in original).
48. See Armitage, "The Declaration of Independence and International Law," 43.
49. Viscardo, *OC*, 205. "Nuestros Padres . . . [conquistaron las Indias] a costa de las mayores fatigas, peligros y gastos personales. . . . pero la inclinación natural hacia el país natal los llevó a hacerle el más generoso homenaje de sus inmensas adquisiciones, sin tener motivo para dudar que un servicio tan importante y gratuito les valiera un reconocimiento proporcional según la costumbre española de recompensar en España a todos los que habían contribuido a extender los dominios de la Nación."
50. Ibid., 206. "Todo lo que hemos prodigado a España, lo hemos sustraído contra toda razón a nosotros mismos y a nuestros hijos."
51. Ibid.
52. Ibid (emphasis added). "Al haberse frustrado las legítimas esperanzas y derechos de los conquistadores, sus descendientes y los de otros Españoles que fueron llegando progresivamente a América, y a pesar de que sólo reconocemos a ésta como nuestra Patria, y que toda nuestra subsistencia y la de nuestra descendencia se fundan en ella, hemos respetado, conservado y venerado sinceramente el cariño de nuestros Padres por su primera Patria; por ella hemos sacrificado infinitas riquezas de todo tipo, sólo por ella hemos resistido hasta aquí, y por ella hemos en todo encuentro vertido con entusiasmo nuestra sangre."
53. Ibid. "Nuestra necedad nos ha hecho cargar cadenas."
54. Ibid. "Un inmenso imperio, tesoros más grandes que todo lo que la imaginación hubiera podido desear en otras épocas, gloria y poderío superiores a todo lo que la antigüedad había conocido, he aquí los grandes títulos que nos hacen merecedores a la gratitud de España y de su gobierno

y a la protección y la benevolencia más distinguidas. Nuestra recompensa ha sido la que la más severa justicia hubiera podido dictar si hubiéramos sido enteramente culpables de los crímenes opuestos, exilándonos del antiguo mundo, alejándonos de la sociedad a la que estábamos tan estrechamente ligados."

55. Ibid., 209. "Consultemos nuestros anales de tres siglos y después de la ingratitud, la injusticia y el incumplimiento de la Corte de España para con los compromisos que había contraído, primero con el gran Colón y luego con los otros conquistadores que le dieron el imperio del Nuevo Mundo bajo condiciones solemnemente estipuladas, encontramos en sus descendientes solo los efectos del desprecio y del odio con que fueron calumniados, perseguidos y arruinados."

56. Ibid., 211. "Después de la época memorable en que el poder arbitrario y la injusticia de los últimos Reyes Godos llevaron a la ruina el imperio y la nación española, nuestros ancestros, durante el restablecimiento de su Reino y de su gobierno, no pensaron en nada tan cuidadosamente como en premunirse contra el poder absoluto, al que han aspirado siempre nuestros Reyes."

57. Ibid., 212. "Por medio de la reunión de los Reinos de Castilla y Aragón, de los tesoros de las Indias, y de otros grandes estados, que casi al mismo tiempo les tocaron en suerte a los Reyes de España, la corona adquirió tanta preponderancia y tan imprevista, que en muy poco tiempo echó abajo todas las barreras con que la prudencia de nuestros abuelos había pensado asegurar la libertad de su descendencia; la autoridad Real inundó como el mar toda la Monarquía y la voluntad del Rey y de sus ministros se convirtió en la única ley universal."

58. Ibid., 211. "el noble espíritu de la Libertad."

59. See Conway, *The Cult of Bolívar*.

60. See Ardao, *La idea de la Magna Colombia*, 16–20. "Como su gloria depende de tomar a su cargo la empresa de marchar a Venezuela, a libertar la cuna de la independencia colombiana." Bolívar, *Doctrina del Libertador*, 17.

61. Bolívar, *Obras completas*, 3:596.

62. Bolívar, *Doctrina del Libertador*, 72.

63. This nation was formed at Angostura in 1819, and it ceased to exist in 1830 when New Granada, Venezuela, and Ecuador became independent nation-states. Because New Granada assumed the name "Colombia" in 1863, the first Colombia (1819–30) is often referred to retrospectively as Greater Colombia (la Gran Colombia) to distinguish it from its later counterpart.

Here, since I do not deal with the second "Colombia," I do not use the retrospective term "Greater Columbia."
64. Bolívar, *Doctrina del Libertador*, 70.
65. O'Leary, *Memorias*, 2:20.
66. Regarding the manner in which Las Casas was incorporated into independence discourses, see Arias, "Las Casas as Genealogical Keystone" and Arias, *Retórica, historia y polémica*, 3–4.
67. Las Casas unambiguously supported the Catholic kings' effort to construct a universal Christian empire.
68. Washington, *The Writings of George Washington*, 1:572; 8:424, 563; 11:392, 399; 12:266.
69. For a discussion of how settlement patterns in Spanish America changed in the mid to later nineteenth century, see Butland, "Frontiers of Settlement in South America."
70. The translation above is found in Miller, *Memoirs of General Miller*, 2:453–545. "Todas las Naciones y todos los Imperios fueron en su infancia débiles y pequeños, como el hombre mismo á quien deben su institucion. Esas grandes Ciudades que todavía asombran la imaginacion, Menfis, Palmira, Tebas, Alexandría, Tyro, la Capital misma de Belo y de Semiramís, y tu tambien sobervia Roma, Señora de la tierra, no fuiste en tus principios otra cosa que una mesquina y miserable Aldea. No era en el Capitolio, no en los Palacios de Agripa y de Trajano; era en una humilde choza, baxo un techo pagizo que Romulo sencillamente vestido, trazaba la Capital del Mundo, y ponia los fundamentos de su inmenso Imperio. Nada brillaba allí sino su genio; nada habia de grande sino él mismo. No es por el aparato, ni la magnificencia de nuestra instalacion, sino por los inmensos medios que la Naturaleza nos ha proporcionado, y por los inmensos planes que vosotros concibiereis para aprovecharlos, que deberá calcularse la grandeza y el poder futuro de nuestra República. Esta misma sencillez, y el esplendor de este grande acto de patriotismo de que el General BOLIVAR acaba de dar tan ilustre y memorable exemplo, imprime á esta solemnidad un carácter antiguo, que es ya un presagio de los altos destinos de nuestro Pais. Ni Roma ni Atenas, Esparta misma en los hermosos dias de la heroicidad y las virtudes públicas no presenta una escena mas sublime ni mas interesante. La imaginacion se exalta al contemplarla, desaparecen los siglos y las distancias, y nosotros mismos nos creemos contemporaneos de los Aristides y los Phociones, de los Camilos y los Epaminondas." *Acta de la instalación del Segundo congreso nacional de Venezuela*, 5.

71. Here I use the English translation reprinted by the John Carter Brown Library in 2002 and originally published in London in 1810, as it foregrounds the notion that Spanish America will be an empire. Viscardo y Guzmán, *Letter to the Spanish Americans*, 85. The Spanish reads: "nuestra noble empresa ha de hacer renacer la gloria nacional en un campo tan vasto y de asegurarles un asilo, donde además de la hospitalidad fraternal, que siempre han encontrado, puedan respirar y actuar libremente de acuerdo a la razón y a la justicia." Viscardo y Guzmán, *OC*, 217.
72. Viscardo y Guzmán, *OC*, 218. "De esta manera ¡por América se acercarían los extremos más alejados de la tierra, y sus habitantes se unirían en los intereses comunes de una sola gran familia de hermanos!"
73. Collier, "Nationality, Nationalism, Supranationalism," 54.
74. Bolívar, *Doctrina del Libertador*, 72. "Es una idea grandiosa pretender formar de todo el Mundo Nuevo una sola nación con un solo vínculo que ligue sus partes entre sí y con el todo . . . ¡Qué bello sería que el Istmo de Panamá fuese para nosotros lo que el de Corinto para los griegos! Ojalá que algún día tengamos la fortuna de instalar allí un augusto congreso de los representantes de las repúblicas, reinos e imperios a tratar y discutir sobre los altos intereses de la paz y de la guerra, con las naciones de las otras partes del mundo."
75. Bolívar, *Obras completas*, 3:665, 1:294, 1:619.
76. Collier, "Nationality, Nationalism, Supranationalism," 49.
77. Lynch, *Simón Bolívar*, 213.
78. Collier, "Simón Bolívar as a Political Thinker," 25.
79. Bolívar, *Doctrina del Libertador*, 178.
80. Collier, "Simón Bolívar as a Political Thinker," 26.
81. Bolívar, *Doctrina del Libertador*, 216.
82. Ibid., 114.
83. Bolívar, *OC*, 2:151, 167.
84. Bolívar, *Doctrina del Libertador*, 218.
85. Bolívar, *El Libertador: Writings*, 53. The original can be found in Bolívar, *Doctrina del Libertador*, 126–27.
86. Bolívar, *El Libertador: Writings*, 30 (trans. modified). "Luego que seamos fuertes . . . se nos verá de acuerdo cultivar las virtudes y los talentos que conducen a la gloria; entonces seguiremos la marcha majestuosa hacia las grandes prosperidades a que está destinada la América meridional; entonces las ciencias y las artes que nacieron en el Oriente y han ilustrado la Europa volarán a Colombia libre, que las convidará con un asilo." Bolívar, *Doctrina del Libertador*, 74.

87. Bolívar, *Doctrina del Libertador*, 4. "La civilización que ha soplado del Oriente, ha mostrado aquí todas sus faces, ha hecho ver todos sus elementos; mas en cuanto a resolver el gran problema del hombre en libertad, parece que el asunto ha sido desconocido y que el despejo de esa misteriosa incógnita no ha de verificarse sino en el Nuevo Mundo. ¡Juro delante de usted; juro por el Dios de mis padres; juro por ellos; juro por mi honor, y juro por mi Patria, que no daré descanso a mi brazo, ni reposo a mi alma, hasta que haya roto las cadenas que nos oprimen por voluntad del poder español!"
88. Bolívar, *OC*, 1:881.
89. Masur, *Simón Bolívar*, 59.
90. Rotker, "El evangelio apócrifo de Simón Bolívar," 42 (emphasis in original).
91. Conway, *The Cult of Bolívar*, 152.
92. O'Leary, *Memorias*, 1:67–68.
93. Wiseman, *Remus*, 114–17.
94. Lynch, *Simón Bolívar*, 26.
95. Bolívar, *El Libertador*, 113.
96. Ibid.
97. Zea, "Imperio romano e imperio español," 11.
98. See, for example, Masur, *Simón Bolívar*, 463n45.
99. Lynch, *Simón Bolívar*, 171.
100. Bolívar, *El Libertador*, 135–36.
101. Grisanti, *Bolívar sí escaló el Chimborazo*, 45.
102. Ibid., 54.

CONCLUSION

1. See Ch.1, n8.
2. Richardson, "*Imperium Romanum:* Empire and the Language of Power," 1.
3. Ibid., 6.
4. A valuable comparative history of the British and Spanish conquests in the New World is Elliott, *Empires of the Atlantic World*.

~ Works Cited ~

PRIMARY SOURCES

Acta de la instalación del Segundo congreso nacional de Venezuela por el Excmo. Señor Gefe Supremo y Capitan-General Simon Bolívar, en la Capital de la Provincia de Guayana, el dia 15 de Febrero de 1819. Angostura: Andrés Roderick, Impresor de la República [1819].

Americus, Sylvanus [Samuel Nevill], ed. "The History of the Northern Continent of *America*." *The New American Magazine* 1 (1758): 8.

Barlow, Joel. *The Columbiad.* London: R. Phillips, 1809.

———. *The Vision of Columbus: A Poem in Nine Books.* Hartford, CT: Hudson and Goodwin, 1787.

Berkeley, George. "An Essay towards Preventing the Ruin of Great Britain." In *The Works of George Berkeley*, 2:185–98. 2 vols. London: Printed for T. Tegg, 1843.

———. *A Proposal for the Better Supplying of Churches in Our Foreign Plantations and for Converting the Savage Americans to Christianity by a College in the Summer Islands.* London: H. Woodfall. 1724.

———. "Verses on the Prospect of Planting Arts and Learning in America." In *The Works of George Berkeley*, edited by A. Fraser, 4: 365–66. 4 vols. Oxford: Clarendon Press, 1994.

Boccage, Anne-Marie Du. *La Colombiade, ou La foi portée au Nouveau Monde.* Paris: Côté-femmes, 1991.

Bolívar, Simón. *Doctrina del Libertador.* [Caracas]: Biblioteca Ayacucho, 1976.

———. *El Libertador: Writings of Simón Bolívar.* Edited by David Bushnell. Translated by Frank Fornoff. New York: Oxford University Press, 2003.

———. *Obras completas.* Edited by Vicente Lecuna. 2nd ed. 3 vols. Habana: Editorial Lux, 1950.

Bradford, William. *Of Plymouth Plantation, 1620–1647: The Complete Text.* New York: Knopf, 1952.

"Bula *Inter caetera* de 3 de mayo." "Bulas alejandrinas de 1493. Texto y traducción," by Emma Falque, 11–35. In *Humanismo latino y descubrimiento*, edited by J. Gil y J. Ma. Maestre. Sevilla/Cádiz: Universidad de Sevilla/Universidad de Cádiz, 1992.

"Capitulaciones de Santa Fe." In *Las Capitulaciones en Santa Fe (1492-1498)*. Edited by David Torres Ibáñez, 35–36. Granada: Diputación Provisional de Granada, 1993.

Cartagena, Pedro de. *Poesía*. Edited by Ana María Rodado Ruiz. Cuenca: Ediciones de la Universidad de Castilla-La Mancha / Ediciones de la Universidad de Alcalá, 2000.

Cicero, *The Orations of Marcus Tullius Cicero*. Translated by C. D. Yonge. 2 vols. London: G. Bell and Sons, 1917.

Colón, Cristóbal. *Textos y documentos completos*. Edited by Consuelo Varela. Madrid: Alianza Editorial, 2003.

Columbus, Christopher. *Accounts and Letters of the Second, Third, and Fourth Voyages*. Edited by Paolo Amilio Taviani, et al. Translated by Luciano F. Farina and Marc A. Beckwith. Rome: Istituto Poligrafico e Zecca dello Stato, 1994.

———. *The Book of Prophecies Edited by Christopher Columbus*. Edited by Roberto Rusconi. Translated by Blair Sullivan. Berkeley: University of California Press, 1997.

———. *The Journal: Account of the First Voyage and Discovery of the Indies*. Edited by Paolo Emilio Taviani and Consuelo Varela. Translated by Marc A. Beckwith and Luciano F. Farina. 2 vols. Roma: Istituto Poligrafico e Zecca dello Stato, 1990.

Crito [pseud.]. "Peace." *South Carolina Weekly Gazette*. June 21, 1783, vol. 1, no. 19, 4.

Depew, Chauncey. *The Columbian Oration, Delivered at the Dedication Ceremonies of the World's Fair at Chicago, October 21st, 1892*. New York: Edwin C. Lockwood, 1892.

Douglass, William. *A Summary, Historical and Political, of the First Planting, Progressive Improvements, and Present State of the British Settlements in North-America*. 2 vols. Boston: Rogers and Fowle, 1749.

Dwight, Timothy. "America: Or, A Poem on the Settlement of the British Colonies." In *The Major Poems of Timothy Dwight (1752–1817)*, 3–12. Gainesville: Scholars' Facsimiles and Reprints, 1969.

———. "Columbia: An Ode." [Philadelphia, 1794?].

Eden, Richard, trans. *The Decades of the Newe World or West India*. By Pietro Martire d'Anghiera. London: In aedibus Guilhelmi Powell, 1555. Reprinted in *The First Three English Books on America*. Edited by Edward Arber. Birmingham: privately printed, 1885.

Fernández de Navarrete, Martín. *Colección de los viajes y descubrimientos que hicieron por mar los españoles desde fines del siglo XV*. 5 vols. Buenos Aires: Editorial Guarania, 1945.

Franklin, Benjamin. "Observations Concerning the Increase of Mankind, Peopling of Countries." 2:311–21. In *The Works of Benjamin Franklin*. 10 vols. Edited by Jared Sparks. London: Benjamin Franklin Stevens, 1882.

Freneau, Philip. "Columbus to Ferdinand." In *The Poems of Philip Freneau*, 39–41. Philadelphia: Francis Bailey, 1786.

———. *On the Rising Glory of America: Being an Exercise Delivered at the Public Commencement at Nassau-Hall September 25, 1771*. Philadelphia: Joseph Crukshank, 1772.

———. "Pictures of Columbus, the Genoese." In *Poems Written and Published During the Revolutionary War* by Philip Freneau, 1:105–27. 3rd ed. 2 vols. Philadelphia: Lydia R. Bailey, 1809.

Gambara, Lorenzo. *De navigatione Christophori Colombi*. Edited by Cristina Gagliardi. Rome: Bulzoni, 1993.

Hakluyt, Richard, ed. *The Principal Navigations, Voyages, Traffiques and Discoveries of the English Nation*. 12 vols. Glasgow: MacLehose, 1903–5.

Herrera y Tordesillas, Antonio de. *Historia general de los hechos de los castellanos en las islas y tierrafirme del mar oceano o "Decadas."* Edited by Mariano Cuesta Domingo. Madrid: 1991.

Irving, Washington. *The Life and Voyages of Christopher Columbus*. 2 vols. 1828. Reprint, New York: G. and C. and H. Carvill, 1831.

Jane, Cecil, ed. *The Four Voyages of Columbus*. 2 vols. New York: Dover, 1988.

Jefferson, Thomas. *Memoir, Correspondence and Miscellanies from the Papers of Thomas Jefferson*. Edited by Thomas Jefferson Randolph. 4 vols. Charlottesville: F. Carr, 1829.

Las Casas, Bartolomé de. *Historia de las Indias*. 2nd ed. 2 vols. México: Fondo de Cultura Económica, 1965.

———. *Brevísima relación de la destrucción de las Indias*. Madrid: Cátedra, 1982.

———. *Las Casas on Columbus: Background and the Second and Fourth Voyages*. Edited and translated by Nigel Griffen. Repertorium Columbianum 7. Turnhout: Brepols, 1999.

Livy, *The History of Rome: Books 1–5*. Translated by Valerie M. Warrior. Indianapolis: Hackett, 2006.

López de Gómara, Francisco. *Historia general de las Indias*. Caracas: Biblioteca Ayacucho, 1978.

Martire d'Anghiera, Pietro. *The Discovery of the New World in the Writings of Peter Martyr of Anghiera*. Edited by Ernesto Lundardi, et al. Translated by Felix

Azzola. Nuova Raccolta Colombiana. Rome: Istituto Poligrafico e Zecca dello Stato, Libreria dello Stato, 1992.

———. *The Decades of the Newe World or West India*. Translated by Richard Eden. London: In aedibus Guilhelmi Powell, 1555. Reprinted in *The First Three English Books on America*. Edited by Edward Arber. Birmingham: privately printed, 1885.

Mather, Cotton. *Magnalia Christi Americana: Or, The Ecclesiastical History of New-England*. 2 vols. Hartford: Silas Andrus and Son, 1853.

Miller, George. *Memoirs of General Miller, In the Service of the Republic of Peru*. 2nd ed. 2 vols. London: Longman, Rees, Orme, Brown, and Green, 1829.

Miranda, Francisco de. *América espera*. Edited by J. L. Salcedo-Bastardo. Caracas: Biblioteca Ayacucho, 1982.

———. *Archivo del General Miranda*. 24 vols. Caracas: Editorial Sur-América, 1929–50.

Morison, Samuel E., ed. *Journals and Other Documents on the Life and Voyages of Christopher Columbus*. New York: The Heritage Press, 1963.

Morton, Nathaniel. *New-England's Memorial: Or, A Brief Relation of the Most Memorable and Remarkable Passages of the Providence of God, Manifested to the Planters of New-England in America*. Cambridge, MA: S. G. and M. J. [Samuel Green and Marmaduke Johnson], 1669.

O'Leary, Daniel. *Memorias del General Daniel Florencio O'Leary: Narración*. 3 vols. Caracas: Imprenta Nacional, 1952.

Peacock, Thomas Brower. *The Columbian Ode*. [Topeka, Kansas]: Thomas Brower Peacock, 1914.

Robertson, William. *The History of America*. 2 vols. Dublin: Printed for Messrs. Whitestone, et al. 1777.

"Salvoconducto." *Capitulaciones del Almirante Don Cristóbal Colón y Salvoconductos para el descubrimiento del Nuevo Mundo*. Madrid: Dirección General de Archivos y Bibliotecas, 1970.

Seneca, Lucius Annaeus. *Hercules, Trojan Women, Phoenician Women, Medea, Phaedra*. Edited and translated by John G. Fitch. Cambridge, MA: Harvard University Press, 2002.

Sewall, Samuel. *Phaenomena quaedam apocalyptica*. Boston: Bartholomew Green, 1727.

"The Speech of his Grace the Duke of A[rgyle], on the Motion made in the H[ou]se of L[or]ds, for addressing his Majesty to dismiss the Rt. Hon. Sir R. W[alpol]e; so far as it relates to the Management of the War." *Boston Evening Post*. 30 Nov. 1741.

Stella, Giulio Cesare. *Colombeidos libri priores duo*. London: Iohannem Wolfium, 1585.
Thacher, John Boyd. *Christopher Columbus: His Life, His Work, His Remains*. 3 vols. New York: AMS, 1967.
Turner, Frederick Jackson. "The Significance of the Frontier in American History." In *The Frontier in American History*, 1–38. New York: Henry Holt, 1920.
Virgil. *Aeneid*. Translated by Robert Fagles. New York: Viking, 2006.
Virgil's Georgics: Vol. 1, Books 1–11. Translated by Richard Thomas. Cambridge: Cambridge University Press, 1988.
Viscardo y Guzmán, Juan Pablo. *Letter to the Spanish Americans: A Facsimile of the Second English Edition (London, 1810)*. Providence, RI: The John Carter Brown Library, 2002.
———. *Obra completa*. Lima: Banco de Crédito de Perú, 1988.
Washington, George. *The Writings of George Washington*. Edited by Jared Sparks. 12 vols. Boston: American Stationers' Company, John B. Russell, 1837.

SECONDARY SOURCES
Adorno, Rolena. "Washington Irving's Romantic Hispanicism and its Columbian Legacies." In *Spain in America: The Origins of Hispanism in the United States*, edited by Richard L. Kagan, 49–105. Urbana: University of Illinois Press, 2002.
Aldridge, Alfred Owen. *Early American Literature: A Comparatist Approach*. Princeton, NJ: Princeton University Press, 1982.
Anna, Timothy E. Review of *Los escritos de Juan Pablo Viscardo y Guzmán*, by Merle E. Simmons. *Hispanic American Historical Review* 65 (1985): 562–64.
Ardao, Arturo. *La idea de la Magna Colombia, de Miranda a Hostos*. México: Universidad Nacional Autónoma de México, 1978.
Arias, Santa. "Las Casas as Genealogical Keystone for Discourses on Political Independence." In *Approaches to Teaching the Writings of Bartolomé de las Casas*, edited by Santa Arias and Eyda M. Merediz, 167–76. New York: The Modern Language Association, 2008.
———. *Retórica, historia y polémica: Bartolomé de las Casas y la tradición renascentista*. Lanham, MD: University Press of America, 2001.
Armitage, David. "The Declaration of Independence and International Law." *William and Mary Quarterly*, 3rd ser., 59 (2002): 39–64.
———. *The Ideological Origins of the British Empire*. Cambridge: Cambridge University Press, 2000.

Bailyn, Bernard. *The Ideological Origins of the American Revolution.* Cambridge, MA: Belknap Press of Harvard University Press, 1967.

Bancroft, Hubert Howe. *The Book of the Fair.* Chicago: The Bancroft Company, 1893.

Bartosik-Vélez, Elise. "The First Interpretations of the Columbian Enterprise." *Revista Canadiense de Estudios Hispánicos* 33 (2009): 313–34.

———. "The Three Rhetorical Strategies of Christopher Columbus." *Colonial Latin American Review* 11 (2002): 33–46.

———. "*Translatio imperii:* Virgil and Peter Martyr's Columbus." *Comparative Literature Studies* 46 (2009): 559–88.

Bellini, Giuseppe and Dario G. Martini. *Colombo e la scoperta nelle grandi opere letterarie.* Nuova Raccolta Colombiana. Rome: Istituto Poligrafico e Zecca dello Stato, 1992.

Benedict, Burton. "International Exhibitions and National Identity." *Anthropology Today* 7 (1991): 5–9.

Blakemore, Steven. *Joel Barlow's Columbiad: A Bicentennial Reading.* Knoxville: The University of Tennessee Press, 2007.

Bolton, Herbert. "The Epic of Greater America." *American Historical Review* 38 (1933): 448–74.

Boruchoff, David A. "Piety, Patriotism, and Empire: Lessons for England, Spain, and the New World in the Works of Richard Hakluyt." *Renaissance Quarterly* 62 (2009): 809–58.

Brading, David. *The First America: The Spanish Monarchy, Creole Patriots, and the Liberal State 1492–1867.* Cambridge: Cambridge University Press, 1991.

———. *Classical Republicanism and Creole Patriotism: Simón Bolívar (1783–1830) and the Spanish American Revolution.* Cambridge: University of Cambridge, 1983.

———. *The Origins of Mexican Nationalism.* Cambridge: University of Cambridge, 1985.

Brennan, Michael G. "The Texts of Peter Martyr's *De orbe novo decades* (1504–1628): A Response to Andrew Hadfield." *Connotations* 6 (1996/97): 227–45.

Breuninger, Scott. "Morals, the Market, and History: George Berkeley and Social Virtue in Early Eighteenth-Century Thought." PhD diss., University of Wisconsin-Madison, 2002.

Briggs, Ronald. *Tropes of Enlightenment in the Age of Bolívar: Simón Rodríguez and the American Essay at Revolution.* Nashville: Vanderbilt University Press, 2010.

Brinton, Anna Cox. "The Ships of Columbus in Brant's Virgil." *Art and Archaeology* 26 (1928): 83–86, 94.

Brückner, Martin. "The Critical Place of Empire in Early American Studies." *American Literary History* 15 (2003): 809–21.

Burke, John M. *"Buffalo Bill," from Prairie to Palace: An Authentic History of the Wild West*. Chicago: Rand McNally, 1893.

Burton, Antoinette. "Introduction: On the Inadequacy and the Indispensability of the Nation." In *After the Imperial Turn: Thinking with and Through the Nation*, edited by Antoinette Burton, 1–23. Durham: Duke University Press, 2003.

Buscaglia-Salgado, José F. *Undoing Empire: Race and Nation in the Mulatto Caribbean*. Minneapolis: University of Minnesota Press, 2003.

Bushman, Claudia. *America Discovers Columbus*. Hanover, NH: University Press of New England, 1992.

Butland, Gilbert J. "Frontiers of Settlement in South America." *Revista Geográfica* 65 (1966): 93–108.

Cañizares-Esguerra, Jorge. *Puritan Conquistadors: Iberianizing the Atlantic, 1550–1700*. Stanford: Stanford University Press, 2006.

Clay, Diskin. "Columbus's Senecan Prophecy." *American Journal of Philology* 113 (Winter 1992): 617–20.

Cock Hincapié, Olga. *Historia del nombre de Colombia*. Santafé de Bogotá: Instituto Caro y Cuervo, 1998.

Collier, Simon. "Nationality, Nationalism, and Supranationalism in the Writings of Simón Bolívar." *Hispanic American Historical Review* 63 (1983): 37–64.

———. "Simón Bolívar as a Political Thinker." In *Simón Bolívar: Essays on the Life and Legacy of the Liberator*, edited by Lester Langley and David Bushnell, 13–34. Lanham, MD: Rowman and Littlefield, 2008.

Conway, Christopher. *The Cult of Bolívar in Latin American Literature*. Gainesville: University Press of Florida, 2003.

Davidson, Miles H. *Columbus Then and Now: A Life Reexamined*. Norman, OK: University of Oklahoma Press, 1997.

Dennis, Matthew. "The Eighteenth-Century Discovery of Columbus: The Columbian Tercentenary (1792) and the Creation of American National Identity." In *Riot and Revelry in Early America*, edited by William Pencak, Matthew Dennis, and Simon P. Newman, 205–28. University Park, PA: The Pennsylvania State University Press, 2002.

Diffie, Bailey W. and George D. Winius. *Foundations of the Portuguese Empire, 1415–1580*. Minneapolis: University of Minnesota Press, 1997.

Drinnon, Richard. *Facing West: The Metaphysics of Indian-Hating and Empire-Building*. Minneapolis: University of Minnesota Press, 1980.

Dussel, Enrique. "Eurocentrism and Modernity (Introduction to the Frankfurt Lectures)." *boundary 2* 20, no.3 (1993): 65–76.

Edwards, Burton Van Name. Bibliographical note to *Letter to the Spanish Americans: A Facsimile of the Second English Edition (London, 1810)*, by Juan Pablo Viscardo y Guzmán, 89–97. Providence, RI: The John Carter Brown Library, 2002.

Elliott, John. *Empires of the Atlantic World: Britain and Spain in America 1492–1830*. New Haven, CT: Yale University Press, 2006.

———. *Imperial Spain, 1469–1716*. New York: St. Martin's Press, 1963.

Fiering, Norman. Preface to *Letter to the Spanish Americans: A Facsimile of the Second English Edition (London, 1810)*, by Juan Pablo Viscardo y Guzmán, vii–ix. Providence, RI: The John Carter Brown Library, 2002.

Fifer, J. Valerie. *American Progress: The Growth of the Transport, Tourist, and Information Industries in the Nineteenth-Century West*. Chester, CT: The Globe Pequot Press, 1988.

Fisher, John R. *The Economic Aspects of Spanish Imperialism in America, 1492–1810*. Liverpool: Liverpool University Press, 1997.

Fraker, Charles. *The Scope of History: Studies in the Historiography of Alfonso El Sabio*. Ann Arbor: University of Michigan Press, 1996.

Fryd, Vivien Green. *Art and Empire: The Politics of Ethnicity in the United States Capitol, 1815–1860*. New Haven, CT: Yale University Press, 1992.

Gardner, Lloyd C., Walter LaFeber, and Thomas J. McCormick. *The Creation of the American Empire: US Diplomatic History*. Chicago: Rand McNally, 1973.

Gil, Juan. "*Decades* de Pedro Mártir de Anglería: Libros relativos a Cristóbal Colón." In *Cartas de particulares a Colón y Relaciones coetáneas*, edited by Juan Gil and Consuelo Varela, 39–124. Madrid: Alianza Editorial, 1984.

———. "Génesis y desarrollo del proyecto colombino." In *Cristóbal Colón*, edited by Carlos Martínez Shaw and Celia María Parcero Torre, 83–113. [Salamanca]: Junta de Castilla y León, Consejería de Cultura y Turismo, 2006.

———. Introduction to *Textos y documentos completos*, edited by Consuelo Varela, 15–79. 2nd ed. Madrid: Alianza, 2003.

———. "La épica latina quiñentista y el descubrimiento de América." In *Anuario de Estudios Americanos* 40 (1983): 203–51.

Gillman, Susan. "The New, Newest Thing: Have American Studies Gone Imperial?" *American Literary History* 17 (2005): 196–214.

Grisanti, Angel. *Bolívar sí escaló el Chimborazo y escribió su Delirio en Riobamba*. Caracas: Tipografía Principios, 1964.

———. *Miranda: Precursor del Congreso de Panamá y del panamericanismo.* Caracas: Jesús E. Grisanti, 1954.

Gustafson, Sandra M. "Histories of Democracy and Empire." *American Quarterly* 59 (March 2007): 107–33.

Hamilton, Donna B. *Virgil and The Tempest: The Politics of Imitation.* Columbus: Ohio State University Press, 1990.

Hart, Jonathan. *Columbus, Shakespeare, and the Interpretation of the New World.* New York: Palgrave Macmillan, 2003.

Henige, David. *In Search of Columbus: The Sources for the First Voyage.* Tucson: The University of Arizona Press, 1991.

Hofmann, Heinz. "*Adveniat tandem Typhis qui detegat orbes:* Columbus in Neo-Latin Epic Poetry (16th–18th Centuries)." In *The Classical Tradition and the Americas.* Vol. 1 of *European Images of the Americas and the Classical Tradition,* edited by Wolfgang Haase and Meyer Reinhold, 420–656. Berlin: Walter de Gruyter, 1994.

James, Sharon L. "Establishing Rome with the Sword: *Condere* in the *Aeneid.*" *American Journal of Philology* 116 (1995): 623–37.

Kadir, Djelal. *Columbus and the Ends of the Earth: Europe's Prophetic Rhetoric as Conquering Ideology.* Berkeley: University of California Press, 1992.

Kafer, Peter K. "The Making of Timothy Dwight: A Connecticut Morality Tale." *William and Mary Quarterly,* 3rd ser., 47 (1990): 189–209.

Kallendorf, Craig. "Virgil's Post-classical Legacy." In *A Companion to Ancient Epic,* edited by John Miles Foley, 574–88. Malden, MA: Blackwell, 2005.

Kaplan, Amy. *The Anarchy of Empire in the Making of US Culture.* Cambridge: Harvard University Press, 2002.

———. "'Left Alone With America': The Absence of Empire in the Study of American Culture." In *Cultures of United States Imperialism,* edited by Amy Kaplan and Donald Pease, 3–21. Durham: Duke University Press, 1993.

——— and Donald Pease, eds. *Cultures of United States Imperialism.* Durham: Duke University Press, 1993.

Kasson, Joy S. *Buffalo Bill's Wild West: Celebrity, Memory, and Popular History.* New York: Hill and Wang, 2000.

Kicza, John E. "Patterns in Early Spanish Overseas Expansion." *William and Mary Quarterly,* 3rd ser., 49 (1992): 229–53.

Larner, John P. "North American Hero? Christopher Columbus 1702–2002." *Proceedings of the American Philosophical Society* 137 (1993): 46–63.

Limerick, Patricia. *The Legacy of Conquest: The Unbroken Past of the American West.* New York: Norton, 1987.

Liss, Peggy. "Isabel of Castile (1451–1504): Her Self-Representation and Its Context." In *Queenship and Political Power in Medieval and Early Modern Spain*, edited by Theresa Earenfight, 120–44. Aldershot: Ashgate, 2005.

———. *Isabel the Queen: Life and Times*. New York: Oxford University Press, 1992.

López Grigera, Luisa. "Iberian Peninsula." In *A Companion to the Classical Tradition*, edited by Craig W. Kallendorf, 192–207. Malden, MA: Blackwell, 2007.

Loughran, Trish. "Disseminating *Common Sense:* Thomas Paine and the Problem of the Early National Bestseller." *American Literature* 78 (Mar 2006): 1–28.

Lubbers, Klaus. "'Westward the Course of Empire': Emerging Identity Patterns in Two Eighteenth-Century Poems." In *Literatur im Kontext: Festschrift für Horst W. Drescher*, edited by Joachim Schwend, et al., 329–43. Frankfurt am Main: Peter Lang, 1992.

Lunardi, Ernesto, et al., eds. *The Discovery of the New World in the Writings of Peter Martyr of Anghiera*. Translated by Felix Azzola. Rome: Istituto Poligrafico e Zecca dello Stato, Libreria dello Stato, 1992.

Lupher, David A. *Romans in a New World: Classical Models in Sixteenth-Century Spanish America*. Ann Arbor: University of Michigan Press, 2006.

Lynch, John. *Simón Bolívar: A Life*. New Haven, CT: Yale University Press, 2006.

Masur, Gerhard. *Simón Bolívar*. Albuquerque: The University of New Mexico Press, 1948.

Mignolo, Walter. "The Geopolitics of Knowledge and the Colonial Difference." *South Atlantic Quarterly* 101 (2002): 57–96.

Milhou, Alain. *Colón y su mentalidad mesiánica en el ambiente franciscanista español*. Valladolid: Casa-Museo de Colón, Seminario Americanista de la Universidad de Valladolid, 1983.

Moraña, Mabel, Enrique Dussel, and Carlos A. Jauregui, eds. *Coloniality at Large: Latin America and the Postcolonial Debate*. Durham, NC: Duke University Press, 2008.

Morison, Samuel Eliot. *Admiral of the Ocean Sea: A Life of Christopher Columbus*. Boston: Little, Brown, 1942.

———. "The Earliest Colonial Policy Toward America: That of Columbus." *Bulletin of the Pan American Union* 76, no. 10 (Oct. 1942): 543–55.

———. "Texts and Translations of the Journal of Columbus' First Voyage," *Hispanic American Historical Review* 19 (1939): 235–61.

Mortimer, Ruth. "Vergil in the Light of the Sixteenth Century: Selected Illustrations." In *Vergil at 2000: Commemorative Essays on the Poet and His Influence*, edited by John D. Bernard, 159–84. New York: AMS, 1986.

Morwood, James. "Aeneas, Augustus, and the Theme of the City." *Greece and Rome* 38, no. 2 (1991): 212–23.

Muldoon, James. *Empire and Order: The Concept of Empire, 800–1800*. Studies in Modern History. New York: St. Martin's, 1999.

———. *Popes, Lawyers, and Infidels*. Philadelphia: University of Pennsylvania Press, 1979.

Murrin, John M. "A Roof Without Walls: The Dilemma of American National Identity." In *Beyond Confederation: Origins of the Constitution and American National Identity*, edited by Richard Beeman, et al., 333–48. Chapel Hill: University of North Carolina Press, 1987.

Nader, Helen. "The End of the Old World." *Renaissance Quarterly* 45 (1992): 791–807.

Nugent, Walter. *Habits of Empire*. New York: Vintage Books, 2009.

Onuf, Peter. *Jefferson's Empire: The Language of American Nationhood*. Charlottesville: University Press of Virginia, 2000.

Pagden, Anthony. *Lords of all the World: Ideologies of Empire In Spain, Britain and France, c. 1500–c. 1800*. New Haven, CT: Yale University Press, 1998.

———. *Peoples and Empires: A Short History of European Migration, Exploration, and Conquest, from Greece to the Present*. New York: Modern Library, 2001.

———. *Spanish Imperialism and the Political Imagination: Studies in European and Spanish-American Social and Political Theory 1513–1830*. New Haven, CT: Yale University Press, 1998.

Pereyra, Carlos. *Breve historia de América*. México: Aguilar, 1949.

Phillips, J. R. S. *The Medieval Expansion of Europe*. Oxford: Oxford University Press, 1988.

Quijano, Aníbal. "Coloniality of Power, Eurocentrism, and Latin America." *Nepantla: Views from the South* 1 (2000): 533–80.

Quint, David. "Epic and Empire." *Comparative Literature* 41 (1989): 1–32.

———. *Epic and Empire: Politics and Generic Form from Virgil to Milton*. Princeton, NJ: Princeton University Press, 1993.

Racine, Karen. *Francisco de Miranda: A Transatlantic Life in the Age of Revolution*. Wilmington, DE: Scholarly Resources, 2003.

Ramos Pérez, Demetrio. *La primera noticia de América*. Valladolid: Casa-Museo de Colón, Seminario Americanista de la Universidad de Valladolid, 1986.

Regazzoni, Susanna. *Cristoforo Colombo nella letteratura spagnola dell'Ottocento: Storie da vedere, storie da leggere*. Milano: Cisalpino-Goliardica, 1998.

Richardson, John S. "*Imperium Romanum:* Empire and the Language of Power." *Journal of Roman Studies* 81 (1991): 1–9.

———. *The Language of Empire: Rome and the Idea of Empire from the Third Century BC to the Second Century AD*. Cambridge: Cambridge University Press, 2008.

Robertson, William Spence. *The Life of Miranda*. 2 vols. Chapel Hill: The University of North Carolina Press, 1929.

———. *Francisco Miranda and the Revolutionizing of Spanish America*. Extracted from American Historical Association Annual Report, 1907, vol. 1. [Washington: Government Printing Office, 1908].

Romm, James. "New World and 'novos orbes': Seneca in the Renaissance Debate over Ancient Knowledge of the Americas." In *The Classical Tradition and the Americas*, edited by Wolfang Haase and Meyer Reinhold, 2 vols, 1: 77–116. Berlin and New York: De Gruyter, 1993.

Ronnick, Michele Valerie. "A Note on the Text of Freneau's 'Columbus to Ferdinand': From Plato to Seneca." *Early American Literature* 29 (1994): 81–82.

Rosenblat, Angel. *El nombre de Venezuela*. Caracas: Tipografía Vargas, 1956.

Rotker, Susana. "El evangelio apócrifo de Simón Bolívar." *Estudios. Revista de Investigaciones Literarias y Culturales* 6 (1998): 29–45.

Rowe, John Carlos. *Literary Culture and US Imperialism: From the Revolution to World War II*. Oxford: Oxford University Press, 2000.

———. *The New American Studies*. Minneapolis: University of Minnesota Press, 2002.

———, ed. *Post-Nationalist American Studies*. Berkeley: University of California Press, 2000.

Rumeu de Armas, Antonio. *Libro copiador de Cristóbal Colón*. 2 vols. Madrid: Testimonio Compañía Editorial, 1989.

Rusconi, Roberto. "Escatologia e conversione al cristianesimo in Cristoforo Colombo e nei primi anni della colonizzazione europea nelle isole delle 'Indie.'" In *Alessandro Geraldini e il suo tempo: Atti del Convengo Storico Internazionale Amelia, 19–20–21 novembre 1992*, edited by Enrico Menestò, 235–85. Spoleto: Centro Italiano di Studi sull'Alto Medioevo, 1993.

———. Introduction to *The Book of Prophecies Edited by Christopher Columbus*, edited by Roberto Rusconi, 3–51. Translated by Blair Sullivan. Berkeley: University of California Press, 1997.

Rydell, Robert. *All the World's a Fair: Visions of Empire at the American International Expositions, 1876–1916*. Chicago: University of Chicago Press, 1984.

Sacks, David Harris. "Richard Hakluyt's Navigations in Time: History, Epic, Empire." *Modern Language Quarterly* 67 (March 2006): 31–62.

Sale, Kirkpatrick. *The Conquest of Paradise: Christopher Columbus and the Columbian Legacy.* New York: Knopf, 1990.

Sánchez Marín, José and Francisca Torres Martínez. "El poema épico *Columbus* de Ubertino Carrara." In *Humanismo latino y descubrimiento*, edited by Juan Gil and José María Maestra, 205–18. Sevilla/Cádiz: Universidad de Sevilla/Universidad de Cádiz, 1992.

Schlereth, Thomas J. "Columbia, Columbus, and Columbianism." *Journal of American History* 79 (Dec. 1992): 937–68.

Shalev, Eran. *Rome Reborn on Western Shores: Historical Imagination and the Creation of the American Republic.* Charlottesville: University of Virginia Press, 2009.

Shields, David. *Oracles of Empire: Poetry, Politics, and Commerce in British America, 1690–1750.* Chicago: The University of Chicago Press, 1990.

Silverman, Kenneth. *A Cultural History of the American Revolution: Painting, Music, Literature, and the Theatre in the Colonies and the United States from the Treaty of Paris to the Inauguration of George Washington, 1763–1789.* New York: Thomas Y Crowell, 1976.

Simmons, Merle E. *Los escritos de Juan Pablo Viscardo y Guzmán, precursor de la independencia hispanoamericana.* Caracas: Universidad Católica Andrés Bello, 1983.

Slotkin, Richard. "Buffalo Bill's 'Wild West' and the Mythologization of the American Empire." In *Cultures of United States Imperialism*, edited by Amy Kaplan and Donald Pease, 164–81. Durham, NC: Duke University Press, 1993.

Smeall, J. F. S. "The Respective Roles of Hugh Brackenridge and Philip Freneau in Composing *The Rising Glory of America*." *The Papers of the Bibliographical Society of America* 67 (1973): 263–81.

Spengemann, William C. *A New World of Words: Redefining Early American Literature.* New Haven, CT: Yale University Press, 1994.

Spina, Giorgio. *Cristoforo Colombo e la poesia.* Genova: Edizioni Culturali Internazionali, 1998.

Stavans, Ilan. *Imagining Columbus: The Literary Voyage.* New York: Twayne, 1993.

Steiner, Carlo. *Cristoforo Colombo nella poesia epica italiana.* Voghera: Tip. succ. Gatti, 1891.

Tanner, Marie. *The Last Descendant of Aeneas: The Hapsburgs and the Mythic Image of the Emperor.* New Haven: Yale University Press, 1993.

Taviani, Paolo Emilio. "Notes for the Historicogeographical Reconstruction of the First Voyage and Discovery of the Indies." In *The Journal: Account of the First Voyage and Discovery of the Indies*, by Christopher Columbus, 2: 69–423.

Edited by Paolo Emilio Taviani and Consuelo Varela. Translated by Marc A. Beckwith and Luciano F. Farina. 2 vols. Roma: Istituto Poligrafico e Zecca dello Stato, 1990.

Tennenhouse, Leonard. *The Importance of Feeling English: American Literature and the British Diaspora, 1750–1850*. Princeton, NJ: Princeton University Press, 2007.

Torres Martínez, Francisca. Introduction to *Columbus*, by Ubertino Carrara, 11–105. Edited by Francisca Torres Martínez. Madrid: Ediciones Clásicas, 2001.

Trouillot, Michel-Rolph. "Good Day Columbus: Silences, Power and Public History (1492–1892)." *Public Culture* 3 (Fall 1990): 1–24.

Tuveson, Ernest Lee. *Redeemer Nation: The Idea of America's Millennial Role*. Chicago: University of Chicago Press, 1968.

Uslar Pietri, Arturo. *Los libros de Miranda*. Caracas: Comisión Nacional del Cuatricentenario de la Fundación de Caracas, 1966.

Van Alstyne, R. W. *The Rising American Empire*. New York: Norton, 1974.

Varela, Consuelo. "Notes on Paleographic, Linguistic, and Literary Questions." In *The Journal: Account of the First Voyage and Discovery of the Indies*, by Christopher Columbus, 2: 7–65. Edited by Paolo Emilio Taviani and Consulo Varela. Translated by Marc A. Beckwith and Luciano F. Farina. 2 vols. Roma: Istituto Poligrafico e Zecca Dello Stato, 1992.

Voigt, Lisa. *Writing Captivity in the Early Modern Atlantic: Circulations of Knowledge and Authority in the Iberian and English Imperial Worlds*. Chapel Hill, NC: University of North Carolina Press, 2009.

Walker, John Brisben. "A World's Fair, Introductory: The World's College of Democracy." *Cosmopolitan* 15 (Sept. 1893): 517–27.

Waswo, Richard. "The Formation of Natural Law to Justify Colonialism, 1539–1689." *New Literary History* 27 (1996): 743–59.

———. *The Founding Legend of Western Civilization: From Virgil to Vietnam*. Hanover, NH: Wesleyan University Press, 1997.

Weckmann, Luis. *The Medieval Heritage of Mexico*. New York: Fordham University Press, 1992.

Wertheimer, Eric. "Commencement Ceremonies: History and Identity in 'The Rising Glory of America,' 1771 and 1786." *Early American Literature* 29 (1994): 35–58.

Wey Gómez, Nicolás. *The Tropics of Empire: Why Columbus Sailed South to the Indies*. Boston: MIT Press, 2008.

Williams, William Appleman. *Empire as a Way of Life: An Essay on the Causes and Character of America's Present Predicament, Along with a Few Thoughts about an Alternative*. New York: Oxford University Press, 1980.

Wilson-Okamura, David Scott. "Virgilian Models of Colonization in Shakespeare's Tempest." *ELH: English Literary History* 70 (2003): 709–37.
Wiseman, T. P. *Remus: A Roman Myth.* Cambridge: Cambridge University Press, 1995.
Yates, Frances A. *Astraea: The Imperial Theme in the Sixteenth Century.* London: Routledge and Kegan Paul: 1975.
Yruela Guerrero, Manuel. Introduction to *La navegación de Cristóbal Colón*, by Lorenzo Gambara, xvii–lxxix. Madrid: Consejo Superior de Investigaciones Científicas; Alcañiz (Teruel): Instituto de Estudios Humanísticos, 2006.
Zamora, Margarita. *Reading Columbus.* Berkeley: University of California Press, 1993.
Zea, Leopoldo. "Imperio romano e imperio español en el pensamiento de Bolívar." *Nuestra América* 1 (1980): 11–26.
Zunzunegui, José. "Los orígenes de las misiones en las Islas Canarias." *Revista española de teología* 1 (1941): 361–408.

Index

Numbers in italics indicate references to figures.

Achaemenides, 58
Addington, Henry, 111
Advice to Privileged Orders (Barlow), 109
Aeneid (Virgil)
   Achaemenides in, 58
   Barlow and, 77
   Columbus and, 2, 5–6, 44–45, 50–58, 60–65
   Gambara and, 61–62
   Hakluyt and, 68
   Jason in, 39
   translatio imperii et studii tradition and, 5–6, 44–45, 46–48, 50–58, 60
Aldridge, Alfred Owen, 7
Alexander VI (pope)
   Columbus and, 29, 161n59
   crusades and, 18
   Inter caetera and, 20–21, 33
   Spain and, 12
Alfonso X, King of Castile and Leon, 18–19
America (Dwight), 75–76, 80
American Progress (Gast), 91–92, *91*
American Revolution, 81, 108–9
Americus, Sylvanus (Samuel Nevill), 69, 77
Anna, Timothy E., 172n41
Ardao, Arturo, 118, 128
Argonauts, 39–42, 63–64
Arias, Santa, 12
Aristotle, 3, 11
Armitage, David, 81
Augustine of Hippo, 19
Augustus (Roman emperor), 47

Barlow, Joel, 67, 69–70, 76–77, 109, 150–51
Bello, Andrés, 108, 117
Benedict, Burton, 99
Benedict XIV (pope), 63
Bentham, Jeremy, 117
Berkeley, George, 77–79
Bible, 11, 17, 18
Black Legend, 69, 86, 161n64
Blakemore, Steven, 77
Bobadilla, Francisco de, 58
Bolívar, Simón
   Columbus and, 14, 129–30
   empire and, 131, 133–34, 148–49
   Miranda and, 108, 117, 119, 127–28
   use of "Colombia," 128–30, 137
Bolívar, Simón: writings
   Cartagena Manifesto, 128
   Jamaica Letter, 128, 134, 137
   "My Delirium on Chimborazo," 142–43, 150–51
   "Oath Taken in Rome," 137–41, 150–51
   "Thought on the Congress of Panama," 136
Bolton, Herbert, 6
Book of Prophecies, The (Columbus), 35–36, 40–41
Boston Evening Post, 13
Brackenridge, Hugh Henry, 72
Bradford, William, 166n2

Brading, David, 42–43, 107, 122
Brant, Sebastian, 44–45, 48
Brevísima relación de la destrucción de las Indias (las Casas), 12
Briggs, Ronald, 7
Brinton, Anna Cox, 44–45
Brumidi, Constantino, 88–90, *89, 90*
Buffalo Bill (William Frederick Cody), 103–4
Buil, Bernardo, 58
Burke, John, 104
Burton, Antoinette, 7
Bushman, Claudia, 69

cabinets of curiosities, 101
Calancha, Antonio de la, 13
Cañizares-Esguerra, Jorge, 6
Capitulaciones de Santa Fe
    Columbus and, 15–16, 24, 31–32
    mercantile expectations of, 22–23, 26
Carrara, Ubertino, 62–63
Cartagena Manifesto (Bolívar), 128
Charles I (Roman emperor), 5
Charles III (king of Spain), 121
Charles V (Roman emperor), 39–40, 49, 155n2
Cicero, 55, 108
Clay, Diskin, 41
Cock Hincapié, Olga, 13
Cody, William Frederick (Buffalo Bill), 103–4
Collier, Simon, 128–29, 133–35
Colombeidos libri priores duo (Stella), 62
Colombia
    use of term by Bolívar, 128–30, 137
    use of term by Miranda, 109–14, 117–18, 146
    use of term in Spanish America, 106
Colombia (state), 135, 136–37
Colombiade, La (Du Boccage), 63–64
Colombiano, El (serial), 117

Columba/Columbo, 11
Columbia
    as allegorical female figure, 90, 91–92
    use of term, 13–14, 90–91, 109–14
"Columbia" (Dwight), 80
Columbiad, The (Barlow), 76–77, 150–51
Columbian Fountain, The (MacMonnies), 98, *100*
Columbian Ode, The (Peacock), 95–97, 150–51
Columbian Oration, The (Depew), 94–95
Columbus, carmen epicum (Carrara), 62–63
Columbus, Christopher
    as Aeneas, 44–45, 50–58, 60–65
    in American colonial literature, 68–80, 150–51
    as Christ-bearer, 19–33, 35–36
    legacy of, 1
    letters to Ferdinand and Isabel, 26–32, 33–35, 41–42
    as martyr and victim, 36–38, 57–59, 82, 118–19, 129–30
    Medea (Seneca) and, 19, 38–43, 72, 85
    as national symbol in the US: in literature, 84–87; overview, 66–67, 81–84; in painting and sculpture, 87–90, *88, 89, 90*; at World's Columbian Exposition, 4, 14, 67, 94–98, *99, 100*, 103–5
    as racial and cultural link to Europe, 147
    self-representations of, 15–16, 19–38, 42–43, 48
    Spanish imperial discourse and, 19–38, 42–43
    as symbol of Catholicism, 147
    as symbol of empire for Spanish America: Bolívar and, 127–30, 133–34, 137–43, 148–49, 150–51; Miranda and, 107–21; overview,

3–4, 10, 106–7; *translatio imperii* and, 10, 130–43; Viscardo y Guzmán and, 121–27
as symbol of Europe's imperial conquest, 1–2
translatio imperii et studii tradition and, 19–20, 38–39, 44–45, 48–57, 59–65, 130–43
use of the word "Columbus" for Colombo/Colón, 8–9
Columbus, Christopher: writings
Book of Prophecies, The, 35–36, 40–41
Diario, 23–26, 32
"Letter on the Discovery," 44
Columbus, Ferdinand
Book of Prophecies, The, and, 35–36
Columbus's writings and, 15
Miranda and, 108
as source, 50, 81, 84, 107
Columbus and the Indian Maiden (Brumidi), 89–90, 90
Columbus Doors (Rogers), 88
Columbus Quadriga, The (French and Potter), 98, 99
"Columbus to Ferdinand" (Freneau), 72
Common Sense (Paine), 121
Continental Journal (newspaper), 110
Conway, Christopher, 138–39
Cortés, Hernán, 122
Cosmographiae (Münster), 8–9
Crofutt, George A., 91–92
Crofutt's Western World (magazine), 91–92
Crusades, 17–18, 20, 39–40
Crystal Palace Exhibition (London, 1851), 93

De lege agraria (Cicero), 55
De navigatione Christophori Columbi libri quattuor (Gambara), 60–62
De orbe novo (Martyr)
Columbus as Aeneas in, 50–58

Columbus as martyr in, 57–59, 82
Georgics and, 55–56
as source, 8–9, 49–50, 60–61, 66, 68–69, 84, 107, 108
translatio imperii tradition and, 20, 50–58, 59–60
Décadas (Herrera y Tordesillas), 107
Depew, Chauncey, 94–95
Diario (Columbus), 23–26, 32
District of Columbia, 2
Du Boccage, Anne-Marie, 63–64
Dussel, Enrique, 153n1
Dwight, Timothy, 67, 75–76, 80

Eden, Richard, 8–9, 66, 68, 108
Elliott, John, 6, 21–22
Emerson, Ralph Waldo, 8
empire
in late fifteenth-century Spain, 16–20
origin and use of term, 4–5, 82, 147–48, 153n4
See also *translatio imperii* (transfer of empire)
Empires of the Atlantic World (Elliott), 6
encomiendas, 122
Epic and Empire (Quint), 47, 166n49
"Essay Towards Preventing the Ruin of Great Britain, An" (Berkeley), 78
evangelization, 24–33
"Experience" (Emerson), 8

Ferdinand II (king of Aragon)
Columbus and, 32–33, 82, 85–86
Peter Martyr and, 49
Spanish imperial discourse and, 16–18, 19, 20–23
Fernández de Navarrete, Martín, 84
Fiering, Norman, 172n41
Founding Legend of Western Civilization, The (Waswo), 46
Franklin, Benjamin, 82

French, Daniel C., 98, 99
Freneau, Philip, 67, 72–75, 79–80, 82
Frieze of American History (Brumidi), 88–89, *89*
Fryd, Vivien Green, 87–88
Fuller, Nicholas, 13

Gambara, Lorenzo, 60–62
Gast, John, 91–92, *91*
Gazeta de Buenos Aires (newspaper), 117
Gazeta de Caracas (newspaper), 117–18
Georgics (Virgil), 55–56, 62
Gil, Juan, 62, 160n49
Godoy del Pozo y Sucre, José, 171n19
Gorricio, Gaspar, 35–36
Gramática de la Lengua Castellana (Nebrija), 108
Gramsci, Antonio, 93
Granada, fall of, 18, 19, 23–24, 27, 49
Grenville, William Wyndham, 111
Grisanti, Angel, 143
Gual, Manuel, 113

Habits of Empire (Nugent), 83
Hakluyt, Richard, 68, 69, 108
Hamilton, Alexander, 113–14
Hamilton, Donna, 47
Harrington, James, 81
hegemony, 93–94
hemispheric studies, 6–7
Henige, David, 157nn29–30
Herrera y Tordesillas, Antonio de, 50, 107, 108
Historia de las Indias (las Casas), 12, 84, 108, 154n15
Historia de regibus Gothorum, Wandalorum, et Suevorum (Isidore of Seville), 17
Historia general (Historia de las Indias occidentales) (Herrera y Tordesillas), 108
history, 3

History of America, The (Robertson), 50, 69–70, 77, 107, 108, 110
History of Rome (Livy), 139, 153n5
"History of the Northern Continent of America, The" (Sylvanus Americus), 69, 77
Hofmann, Heinz, 61, 62
Homer, 61, 63, 77

Inter caetera (bull), 20–21, 33
inter-Americanist literary studies, 6–7
Irving, Washington, 42, 50, 67, 69, 84–87
Isabel I, Queen of Castile
 Columbus and, 32–33, 85–86
 Peter Martyr and, 49
 Spanish imperial discourse and, 16–18, 19, 20–23
Isabela (city), 52–53
Isidore of Seville, 17, 19
Italian Americans, 147
Iturbide, Agustín de, 149

Jamaica Letter (Bolívar), 128, 134, 137
Jason and the Argonauts, 39–42, 63–64
Jefferson, Thomas, 3, 81, 113
Jerusalem, 17–18, 19, 25–26, 39–40
Jesuits, 121
Jews, 19, 23–24
João II (king of Portugal), 30
Johnson, Samuel, 13
juramento en el Monte Sacro, El (Salas), 139, *140*

Kadir, Djelal, 7
Kallendorf, Craig, 47–48, 60
Kaplan, Amy, 7
Knox, Henry, 113

Laetus, Pomponius, 49
Landing of Columbus (Vanderlyn), 87–88, *88*
Language of Empire, The (Richardson), 147–48

las Casas, Bartolomé de
  Bolívar on, 130
  Catholic kings and, 175n67
  on Columbus, 11–14, 106–7
  Columbus's writings and, 15
  De orbe novo (Martyr) and, 50
  Irving and, 84, 85–86
las Casas, Bartolomé de: writings
  Brevísima relación de la destrucción de las Indias, 12
  Historia de las Indias, 12, 84, 108, 154n15
Leander expedition, 114–16, 118, 121–22
Leo III (pope), 5
Lepanto, Battle of (1571), 40
"Letter on the Discovery" (Columbus), 44
Letter to the Spanish Americans (Viscardo y Guzmán), 118, 121–22, 123–27, 132–33
Life and Voyages of Christopher Columbus, The (Irving), 42, 50, 67, 84–87
Limerick, Patricia, 10
Liss, Peggy, 17, 19, 155n2
Livy, 139, 153n5
López de Gómara, Francisco, 21
López de Mendoza, Iñigo, 49
López Méndez, Luis, 117
Lords of all the World (Pagden), 6
Lunardi, Ernesto, 55, 57
Lynch, John, 134, 139

MacMonnies, Frederick, 98, 100
Magnalia Christi Americana (Mather), 110
Malvenda, Tomás, 13
manifest destiny, 83–84
Margarit, Pedro de, 58
Martyr d'Anghiera, Peter, 15, 20, 48–49
  See also *De orbe novo* (Martyr)
Mason, Otis, 99–100
Massachusetts Spy (newspaper), 110
Masur, Gerhard, 138

Mather, Cotton, 110
Medea (Seneca), 19, 38–43, 72, 85
Meigs, Montgomery C., 88–89
Merlin, 19
Mexican Empire (1821–1823), 149
Milhou, Alain, 24
Mill, James, 117
Miranda, Francisco de
  Bolívar and, 108, 117, 119, 127–28
  Columbus and, 113, 114–19
  early life and readings, 107–9
  empire and, 120–21, 131
  use of "Columbia" and "Colombia," 109–14, 117–18, 146
  Viscardo and, 118, 121–22, 133
Monarquía de España, 13
Monroe, James, 85
Morison, Samuel E., 156n20
Morton, Nathaniel, 166n2
Morwood, James, 52
Mosquera de Barnuevo, Francisco, 13
Muldoon, James, 21
Münster, Sebastian, 8–9
"My Delirium on Chimborazo" (Bolívar), 142–43, 150–51

Nader, Helen, 156n20
Native Americans, 103–4
La Navidad (settlement), 53–54
Nebrija, Antonio de, 18–19, 108, 164n17
Nevill, Samuel (Sylvanus Americus), 69, 77
New American Magazine, 69
New Americanism (new imperial studies), 7–8, 145
New Laws (1542), 122
New York Gazette (newspaper), 69
New York Mercury (newspaper), 69
Nugent, Walter, 83, 92
Numantina (Mosquera de Barnuevo), 13

"Oath Taken in Rome" (Bolívar), 137–41, 150–51

Observations Concerning the Increase of Mankind (Franklin), 82
Octavian (Roman emperor), 56
Odyssey (Homer), 61, 63
O'Higgins, Bernardo, 134
O'Leary, Daniel Florencio, 129, 139
On the Rising Glory of America (Freneau), 72–75, 79–80, 82
Onuf, Peter, 81
Order of the Golden Fleece, 39–40
Ovando, Nicolás de, 122

Pagden, Anthony, 6, 153n4, 155n2
Paine, Thomas, 121
Panama Congress (1826), 133, 135
Paris Exposition (1889), 99–100
Patriota de Venezuela, El, 117–18
"Peace" (poem), 110
Peacock, Thomas Brower, 95–97, 150–51
Pease, Donald, 7
Pereyra, Carlos, 172n40
Philip II (king of Spain), 39–40, 48
Philip the Good, 39
Phillips, J. R. S., 23
"Pictures of Columbus" (Freneau), 75, 82
Pitt, William, 111, 112, 120, 122
Pizarro, Gonzalo, 122
Poem, on the Rising Glory of America, A (Freneau), 72–75, 79–80, 82
poetry, 3
Política Indiana (Solórzano Pereira), 110
Potter, E. C., 98, 99
Principal Navigations, Voyages, Traffiques and Discoveries of the English Nation, The (Hakluyt), 68
Proclamación a los Pueblos del Continente Colombiano, alias Hispanoamérica, 112
Proposal for the Better Supplying of Churches in Our Foreign Plantations, A (Berkeley), 78–79
Pueyrredón, Juan Martín de, 134
Purchas, Samuel, 69

Quint, David, 47, 52, 60, 94, 166n49

Racine, Karen, 109, 115, 119, 120, 121
Ralegh, Walter, 167n6
Ramos Pérez, Demetrio, 26, 30
Reconquista, 17–18, 20–33, 49
Richardson, John S., 147–48, 149
Rising American Empire, The (Van), 70–71
Robertson, William, 50, 69–70, 77, 82, 107, 108, 110
Robertson, William Spence, 114–15, 120–21
Rodríguez, Simón, 138–39
Rogers, Randolph, 88
Roman Empire, 4, 5, 17–18, 76, 141–42, 147–48
Roman Republic, 5, 141–42
Rome Reborn on Western Shore (Shalev), 3
Romm, James, 40–41, 42
Rosenblat, Angel, 112
Rotker, Susana, 138
Rusconi, Roberto, 41–42
Rydell, Robert, 93

Salas, Manuel José de, 171n19
Salas, Tito, 139, *140*
Salazar de Mendoza, Pedro, 13
Sale, Kirkpatrick, 50, 170n1
Sallust, 78
San Martín, José de, 108
Sánchez Marín, José, 63
Seneca, Lucius Annaeus, 19, 38–43, 72, 85
Shalev, Eran, 3
Shields, David, 168n30
"Significance of the Frontier in American History, The" (Turner), 92–93
Silverman, Kenneth, 78
Sketch Book of Geoffrey Crayon, Gent. (Irving), 84

Slotkin, Richard, 104
Solórzano Pereira, Juan de, 13, 110
South Carolina Weekly Gazette (newspaper), 110
Spengemann, William C., 8, 9–10
Stella, Giulio Cesare, 62

Tanner, Marie, 39, 155n2
"Thought on the Congress of Panama" (Bolívar), 136
Torre, Juana de la, 37–38
Torres, Antonio, 37
Torres Martínez, Francisca, 62–63
translatio imperii (transfer of empire)
  Aeneid and, 44–45, 46–48, 50–58, 60
  in American colonial literature, 72–80, 82–84
  Columbus and, 19–20, 38–39, 44–45, 48–57, 59–65, 72–80
  overview, 4–6, 45–46
  Peter Martyr d'Anghiera and, 20, 50–58, 59–60
  Philip II and, 40
  in Spanish America, 10, 130–43
  Spanish imperial discourse and, 18–19
  in the United States, 81–84
translatio studii (transfer of culture)
  Aeneid and, 44–45, 46–48
  American colonists and, 79–80
  in *American Progress* (Gast), 92
  Bolívar and, 137
  Columbus and, 38–39, 48
  overview, 5, 45–46
  Peter Martyr d'Anghiera and, 52
Turner, Frederick Jackson, 92–93
Tuveson, Ernest Lee, 168n23

Van Alstyne, R. W., 70–71
Vanderlyn, John, 87–88, *88*

Vansittart, Nicholas, 111
Varela, Consuelo, 36, 38, 157n30
"Verses on the Prospect of Planting Arts and Learning in America," (Berkeley), 77–78, 79
Vespucci, Amerigo, 11, 90–91, 109–10
Virgil
  Brant's edition of, 44–45, 48
  Miranda and, 108
  prophecy on Rome, 18
  See also *Aeneid* (Virgil); *Georgics* (Virgil)
Viscardo y Guzmán, Juan Pablo, 118, 121–27, 132–33
Vision of Columbus, The (Barlow), 69–70, 76–77, 109
Voigt, Lisa, 7

Waldseemüller, Martin, 90
Walker, John Brisben, 102
Washington, George, 2–3, 67, 130
Waswo, Richard, 46
Weckmann, Luis, 21
Wey Gomez, Nicolás, 33
Wheatley, Phillis, 67
Wild West Shows, 103–4
Wilson-Okamura, David Scott, 45
World's Columbian Exposition (Chicago, 1893)
  Columbus as national symbol at, 4, 14, 67, 94–98, *99*, *100*, 103–5
  ethnological villages and Wild West Shows at, 98–104, *101*
  overview, 93–94

Yates, Frances A., 155n2
Yruela Guerrero, Manuel, 61

Zamora, Margarita, 22, 26, 30, 157n30
Zea, Leopoldo, 131–32, 142

www.ingramcontent.com/pod-product-compliance
Lightning Source LLC
Chambersburg PA
CBHW030111010526
44116CB00005B/199